People in Society

People in Society

Second Edition

P. J. North

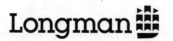

LONGMAN GROUP LIMITED
Longman House,
Burnt Mill, Harlow, Essex, CM20 2JE, England.

First published 1973
Second edition 1980
Second impression 1982

ISBN 0 582 33069 6

Printed in Hong Kong by
Wilture Enterprises (International) Ltd.

To Judy

Preface

Since the first edition of *People in Society* was written there have been substantial developments in the field of sociology, in the way in which it is taught in schools and colleges and in the way in which it is examined. This revised edition takes account of these changes.

Much of the material in the first edition has been revised and updated. A number of new sections have been added and amendments have been made throughout to bring the text into line with new ideas and new approaches within sociology.

The focus of this book is on the student who is coming to sociology for the first time in school or college. It aims to present a broad coverage of the major areas of the subject, introducing the reader to the ways sociologists undertake research and to the theories and concepts they use. *People in Society* provides a basis for the study of sociology. The student should supplement this basis with other material—films, television documentaries, newspapers and journals such as *New Society*. Whenever possible students should engage in enquiries of their own. They should make use of some of the excellent published resource material now available. The Longman Social Science Studies Series, edited by Richard Cootes, provides a wide range of excellent topic books which can be used to supplement the basic text.

This text owes much to the help and advice of my colleagues, especially those who are active within the Association for the Teaching of the Social Sciences, and to the joint experience of those of us who were engaged in the Joint Feasibility Study for a Common Examination at 16+. It also owes a great debt to the students of Crown Woods School and Kidbrooke School whose attempts to grapple with many of the ideas contained herein contributed greatly to its final form.

P. J. North
1979

Contents

Acknowledgements

We are grateful to the following for permission to reproduce copyright material:

The Associated Examining Board for Sociology 'O' level questions from past papers, Q 2, 3, 7 and 12 from November 1975; Q 4, 6 and 11 from June 1976; Q 6, 9 and 11 from November 1977; Q 2, 3, 7, 8 and 9 from June 1978; Q 3, 4 and 5 from Alternative Paper June 1978; Q 3, 7, 8, 11 and 12 from November 1978 and Q 1, 3 and 4 from June 1979; Fabulous Music Ltd (part of The Essex Music Group) for first verse 'My Generation' by Pete Townshend (lyrics only) © 1965 Fabulous Music Ltd; New Left Review for an adapted extract from *Work 2* by Jack Pomlet and Ronald Fraser; Penguin Books Ltd for an adapted extract from p 132 *Just Like a Girl* by Sue Sharpe, 1976; Routledge and Kegan Paul Ltd for extracts from pp 1, 8, 9, 93, 94 and 101 *Power Persistence and Change* (A Second Study of Banbury) by Stacey, Batstone, Bell and Murcott, 1975; the author, Margaret Stacey for extracts from *Tradition and Change* published by Oxford University Press, 1960.

We are grateful to the following for permission to reproduce artwork:

Blondel, *Voters, Parties and Leaders,* Penguin Books Ltd, figures 44, 45; British Library, figure 58; Coates and Silburn, *Poverty, the Forgotten Englishman,* W. Murray figure 50; Controller of Her Majesty's Stationery Office, figures 3, 11, 13, 15, 16, 17, 18, 19, 20, 21, 24, 26, 27, 28, 33, 36, 48, 49 and tables 13, 16, 17, 20, 21, 22, 30, 33; Douglas, *The Home and School,* Hart Davis, MacGibbon Ltd figure 30 and table 23; Hargreaves, *Social Relations in a Secondary School,* figure 31 and Young and Willmott, *The Symmetrical Family,* figure 68, Routledge and Kegan Paul; Hoineville and Jowell, *Survey Research Practice,* Heinemann Educational Books Ltd, figure 8; Independent Broadcasting Authority, figures 65, 67; Inner London Educational Authority, Research and Statistics Group, figure 34; R. K. Kelsall, *Report on an Inquiry into Applications for Admissions to Universities,* Association of Commonwealth Universities, 1957, figure 29; W. Murray, *Boys and Girls,* Ladybird Keywords Reading Scheme, Ladybird Books, 1964, figure 35; National Union of Mineworkers, figure 46; Ann Oakley, *The Sociology of Housework,* Martin Robertson, 1974, tables 21, 26, 27; C. Shaw and Henry McKay, *Juvenile Delinquency in Urban Areas,* The University of Chicago Press, 1969, figure 59.

Introduction
Doing Sociology

A good way to start doing sociology is to take a close look at the ordinary, everyday things that surround you. Perhaps the most exciting thing about sociology is the way it helps us to look at the things we normally take for granted. Someone once compared it to watching people playing a game the rules of which are unknown to you. As you watch you begin to get an idea of the rules and the different parts the players play. Sociology is rather like that but it is more as well. Above all we must remember that the sociologist is not only an observer watching the game. He, or she, is also a player who has played similar games with similar rules. None of us can escape from being in the world we try to understand.

As you work your way through this book and other books about the social world you will build up an idea of what sociologists do, the questions they ask, the methods they use and the subjects that interest them. In Chapter 1, we are going to look at one particular group of sociologists and the work they did. In Chapters 2 and 3 we will consider some of the concepts and theories which help us to understand that particular piece of sociology. Chapter 4 is concerned with the methods which sociologists use. The remainder of the book considers some of the main features of life in modern Britain starting with the pattern of population. Later chapters consider the family, schooling, work, government, rich and poor, crime and deviance and religion.

Banbury – A Case Study

Banbury is in Oxfordshire, very close to the centre of England. There has been a settlement on the site for nearly two thousand years. For the last eight hundred years, since a Norman baron built a castle there and the country people came for protection, Banbury has been an important centre for farmers in the area. For four hundred years it has been a market town and farmers would come on market day to buy and sell, and to gossip. The town is situated at the centre of a triangle of towns made by Stratford-upon-Avon to the north-west, Oxford to the south and Northampton to the north-east. The River Cherwell rising on the high ground away towards Northampton flows south through a long valley before it reaches Oxford to join the River Thames. At the centre of that valley is the town of Banbury. In the early 1950s when the town was studied by a team of sociologists many things could be seen to remind them of the town's past, and many things had changed.

In 1830 there were 6 400 people living within the borough of Banbury; most of them made their living by some form of trade, usually connected with the weekly market. The majority of the remainder were craftsmen – wheelwrights, blacksmiths, millers and harness-makers – closely linked to the needs of agriculture. In 1848 a new industry came to the town. A factory making farming implements was set up and soon afterwards the railway arrived. These new developments required a new kind of worker. They did not need the craftsmen employed in earlier times. They needed engineers, machine workers and factory hands. Many of these new workers came in to the town from outside. New cottages were built to house them. These were not the traditional stone cottages which may still be seen in the villages of Oxfordshire. They were built of red brick, in long lines, by the side of the canal or the railway.

The new industries did well and expanded. The population of the town also expanded as more and more workers were needed. In 1841 the town's population stood at 7 200; by 1871 it had risen to 11 700.

This growth was not continued. The foundry, which at its height employed 2 000 people, fell on hard times and in 1920 the town's population scarcely reached 13 000. New inventions, changes in fashion, and declining markets meant that Banbury was in danger of becoming a depressed area. Jobs were scarce.

In 1929 a worldwide aluminium company showed an interest in a site for a new factory, just outside of the town. A group of leading citizens joined together to give support to the idea and four years later the factory opened. Two thousand jobs were created and the whole pattern of life in the town began to change. 'The Ally' had arrived, and with it came many people in search of work. The demand for labour was such that workers were attracted from all over the country. The ripples of population began to flow inwards towards Banbury.

The town began to grow and in the 1950s and 60s more industries moved in. Most important of these was a food manufacturing plant and a large car-parts factory. The 'ripples' were replaced by large movements of people encouraged by overspill agreements between the Banbury council and councils in London and Birmingham.

By the early 1950s the population of the town had reached 19 000. At the end of the 1960s it was over 40 000. The old market town had become a modern, bustling, industrial centre no different from many other towns in Britain.

THE SOCIOLOGISTS AND CHANGE

Banbury first attracted the interest of sociologists shortly after the end of the Second World War. A team of researchers led by Margaret Stacey went to live in the town for three years to attempt to build up a picture of life there and of the ways in which it was changing. Their report *Tradition and Change* (the first study) was the result of three years' field work and six years spent analysing and sifting the data. The purpose of the research was to study Banbury and the effect of the introduction of large-scale industry on the town.

While the research was being done the members of the team made their homes in or near Banbury. Participation in the life of the town was the main method of the work. Each research worker took part in a different sphere.

But participation and discussion with people met in everyday life are by themselves not enough to give you a full picture of a town the size of Banbury. The published records about Banbury were analysed. A pilot questionnaire followed by a more detailed survey of over a thousand households was used to determine the population pattern, family and household composition, and the religious and political groups to which people belonged. All the leading members of the community were interviewed. All the local organisations were studied by an analysis of their records. The aim of these investigations was to examine the composition of the leadership and membership of the various organisations, to show to what extent their leaderships overlapped and to what broader social group the organisations were connected. Margaret Stacey recorded the changes:

The years around 1930 represent a divide. Life in Banbury before then would have been more easily recognisable to a man who had lived a hundred years earlier than to one living at the present day, only twenty years after (1950). Speak to any born Banburian of middle age or older and he will recall a town and a way of life which seem very remote. He will tell of the scores of carriers' carts which came rattling and rumbling in from the villages; of steaming cattle tethered in the streets; of the shouting drovers and the muck on the pavements. He will tell of the dark ill-lit streets of tiny family shops, of the drunkenness and brawling at night, and of the constable waiting in the shadow outside at closing time with his truncheon ready to help laggards on their way with a whack on the backside.

The market place now has a tarmac surface on which iron-mongers display their goods, patrons of the cinema park their cars and the St. John Ambulance stands ready. Where children used to play marbles at the Cross there are zebra crossings. Traffic streams past it along the north-south road between London and the south and the conurbations of the Midlands. A modern cinema looks on to the Horsefair car park. The shops in the brightly lighted High Street have plateglass windows and, though a few remain as family concerns, in this part of town most are branches of national chains, run by managers: Woolworths has taken the place of the 'Red Lion', farmers who used to do business at the bar have given place to young mothers with their prams. W. H. Smith stands in place of 'The Fox' where at fair times, and not only then, the fights were bloody and blasphemous. While, out of sight in the green fields beyond the town, surrounded by ten feet of barbed wire, immaculate flower beds, orderly bicycle ranks and lines of neatly parked cars, lies the aluminium factory. (Stacey 1960)

The coming of the aluminium factory in the 1930s changed more than just the market place and the High Street. There were far deeper changes in the pattern of life in the town, in the fabric of the community and in people's social relationships.

BANBURY PEOPLE

Four people typical of Banbury as it was in the past are Sir William, Mr Shaw, Mr Grey, and George. Margaret Stacey describes them:

> Everyone looks up to Sir William, who comes of an old local family and who has lived in the same village, just outside Banbury, for the past thirty years. They acknowledge his public service and his work for charity. Sir William accepts his status. He is an active councillor because he regards 'public service as a duty which a man in (his) position owes'. He feels, too, that he should 'set an example' and is, therefore, punctilious in his dress and manners. He is a member of the church council in the village and reads the lesson at Matins. In the town itself, Mr Shaw, a prosperous tradesman who owns a business which has been in the family for three generations and in which his son also works, is an acknowledged leader. He, too, knows where he stands in the old-town society and accepts his position. Like Sir William, he considers that 'service to the community' is a duty. He has been Mayor of the town and gives freely to local charity. Mr Grey, another of the leading trades-people, is very like him in his social position and in many of his attitudes. But Grey is a 'pillar of the Methodist Church' and a Liberal in politics, while Shaw is a sidesman at the parish church and a member of the Conservative Association.
>
> George is an example of a traditional worker in Banbury. He has been employed at one of the old family businesses for twenty-five years. He accepts the leadership of Sir William and of the Shaws and Greys in the town. For he feels that 'the ordinary working man hasn't got the education' and that 'it's better to leave things like that to people who know about them'. So he does not belong to a trade union and avoids political discussion. He votes Conservative and is 'Church', but his neighbour, a native of Banbury like himself, with a similar job, is a staunch Baptist and a Liberal.
>
> Thus, Sir William rides with the Hunt. Shaw and Grey play bowls with the Chestnuts, while George and his neighbour belong to the Borough Bowls. Shaw drinks at the 'White Lion' in the town centre, but George goes to the pub at the end of the street. Grey, like George's neighbour, does not drink. George is a member of the British Legion (Sir William is its president). (Stacey 1960)

To men like these Banbury was the centre of their life. They could look back on Banbury as it was. Their ideas of politics, of religion and of life gave them security. Theirs was an established order in which each man 'knows his place'. To them the most important question to ask of a man was 'Who is he?'

But, since the prewar expansion of Banbury, people who do not recognise such traditions have been drawn to the town. Men whose ideas and values are 'non-traditional'; whose roots are often far away. To them the key question is not 'Who is he?' but 'What does he do?'

Sir William is matched, for example, by Lord A. who was chairman of a group of engineering companies. Lord A. owns a hall in the district, but he is not often there because his work takes him to various parts of the country, to London, to the United States. He has no roots in the locality and belongs rather to an international society. He does not belong to the traditional status system, for he derives his status, not from his family as Sir William does, but from his position in industry.

Mr Shaw and Mr Grey are matched by Mr Brown. He is a technologist on the staff at the aluminium factory. He is a graduate from a provincial university. Like Lord A. he did not inherit his position but earned it on merit. He came to Banbury to work and if he does not get promotion in the factory, he will apply for a better post elsewhere.

George is matched today by people like Ted, who was brought up in an industrial city. He, like his father, has been a 'union man' ever since he started work. He is a Labour councillor. The class system for him is a matter of worker or not worker. He accepts his status as a worker and is proud of it, but, unlike George, he will not receive patronage from his 'betters'. 'The workers look after their own', he says. He does not accept that he has 'betters' like Sir William, Shaw and Grey. He supports the Labour Party. He wants to improve the lot and the chances of the workers as a class. (Stacey 1960)

THE SECOND STUDY

In 1966 Margaret Stacey returned to Banbury with a new team of sociologists.

The first field-work team left Banbury before the end of the age of austerity which followed the 1939-45 war: food was still rationed, hardly any post-war private houses had been built. In the period between the two studies the 'affluent society', the 'permissive society', the age of the pop group and youth culture all emerged. Communications were radically altered: television was in wide-spread use by the time of the restudy and the once-empty Oxfordshire lanes filled with cars faster than most that were on the road when the first study was made. These, of course, were technical and cultural changes that affected the whole nation. They have un-doubtedly reduced the relative isolation of Banbury in a number of

7

ways. Once distant neighbouring towns, already nearer by road in 1950 than they had been in 1900, were now nearer still. Furthermore, the improved communications, both TV and motor car, were shared by large sections of the population. They were not the privilege of the few. At the same time rail 'improvements' have reduced the connections of Banbury with the outside world.

The town itself now sprawls over a much wider area. Its cattle market, under cover and discreetly hidden, bears little resemblance to the old cattle market in the open streets about which people still talked in the late forties. Highly capitalised and organised, the market has progressed from being the 'largest in southern England' to the 'largest in England' and now, they claim, is the 'largest in Europe'. Despite this, and the twice-weekly street market, Banbury by 1966 had much more the air of an industrial town than of a market town. Along the road north out of Banbury there is a complex of factories where once the aluminium factory stood in splendid isolation among the fields.

To a field-worker returning from the first study the most dramatic visual change is the many acres of erstwhile fields now covered in new housing estates. The land between the main roads has been progressively filled in: the Council Estate between the Broughton and Warwick roads, the superior private housing between the Broughton and Bloxham roads, and the less expensive housing between the Bloxham and Oxford roads. All the country walks, at one time so close to the town centre, seem to have disappeared and with their disappearance the character of the town seems to have changed. There are no longer tongues of open country penetrating wedge-shaped behind the ribbon development which fronted each main road in the thirties, forties and early fifties.

Some inhabitants express a mixture of awe, horror and pride as they point out to those returning on a visit to the town the 'acres' of new houses. One elderly Banburian, talking with nostalgia of the pre-war days, said, 'One thing I regret is the growth of Banbury; life in old Banbury made people terribly matey.' Another, having stated her disapproval of the rapid growth of the town which had already taken place, retorted with regard to the proposals for further expansion of the town, 'They might as well build a New Town, it won't be Banbury any more.' (Stacey and others 1975)

To the sociologist looking at Banbury in 1950 the most obvious feature of the town was the division between the traditional way of life of the old market town and the new developments which followed the growth of industry. By 1965 much of the old Banbury had dis-

8

appeared. It was not only shops and buildings that had changed with housing estates covering what were once green fields. Attitudes changed. Men like Ted and Mr Brown became the majority. Whereas in 1950 they were newcomers, fifteen years later they were established members of the community. Margaret Stacey describes two streets in 1950.

Tracey Avenue is known locally as 'Little Rochdale' because of the origin of its residents. Most of the men came from the depressed areas during the 1930s to look for work. When they found it they looked for houses for their families. Tracey Avenue was just being completed and naturally attracted them. This 'community within a community' was a much more comfortable setting for the immigrant than being surrounded by neighbours who were natives of the town.

In Sonniton Street, a street mainly of Banburians, a middle-aged woman from the north found it impossible to get into the charmed circle of 'respectable' people, even though she attended the local church and joined the local Conservative Women's Association. In the same street a Scots family lived in complete isolation from other residents because they thought them 'unfriendly'. Their problem was undoubtedly increased because Sonniton Street is an established street with a defined structure. A substantial number of its residents have lived there for thirty or forty years. (Stacey 1960)

In the second study of Banbury the researchers looked closely at One End Street, a terrace of small Victorian houses, and Little Newton, a new housing estate on the edge of town.

Although the personnel of the Little Newton estate was in many ways so different from that of One End Street, particularly in being younger, non-Banburian and better-off, the sociological determinants of neighbour relations appeared to be essentially the same. Thus it was seen in One End Street that those neighbours who interacted with each other as neighbours were those who had other roles in common: kinship; common stage in the family circle; having children at home; place of origin, especially residence in the area. So it was in Little Newton, although there was some variation in the roles which were held in common.

In One End Street long residence together and especially having been born in the street, tended to lead residents to be friends as well as neighbours. In Little Newton everyone was a relative newcomer. Common place of origin in a sense replaced long residence together as a basis for developing neighbour relations. Thus it was noticeable that Banburians were friendly with each other: some had been to the same school, others had been brought up in the same part of Banbury before they came to Little Newton.

In Little Newton, as in One End Street, availability to neighbour, i.e. being about in the locality, was important. Thus those who were around the house for long periods of time were in a position to develop neighbour relations. As in One End Street, among domestic groups where the wife went out to work there were few

Fig. 1. *Reasons for moving to Banbury*

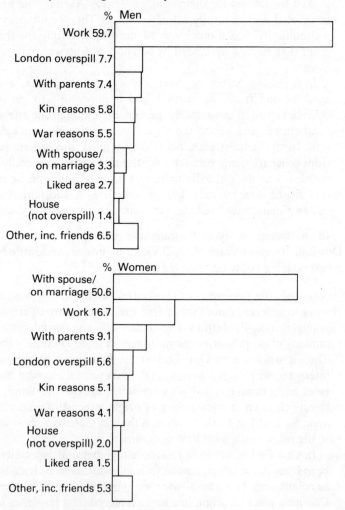

Source: Stacey and others 1975

neighbour relations compared with those where she was at home. In Little Newton the men were younger and at work for the most part. Neighbouring for the men, as for the working wives, was thus largely confined to exchanges in the evening or at the weekends. The neighbour relations of working women and men were largely of the coincidental kind, superficial exchanges when working in the garden, hanging out the clothes, or cleaning the car. Without other over-lapping roles, such exchanges seemed rarely to develop into any other form of interaction. In contrast, those women who did not work and more particularly those who were the mothers of young children (and these categories overlapped very largely) were not only available in the locality for a great many hours, but also had the mother-role in common and children who played together and/or went to school together. For them the chances of establishing interaction with neighbours were higher because availability and overlapping roles coincided. (Stacey and others 1975)

As well as these small-scale studies of particular neighbourhoods (in which some of the researchers lived while working on the study), the team also collected evidence on the town as a whole.

Table 1. *Employment in Banbury*

	1967 %
Metal manufacture	10.0
Distribution	12.3
Transport	8.3
Clothing	2.4
Government	5.1
Building	10.7
Services except professional	8.7
Professional and commercial services	13.0
Food and drink	9.7
Woodworking	0.6
Electrical machinery, engineering	7.5
Printing	2.7
Agriculture	3.4
Gas, water, electricity	1.2
All other	4.4
Total	100.0

Source: Stacey and others 1975

They investigated the reasons people moved to Banbury in the first place.

From the census they discovered how many people lived in Banbury, their age and sex. They considered the industries in which people worked.

They collected evidence on religion in the town and the membership of the various churches.

Table 2. *Church members: 1950 and 1967*

Denomination	Denominational % of Church members	
	1950	1967
Church of England	36.5	27.7
Methodist	23.3	21.1
Baptist	4.6	7.2
Salvation Army	3.7	4.8
Congregational	3.7	2.8
Roman Catholic	28.2	36.4
Total	100.0	100.0
Total in sample	1 939	2 489

Source: Stacey and others 1975

They examined the links between people's jobs and their involvement in clubs and societies.

Table 3. *Occupation and voluntary associations*

Number of associations belonged to	Non-manual workers %	Manual workers %
None	36	46
One	24	29
Two or more	40	25
Total	100	100

Source: Stacey and others 1975

They looked at the way people voted.

Table 4. *Voting of non-manual and manual workers, by date of arrival in Banbury*

Non-manual

Date of arrival	Since 1945 %	1930–45 %	Before 1930 %	Banbury born or brought up %	Total %
Conservative	55.0	49.2	75.0	55.7	55.4
Labour	18.1	37.3	12.5	13.5	18.2
Liberal	8.4	4.5	8.3	6.5	7.2
Did not vote	12.0	1.5	4.2	16.5	12.3
Rest	6.4	7.5	0.0	7.8	6.8
Total	99.9	100.0	100.0	100.0	99.9

Manual

Date of arrival	Since 1945 %	1930–45 %	Before 1930 %	Banbury born or brought up %	Total %
Conservative	25.7	25.8	34.7	28.1	27.5
Labour	44.0	46.4	38.8	40.3	42.0
Liberal	5.2	5.1	4.1	6.5	5.8
Did not vote	19.4	13.4	12.2	18.4	17.8
Rest	5.6	9.3	10.2	6.7	6.8
Total	99.9	100.0	100.0	100.0	99.9

Source: Stacey and others 1975

What is Sociology?

The two studies of Banbury provide a unique picture of life in an English town over a period of twenty years. They also provide an indication of the sort of things sociologists are interested in and how they study them.

Having read about Banbury and the research that was done there you may be wondering why it is called sociology. A great deal of what you have read could have been history or geography. Sociology, history and geography are similar subjects and they overlap. They are all social sciences. Sociologists often use historical or geographical material in their work. The content of their studies is often similar. They are all concerned with aspects of man's life on earth. The differences appear when you consider how the content, the raw material, is used by the different subjects. Any subject that you study at school, college or university is more than a list of topics. It also includes methods – the ways in which evidence is collected and used, and concepts – ideas which are used to put the evidence into some kind of order. Sociologists also use theories which guide and influence the way they work. We shall be considering methods in much more detail in Chapter 4.

A concept: community

A sociological concept which is central to the Banbury studies is 'community'. It is fairly typical of many ideas used in sociology. Firstly it is a word which has an everyday meaning outside of sociology. Sociologists use it in a similar way but try to be more precise. Secondly, in everyday use 'community' has a number of meanings and they overlap. Think about the differences of meaning in these uses of the word 'community':

   – local community

- community spirit
- Community Centre
- the school community

'Local community' refers to a geographical area; a town, or village, or even a collection of streets like those around Tracey Avenue or One End Street in Banbury. 'Community spirit' is what you might expect to find in 'a community'. It is made up of attitudes of people towards each other and their relationships. It need not be tied down to a geographical area. 'Community Centre' is a place, in a local community, where community spirit is expected to develop. You do not need a Community Centre to develop 'community spirit' and even if you do have one there is no guarantee that it will. In reality a Community Centre may be little more than the place where they hold whist drives and playgroups. 'The school community' also involves the idea of 'place' except that it is the place you go to, rather than the place where you live. School community is usually used to refer to the relationships which exist within the school.

Thirdly, because 'community' can be understood in a number of ways both in everyday use and by sociologists there are often debates and arguments about exactly what it does mean and how it is being used. These debates are an important part of sociology.

Fourthly, as long as we are clear about the ways in which we use the word 'community' it can help us to organise our knowledge. In sociology similar events and actions from real life are grouped together as examples of particular ideas, or concepts. For example, in Banbury we can find evidence for the existence of some kind of community relationship within both One End Street and Little Newton. People know each other, they help each other out, they share experiences. This helps us to build up some kind of pattern. We can link particular behaviour or particular ways of life to particular situations. By observing such patterns in everyday life we are able to predict what could happen in the future. Human social life is so complicated that we could never hope to be one hundred per cent accurate in our predictions but we can get some idea of what *might* happen.

Fifthly, the concept of community helps us to make comparisons. We can compare Tracey Avenue in 1950 and Little Newton in 1965. One is a street of people with a common background who have shared many common experiences over nearly twenty years, the other is a new estate made up of people who had very little in common before they moved there. You could go on to compare them with other districts including your own. Comparison such as this is useful to the sociologist because it enables him or her to get a more precise picture of how social life fits together.

15

Community and association

A sociologist who was particularly interested in the way communities changed was Ferdinand Tonnies. He was German and lived from 1855 to 1936. His most important work was a book entitled *Gemein-schaft und Gesellschaft*. In this book Tonnies describes two patterns of social life which he called Gemeinschaft and Gesellschaft. These two German words are translated into English as 'community' and 'association' but many sociologists still prefer to use the original words.

An important feature of change in society is the movement from societies which are *gemeinschaft* or communities, to those which are mainly *gesellschaft* or associations. This is not just a change in the size or scale of the society, it is a change in the way people behave towards each other.

GEMEINSCHAFT

A *gemeinschaft* type of society, or community, would be fairly small. It would not contain many people. The people within such a community would recognise each other when they met 'face-to-face'. They may not have a very close relationship but they would know a little about each other and, as in Banbury in the old days, 'everyone would know their place'. This often amounted to knowing the positions and duties each individual held within the community.

GESELLSCHAFT

Gesellschaft is only a partial society. It does not attempt to provide for all of the needs of its members. It usually has very precise and limited aims which only concern part of people's lives. Its membership may be larger than the membership of a *gemeinschaft* type of society but its members do not stay for ever. People come and go. Membership is temporary, not permanent. The relationships which exist under *gesellschaft* are sometimes called 'associational relationships'. People only come into contact with each other for specific purposes and relationships tend to be formal. There are often rules about how people should communicate with each other; these are sometimes referred to as 'the proper channels'. A large business concern, or a government department provides examples of *gesellschaft* or association. Modern city life is made up of a network of such associational relationships which interlock through the members of the society.

A village in the country

We can see some of the features of *gemeinschaft* if we look at life in a country village. In 1940 Alwyn Rees lived for a time in the parish of Llanfihangel-yng-Ngwynfa in mid-Wales. His description of this little community can be found in his book *Life in a Welsh Countryside*.

It would not be quite accurate to call Llanfihangel a village. It is a parish of three small hamlets and scattered farms spread over an area of 15½ square miles of Montgomeryshire. When Rees was there the population of the parish was about five hundred people and all but fifty of these lived in farms and cottages spread across the countryside. The largest of the three hamlets, Llanfihangel itself (known locally as the Llan), contained less than a dozen buildings. As well as the church and the rectory, the school and the school-house, there were two shops, a post-office, a village hall and two cottages.

Within eleven miles of the cluster of dwellings that made up Llanfihangel were the boundaries of eight other parishes, making a total of 177 square miles of countryside. Within these nine parishes 75 per cent of the householders of Llanfihangel were born, and 85 per cent of their wives. It was within these 177 square miles that the majority of the inhabitants lived out their entire lives.

There was a time when the farms were self-sufficient. Growing their own food and only trading outside when they had a surplus. This had changed by the time of Rees's study. The isolation of the parish had been broken. The farmers now reared stock for the market away in Oswestry and shops-on-wheels were regular callers at even the most isolated farms. Over the years the parish had become more closely linked with the life of mid-Wales and the Borders.

In the Llan household the father combines many roles. He is father, employer, manager and workman, as well as husband. In years past he was also expected to lead the family in prayer and organise family entertainment. In most of the farmhouses 'the family' would include hired labourers who lived under the same roof and ate at the same table. These were often young men, sons of neighbouring farmers, who would one day have farms of their own. Local families were often closely linked together. Two-thirds of the households studied had members whose close kin (parents, brothers, sisters, sons or daughters) lived elsewhere in the parish. One-third of the households were linked with two other households in this way. At sheep-shearing time these kin, and others from farther afield, would be expected to come and lend a hand. Thus, whereas in Banbury the question might be asked of a man, 'who is he?' or 'what does he do?' in Llanfihangel the question would be, 'who are his family?'.

Within the family each member would have a special task. The men would work in the fields under the direction of the father. The women would work around the house and concern themselves with the poultry and the dairy.

Within this community each individual has many roles.

A shopkeeper interests himself in cures and his advice is sought in case of illness. He also takes a lead in the organisation of sports and coaches the local teams, while his wife plays the piano and has now succeeded her father as church organist. The latter, a retired blacksmith and part-time postmaster, was very well read, and good use was made of his literacy not only by his immediate neighbours but also by the inhabitants of the surrounding district. The postman makes walking sticks in return for which farmers give him presents of tobacco, and he is also the church bellringer and organ blower. (Rees 1950)

Llanfihangel provides a good example of *gemeinschaft*. It is a small community in which the inhabitants meet face-to-face. Each individual participates in the community in many ways, acting out many different roles, over a whole lifetime. It is not a 'pure' example of *gemeinschaft*. Some elements of *gesellschaft* come into it. The farmers trade with buyers from far away; their sheep end up on the dinner tables of Birmingham and London; the post office exists to maintain contact between the hamlet and the world outside; the school is part of a wider county education service, as is the mobile library. Few communities today are completely isolated and self-contained.

Ted

A single community does not give us a clear picture of the nature of *gesellschaft*. We can see it better if we follow one man around on a fairly normal day of his life. One of the people we met in Banbury was Ted. Ted was not born in Banbury. His parents lived in Birmingham and after school Ted got an apprenticeship as a sheet metal worker. After a few years he married and when his apprenticeship was finished he applied for a job with one of the newer firms in Banbury. He and his wife, Irene, moved out to Banbury and, after a year or so, managed to get a council house in the southern part of the town. When Ted is at work he wears a boiler-suit to protect his clothes. His foreman wears a white overall. Ted has a lot of contact with the foreman and with the works manager because he is the shop steward for his part of the factory. Ted's relationship with both these men is determined by the rules drawn up over many years by the firm and the unions together. Their relationships are also affected by the accepted manner of behaviour in the works. Ted, the foreman, and the works manager, all have expectations of how each should behave in the work situation. These rules and expectations do not apply to Ted when he is in the canteen with his mates, or at a union meeting. In Llanfihangel most of the farmers were there because that was where their families had always farmed. It seemed the natural thing for them to do. Ted works at the factory, and is a shop steward in the union, by choice. He does not have to join in these particular 'associations'. He could work elsewhere and he could belong to another union.

When Ted leaves the factory at five-thirty he leaves his 'factory life' behind him. On the way home he enters into other relationships of a partial kind. He gets on the bus and buys a ticket, making a short-term contract with the bus company through their appointed agent, the bus conductor. If Ted wanted to he could determine the precise nature of his 'contract' by reading the bus company's by-laws. He stops to buy an evening newspaper, and then some cigarettes. Each time he enters into an associational relationship with another individual. Each time the aim of the relationship is very specific – to travel home, to exchange money for newspaper or cigarettes, and the relationship is limited. Ted never meets the bus conductor anywhere else. He knows nothing about the tobacconist except that he stocks his brand.

When Ted gets home he enters into the nearest thing in his life to *gemeinschaft*. His family is close, and membership is natural rather than voluntary. It is a situation of face-to-face relationships. In the evening he goes out to the pub where he meets yet another group of people in yet another situation. Some evenings he has to attend council meetings, for he was elected to the local council a couple of years back. In the council chamber Ted's relationships with the Mayor and the other councillors are very formal. He is always addressed as 'Councillor Smith', and in turn he has to address all his remarks through the Mayor. As a councillor Ted often has to sort things out for ratepayers in his ward. This may involve contacting council officials, again 'working through the proper channels' in a particular role.

Ted is a fictional example of someone who could well exist. Most people in a modern city live lives not unlike Ted's. Moving from one limited relationship to another, seldom allowing relationships in different situations to overlap. In advanced industrial societies people live their lives at the centre of a large number of *gesellschaft* or 'associational' relationships.

Social roles

While considering the idea of community we have been using another important sociological concept, that of social roles. The word 'role' is borrowed from the theatre and describes the behaviour which is expected from people in particular social positions. We have already seen that in Llanfihangel individuals play a number of different roles in village life. Ted also has a number of different roles to play but he plays them to different audiences. Sociologists would say that in Llanfihangel each individual plays a number of roles to the same role-set while Ted plays different roles to different role-sets. In everyday life some roles are more clearly defined than others.

When you get on a bus you expect the bus conductor to sell you a ticket, possibly to tell you when you get to your destination and, if you are an old lady, to help you off the bus. You do not expect him to come round selling ice-cream, or to sing a selection of hit songs from *The Sound of Music*. A bus conductor's role is clearly defined. People know what sort of behaviour to expect from him. We can say that his role is 'specific'. But not all social roles are like this. If you tried to write down a list of the 'role content' of the role of 'mother' you would get a very long list. Our expectations of the behaviour involved in performing roles like 'mother', 'father', 'son', 'daughter', are not at all specific. We would say that they are more diffuse.

Richard Hoggart describes some of the things expected of mothers when he was young.

> Partly because the husband is at work but also because women are simply expected to look after such things, it will be the mother who has the long wait in public places, at the doctor's for 'a bottle', at the clinic with a child who has eye trouble, at the municipal offices to see about the instalment on the electricity bill. (Hoggart 1957)

In some situations roles are clearly defined. We can understand that bus conductors don't sell ice-cream because we accept a basic definition of the role of bus conductor. This is close to the way 'role' is used in the theatre to describe a part someone plays from a script.

In many situations roles are not defined at all and we have to decide for ourselves what roles are being played. Usually we can rely on clues about the roles people play. A bus conductor has a uniform which symbolises the role and a setting – his bus – in which to perform it. Take these away and you are left with very few clues. Should you meet a total stranger you would search for clues which might indicate who they are and what they are doing there. Often we are able to use our experience of similar situations in the past to help us.

20

William and Charlotte Wiser describe the problems faced by the people in an Indian village when they arrived in the village intending to carry out a sociological study.

Our assistant brought in the news that after observing our camp, and considering the various rumours that had arrived in advance, the leaders of the village had concluded that the Sahib must be the settlement officer come to check the landholding and revise rents. They knew that he was not the district magistrate nor a deputy; neither was he a public official. There had been missionaries here before, and he might be classified as such. But he had secured maps of the area and had access to records of landholdings. Who would want these but someone interested in taxes? (Wiser and Wiser 1969)

As the villagers got to know the 'Sahib' and 'Memsahib' better they changed their ideas about who they were and what their role was. The original idea about their roles was redefined.

Each year has bound us closer to the life of the community. Some of our neighbours have grasped the idea of our survey and are willing to cooperate in its preparation. Others have accepted us simply as friends. (Wiser and Wiser 1969)

We approach any new situation with a basic stock of knowledge about the behaviour that would be appropriate. As we gain more knowledge of the situation we are able to change our ideas and re-model our understanding of roles. It is important to remember that in real life, social roles are not fixed like the roles in a play. They are frequently 'negotiated' by the people concerned.

Social roles therefore concern the behaviour that is expected of people in certain situations. The behaviour that fits the role needs to be learned and we learn what to expect in the performance of certain roles. But roles may also change and can be 'renegotiated' in the way individuals interact in real life.

The Banbury studies can also show us the different levels at which sociologists work. When Margaret Stacey describes life in Tracey Avenue or Little Newton she is describing the face-to-face relationships of people in their everyday lives. We would call this 'interaction'. It is the basic level of social life. However, when Stacey describes things like voting patterns, or church membership she is moving away from the individuals towards the larger social group. It is rather like a zoom lens at a football match. One moment you are focused right in on a handful of supporters and then you are zooming out to view stands packed with thousands of people. Some sociologists prefer the 'close-up' view while others study the large mass. Of course, they are not really

21

very different. The great mass of fans in the long shot is made up of many small groups of supporters which may require different methods of study and may lead to different kinds of theories.

Trying it out

Margaret Stacey spent thirteen years working on her two studies of Banbury. She was helped by a team of researchers, typists and others. You do not need that much time and all of those resources to do sociology. You can start from where you are at the moment. For example why are you bothering to read this book. Is it because you want to or because you have been made to? Are you reading it because you are interested in sociology and hope to learn more about it or because you want to pass an exam? If you are reading it out of interest, why pick on sociology? Why not Greek drama or nuclear physics? Why do an exam in sociology, and what is the exam for anyway?

The answers to questions such as these are likely to be connected in some way with the social world in which you live. The decision to read this book was unlikely to have been taken on the spur of the moment. The fact that you are reading it may reflect the power situation in which you find yourself, the need to pass examinations, relationships with particular people and so on. Sociologists often theorise in this way, suggesting possible reasons for behaviour on the basis of what they know about the social world.

You could go on asking questions about your reasons for reading this book. You could relate this one activity to a whole range of other ideas – career, qualification, interests, learning, and so on.

Another way of doing sociology would be to go back to the statistics and to look more carefully at Margaret Stacey's evidence. What concepts or ideas can we gain from the tables of voting behaviour, or from the link between social class and membership of voluntary associations? What kind of a town was Banbury and how has it changed?

You could move on from Banbury and look at some other research from the area of community studies. Additional reading is listed at the back of this book.

Finally you could even go out and do some research of your own. Decide on an area you are going to study. See how much evidence you can collect from information in the local library – local histories, census figures, election results, etc., or from the local newspaper. Go out and talk to people either as part of a properly planned survey or by meeting people with special knowledge – local councillors, policemen, or old people who have lived there all of their lives. Look at the way the streets and houses vary by asking estate agents about house prices in different areas and by direct observation. A camera can be a useful tool in such studies.

When you have completed your study find some way of presenting it – either as a written report or on exhibition or even as a tape-slide presentation or a talk on local radio.

Throughout your study keep asking yourself 'why is life here organised the way it is?'. You may not discover the whole answer but trying to find out will be a valuable exercise.

In Chapter 4 we look in more detail at the methods you might use.

3

Class, Status and Power

If you stand a short way away from the bottom of a cliff you can often see lines running along the cliff-face indicating the various geological layers, or strata. Sociologists have borrowed this term 'strata' from the geologists and use it to describe levels which exist in society. Social stratification refers to the division of society into a number of levels placed above and below each other. You are probably familiar with the idea of 'social classes' but before we go on to examine the idea of class we must consider certain other forms of social stratification.

Social stratification

FEUDAL ESTATES

In medieval England society was divided into feudal estates. These were divisions based on land-holding and the obligation to fight for your lord.

> At the top stands a royal family and a landholding, hereditary military aristocracy, closely followed by an allied priesthood, ranking on a par with the secular nobility. Below them are merchants and craftsmen while free peasants and unfree serfs form the broad bottom strata. (Mayer 1955)

They were essentially man-made divisions for both king and nobles had the power to promote someone of low estate to a higher position. Each estate had its part to play in the life of the nation. 'The nobility were ordained to defend all, the clergy to pray for all and the commons to provide food for all.' It was a part of the system of a feudal society and when that form of society went into decline the system of estates went with it. In Sweden the four estates of nobles, clergy, citizens and peasants survived until 1866, but it had died out in most other parts of Europe well before then.

Estates divided up the power in society and restricted each individual's ability to change his status. Because position, power and

status were given at birth we would say that they were 'ascribed' (see
page 30). Very few people were able to improve themselves by their
own efforts. Only the most exceptional achieved the distinction of
ennoblement by the king. People had to be satisfied with their position
in the society. In the words of the Victorian hymn:

> The rich man in his castle,
> The poor man at his gate,
> God made them high and lowly,
> And ordered their estate.

Another hangover from the days of estates can be seen in the division
of Parliament into Lords and Commons.

CASTE

In India a very different form of social stratification operates. This is a
system of 'caste'. Each Hindu belongs to one of the four main castes or
is casteless, an untouchable. As in the system of estates position, status
and power are ascribed at birth. Caste is inherited and advancement in
this life at least is limited. You cannot work your way up in a caste
system. It is also difficult to marry into another caste. Indian society is
endogamous (see page 96), you may only marry someone of your caste.
Caste is supported by the religions of India. Hindu religious culture has
evolved rules, or *dharma*, which restrict contact between those of
different caste. These religious rules affect ordinary social contact as
well as marriage. A strict Brahmin, a member of the highest caste,
would take care not to come into contact with a lower caste such as the
Sudras, or with an untouchable. He would take care not to sit in the
same seat or drink from the same cup, or even be touched by his shadow.
Should he come into contact with someone of lower caste he would
ritually wash himself as an act of purification.

In recent years the Indian Government has tried very hard to remove
the worst injustices of the caste system. Mahatma Gandhi, the great
Indian reformer, called the untouchables 'Harijans' or 'God's people'
and they have now been given many social and political rights which
were once denied them. Despite this the system still exists. In any part
of India there might still be as many as 2 500 *jatis*, or subcastes, each
centred on a particular occupation, restricted by the rules of endogamy,
maintaining ritual distance from other *jatis* and obeying the *dharma*. By
such obedience the Hindu believes that he will attain a good *kharma*
and ensure rebirth into a higher caste in his next life.

THE IDEAS OF MARX

Much of our thinking about class originates in the writings of Karl
Marx who lived from 1818 to 1883. Marx held that class was based on

25

the organisation of production. The economic system of capitalism gave power to those who owned wealth and property. Marx pointed out that every aspect of life depended ultimately on how men provided themselves with 'material' things like food, clothing and shelter. In capitalist societies men and women provided for their material needs by selling their labour power to others who owned or controlled the forces of production. These forces of production included raw materials, factories, machines and the skills needed to use them. Various forms of production created particular relationships between the people involved. In a factory we find managers, foremen, charge hands, shop stewards, clerks, and many other types of worker. The social relationships between these different groups arose out of the way things are produced and Marx called these relationships the social relations of production.

For Marx the most important division of society created by the social relations of production was that between those who owned or controlled the forces of production – the capitalists – and those who sold their labour power – the workers or the proletariat. The differences of interest between these two groups inevitably led to conflict. In *The Communist Manifesto*, which Marx published with his friend Friedrich Engels in 1847, he wrote:

> The history of all hitherto existing society is the history of class struggles.
>
> Freeman and slave, patrician and plebeian, lord and serf, gild-master and journeyman, in a word oppressor and oppressed, stood in constant opposition to one another, carried on an uninterrupted, now hidden, now open, fight, a fight that each time ended either in a revolutionary reconstitution of society at large or in the common ruin of the contending classes.

In this approach to social class Marx introduced a further important idea. It is not enough for a class to exist simply because people share a similar position in society. People should also be conscious of their shared position. Marx distinguishes between the *objective* view of 'a class in itself' in which groups and individuals can be seen to have things in common and the *subjective* 'class for itself' in which people have an awareness of themselves as a class.

Class and status

Marx's view of social class focused on the relationship to the means of production and provides a valuable way of understanding the basic divisions of society. The Marxist approach is particularly useful when considering problems of the distribution of power and wealth in a society.

In our everyday use of the idea of class, however, we link these basic ideas of social and economic relationships to ideas of status and prestige. How do ordinary people see social class and how do they place others in a social class pattern? How, for example, would you 'class' the following occupations: tractor driver, carpenter, railway porter, barman and dock labourer? Are they all working class, or proletariat, and therefore all at the same level, or would you say that a carpenter has a higher position than a barman, or vice versa? How would you decide? Obviously a system based only on an individual's job is not adequate. It does not fully explain how people really see social differences. We must clearly take other factors into account.

We must, in fact, consider the individual's status in society. If social class is derived from how you earn your money then social status depends on how you spend it. One refers to the individual as a producer, the other to the individual as a consumer. Society is made up of a series of levels or status groups.

Each individual's status depends on a number of things. Occupation is obviously important. A doctor has higher status than a road sweeper largely because of his job. But status also takes into account education, level of income, style of life, patterns of consumption and so on. If two men sit opposite each other in the morning rush hour they will have a fair idea of each other's status without a word being spoken. If one is wearing a pin-stripe suit, regimental tie, and a bowler hat, and is carrying a rolled umbrella and a copy of *The Times* he would be given a different status from his companion who might be wearing working boots, overalls, a donkey jacket and cloth cap and have *The Sun* newspaper sticking out of his pocket. These visual symbols are very important in enabling us to 'place' people correctly on a scale of status. This is not meant to imply that either individual is any better or worse than the other. Sociology aims to be a value-free science. No doubt if they got talking and found that they had a common interest in cricket, or gardening, or youth work, they would get on very well together. It may be that communication at that level never gets a chance because of the way each man 'reads' the symbols of dress and accent.

We can get an even clearer picture of class and status if we take a closer look at Margaret Stacey's work on Banbury described in Chapter 1.

Class and status in Banbury

Each of the individuals described in the first Banbury study recognised the existence of class and status in some form or another. They did not always agree, but they felt themselves to be part of a stratified system. If we consider their ideas closely we will find that they are more aware of status difference than they are of social class. We would also find that they had two different ways of thinking of class and status, something which arose out of the situation in Banbury at the time of the study.

Sir William, Shaw and Grey, George and his neighbour would have accepted a view of class and status which is based on tradition. Lord A, Mr Brown and Ted held a non-traditional view. The traditional view is shown in Table 5.

A TRADITIONAL VIEW

Table 5. *The traditional pattern of class and status*

Class	Status group
Upper	1. County
	2. Gentry
Middle	3. Upper middle
	4. Middle
	5. Lower middle
Working	6. Respectable working
	7. Ordinary working
	8. Rough working

Source: Stacey 1960

All those in the 'working-class' group were wage earners. They earned their living with their hands. George, for example, is likely to have been employed as a craftsman in a traditional industry – cabinet making, a cooper or a wheelwright – or as an unskilled labourer – on a building site or in a flour mill. The job he does determines his social class. Manual work puts a man into the working-class group. Sociologists often speak of 'manual working class' when referring to this group.

Within the working class there are subgroups whose membership is based more on 'how you live' than on 'what you do'.

Within the working class in Banbury there are three status groups: the 'rough', the 'ordinary', and the 'respectable'. The 'roughs', often the poorest families, would like to lean heavily on their neighbours but they are discouraged. Their personal appearance and the state of their houses add to their unattractiveness as companions. The 'respectables' on the other hand are not expelled: they are 'stand-offish'. They are bent on improving their own social positions and close contact with neighbours is a part of the life of the social class they wish to leave behind. (Stacey 1960)

These groups have different levels of status within the working-class community.

The middle classes

Mr Grey and Mr Shaw are middle-class. Sociologists would say this because they earn their living in non-manual jobs. They have a certain status in the community. They behave in ways which are typical of middle-class people. For example, they live in larger houses than people like George and his neighbour. Shaw and Grey live in an area where many other middle-class people live.

Their houses, sometimes with three bedrooms and sometimes four, are found on the hilly land to the south and west, where there is a prospect of fields and woods. It is here that the more 'well-to-do' live. the larger tradesmen and senior officials. Their houses, owner occupied, are set well back from the road. Some are semi-detached but a noticeable number stand on their own; in either case most have garages. (Stacey 1960)

Such houses are an indication of status. But so also are their other activities. Messrs Shaw and Grey are actively involved in church activities, in politics, and organisations like the Rotary Club and the tennis club.

An examination of class and status in Banbury also reveals a third group – an upper class, which includes men like Sir William. Some people feel that there is no 'upper class' any more. Certainly it is diminishing in the country as a whole. The sort of upper-class groups found in Banbury by Margaret Stacey, owning land and having inherited status, is fast dying out.

A NON-TRADITIONAL VIEW

Alongside this 'traditional' class system there is the non-traditional. Lord A, Mr Brown and Ted are typical examples of people who think of themselves in non-traditional class and status terms. The non-traditional view is shown in Table 6.

It is difficult to link this non-traditional class and status system to the traditional system. There are some similarities – in the working class, for example – but in the middle-class groups there is considerable

Table 6. *The non-traditional pattern of class and status*

Class	Status group
Upper	1. Industrial upper
Middle	2. Senior managers and directors
	3. Newer professions
	4. Industrial technicians
Working	5. Respectable
	6. Ordinary
	7. Rough

Source: Stacey 1960

overlap. And many people would say that there is no 'upper class' in a modern industrial society. Although Lord A and his equals have many of the marks of an 'upper class' – large country houses, wealth, and power in politics as well as industry – they are often men who have 'made their own way in the world', often from quite humble origins. Their wealth, power, status and titles are seldom inherited from their ancestors, as it was for Sir William. In many ways this group merges with the 'upper-middle-class' group in a way which was not possible with the 'traditional' aristocracy.

Status – achieved and ascribed

In a 'traditional' system position in society is established at birth; it is handed on from father to son. This process is termed 'ascription' and the status which is passed on in this way is 'ascribed status'. In more advanced industrial societies status goes to those who have done the most to earn it. It is 'achieved status'. Mr Brown gives us a good example of achieved status. His father was a coal miner in Durham. When 'young Brown' won a scholarship to the grammar school the family scrimped and saved to make ends meet. He did well in his 'A' levels and got to university where he studied metallurgy. He now works in Banbury in the research department of the aluminium factory. His roots are working class but his achievements have put him into the middle class. He is a good example of upward social mobility.

An important feature of advanced industrial society is this ability to move from one class in society to another. It is not something which can happen overnight. It can only be seen clearly when a son's job is compared to his father's. Because status in modern industrial societies is achieved, and depends on 'merit' such societies have been described as 'meritocracies'. This is in contrast to the traditional society which included an 'aristocracy'.

30

Power

The words 'meritocracy' and 'aristocracy' also refer to the way in which power is distributed in a society. In traditional societies 'power' was 'ascribed' and lay in the hands of an inherited 'ruling class'. In Britain today the amount of power a man has depends far more on what he has achieved – on merit. We can see this clearly when we compare Sir William and Lord A in Banbury. Sir William possesses ascribed status and power. His family have been important in that area for generations and in the past have exercised considerable power. Once the entire country was ruled by men like Sir William and by the 'aristocracy'. Today his neighbour Lord A has far more power. Lord A's power is not local; it is national. He is chairman of his own company and on the board of directors of many others. His advice is called for on many matters of national importance and he deals with governments and companies all over the world. Thousands of men's jobs come under his chairmanship, and though his power is not 'absolute' – his shareholders could give him the sack – it is still very considerable. Unlike Sir William, Lord A did not inherit his position. He 'made his own way' in the world, starting from fairly ordinary beginnings. His title came somewhat late in life as a symbol of the recognition of his achievements. His son, who will not continue the title, is expected to make his 'own way in the world', too. His position in life will also depend on his achievements even though he had a far better start than his father.

In reality the division of power in Banbury is more complex. In the second study of the town Margaret Stacey concluded that there was no one group or individual holding complete power. She suggests that a number of elite groups are able to exert influence in different areas of life. Many important decisions for the town were made by politicians in London. Within the town decisions were influenced by a number of different groups: the trades council, the Chamber of Commerce, ratepayers' associations and a range of smaller 'pressure' groups (see Chapter 9).

It is clear, however, that power is not shared equally in Banbury, nor in any other community. Certain individuals and groups have more power to influence events, make decisions or affect the lives of others than do other individuals or groups.

MAX WEBER

These three main ideas – class, status and power – are brought together in the writings of Max Weber, a German sociologist who lived in the early part of this century. Weber's view of 'class' is similar to that of

31

Marx. To Weber, however, 'class' is not simply a matter of owning or not owning capital but also includes the opportunities and advantages a person receives from his or her position in the economic system. A shop-floor worker in a factory is not only a seller of 'labour-power' to a capitalist. He is also a 'worker' as distinct from a 'manager', with different hours, different privileges and different opportunities.

Whereas class concerns the individual's position in a system of production, status is linked to 'consumption'. An individual's status depends on the way other people see them. In Weber's view status is a 'subjective' matter. We can see this in the division of the Banbury working-class groups into 'respectable', 'ordinary', and 'rough'.

Weber's third aspect of social stratification is 'power' which again while linked to class and status is not always so. The Queen is undoubtedly very rich and has very high status but is she more powerful than Parliament or the Prime Minister? Trade union leaders are not the highest paid people in the country, nor do they have great status but in certain situations they have considerable power. Class, power and status may be linked but they may also be quite separate. The barrow-boy who 'makes good' ends up with a chain of supermarkets, may have a large house, a chauffeur-driven Rolls Royce and a yacht at Monte Carlo but need not be accepted by his neighbours as a 'person of class'. Nor might he have power outside of his own business interests.

This chapter began with a view of stratification which compared it to strata on a rock face. We can now see that such a picture is too simple and that social differences depend on a number of different factors. This becomes clearer when we examine how class, status and power change.

SOCIAL MOBILITY

Movement between social classes is described as social mobility. In the Banbury example Mr Brown (page 7) is an example of upward social mobility. In real life very few people go from 'rags to riches' in one generation. 'Log cabin to White House' or 'grocer's shop to 10 Downing Street' may be many a father's dream for his son or his daughter. It seldom happens that way. Most people end up fairly close to the social class from which they set out, moving up or down one step on the ladder, across one frontier.

It is not only the individual who improves or declines in status. Sometimes whole classes of worker change their status.

In 1876 the Secretary of the London and Westminster Bank told a Civil Service inquiry that 'the general social status of clerks' was 'upper middle' and that 'as a rule we would not introduce the sons of shopkeepers' but 'only sons of clergy, military and medical men'. However, a series of surveys in the 1950s showed that between one-third and one-half of clerical workers thought that they were working class and that over 40 per cent were sons of manual workers. The status of clerical workers as a class had declined when compared to the status of skilled manual workers. This does not mean that clerks have become 'working class' or that skilled manual workers have become middle class but that the two groups cannot be separated as clearly as they could in 1876. The clerk's status position has become uncertain. He does not know quite where he stands on the status ladder. His style of life and working situation seem middle class but his pay is often less than that of a factory worker. Sociologists term this 'status ambiguity'. The clerical worker's status is uncertain or ambiguous. He doesn't quite 'know where he stands' (see Chapter 8).

At the same time that the clerk's position has declined, other groups have improved their status. The 'new professions' and 'industrial technicians' in Banbury's non-traditional status system are examples of this. Neither of these groups appears in the traditional pattern of class and status. They are new groups. Such occupations hardly existed at the turn of the century. These groups include research scientists, like Mr Brown, computer programmers, management staff and junior executives, teachers and lecturers, as well as laboratory technicians, supervisors, and junior administrative staff. The status of all of these groups is rising. Modern industry needs their skills. Membership of these groups depends on education and achievement, not on inheritance and ascription. They might be called a 'new middle class' in contrast to the 'old middle class' of men like Mr Shaw and Mr Grey. Mr Brown, with his university education and his 'white-collar' job, is a good example of such a new middle class, and while he individually is making progress in his career he is a member of a profession which is also climbing.

This process by which some sections of the working class seem to merge into the middle class is known as 'embourgeoisement'.

The affluent worker

This idea of 'embourgeoisement' (which means 'becoming bourgeoise', or middle class) has been argued about for many years. It begins with the attempt to explain why the revolution that Marx predicted did not happen in Britain. It has been suggested that modern capitalism, with the help of the Welfare State, has improved everyone's standard of living to such an extent that classes have almost ceased to exist. This

33

is summed up in the phrase 'we are all middle class now'. The old working-class life-styles are supposed to have disappeared with increases in real income, improved living conditions, greater home-ownership, urban re-development and so on. The worker has become affluent.

John Goldthorpe and David Lockwood (1969) did not accept this view. They thought it was too simple and ignored many of the real facts. From 1962 to 1968 they carried out a study of workers in Luton which aimed, among other things, at discovering if embourgeoisement had taken place. They chose Luton because it was an expanding prosperous town where you would expect to find lots of 'affluent workers'. If embourgeoisement was taking place anywhere it would, they argued, be taking place in Luton.

They focused on three aspects of the lives of their sample of 300 industrial workers. Firstly – the work the men did; secondly – the social lives of the men and their families; and thirdly – their hopes for the future and views on life generally.

Not surprisingly they discovered that the work situations of the men had not changed greatly. They were still in the position of selling their skills to the employer and to achieve a 'middle-class' income required considerable amounts of overtime. Social life on the smart new Luton housing estates was seen to be different from traditional working-class life-styles. The differences were not seen as a movement to middle-class ways but as an adaptation of the old working-class patterns. The social networks were more likely to be based on the family and not on friends. Husbands and wives shared fewer friends and they belonged to fewer clubs or associations. Similarly, the affluent workers studied did not seem to have adopted middle-class attitudes.

'Therefore', they concluded, 'we held to the view that the thesis of the progressive embourgeoisement of the British working class was, to say the least, not proven; and that as usually presented, it involved a variety of confused and dubious assertions.'

Measuring social class

It should be clear by now that social class is not easy to define. Sociologists use a variety of different meanings which are very often different from those used in everyday conversation. This becomes a particular problem when social class is a feature of social research. The researcher needs to be able to put individuals into social class categories consistently and reliably. The categories used must also be as close as possible to real life, everyday categories.

THE REGISTRAR GENERAL

One social classification which is very widely used is produced by the Registrar General. It was first used in the 1911 Census and has been revised a number of times since then. It is still used in the ten-yearly Census of Population and in most government reports and surveys. It has a five-point scale with each group based on a particular range of jobs. Group III is often divided into manual and non-manual sections.

Table 7. *The Registrar General's social classification*

Non-manual occupations		
Class I Professional	Doctor, dentist, engineer, scientist, university lecturer, etc	A
Class II Managerial and technical	Manager, librarian, teacher, nurse, other technical occupations: pharmacist, laboratory technician, owner of small business, etc	B
Class III (non-manual) Clerical and minor supervisory	Clerk, commercial traveller, typist, draughtsman, policeman, secretary, shop assistant, etc	C1
Skilled manual work		
Class III (manual) Skilled trades	Carpenter, cook, driver, electrician, fitter, hairdresser, instrument maker, painter, printer, tailor, toolmaker, etc	C2
Semi-skilled and unskilled manual work		
Class IV Semi-skilled work	Assembler, bus conductor, farm worker, machine operator, postman, roundsman, stoker, store-keeper, waiter, etc	D
Class V Unskilled work	Kitchen hand, labourer, messenger, office cleaner, porter, window cleaner, etc	E

Not all Government surveys use the Registrar General's social classification. A number make use of the classification of socio-economic groups. A variation of the classification of socio-economic groups is used by the General Household Survey.

While the social classification tries to arrange people's jobs into some kind of order based on status and skill, the socio-economic groups are merely groups of people whose 'social, cultural and recreational standards are similar'. They are not arranged in any particular order.

Table 8. *The socio-economic grouping*

1. Employers and managers in central and local government, industry, commerce, etc. – large establishments.
2. Employers and managers in industry and commerce, etc. – small establishments.
3. Professional workers – self-employed.
4. Professional workers – employees.
5. Intermediate non-manual workers.
6. Junior non-manual workers.
7. Personal service workers.
8. Foremen and supervisors – manual.
9. Skilled manual workers.
10. Semi-skilled manual workers.
11. Unskilled manual workers.
12. Own account workers (other than professional).
13. Farmers – employers and managers.
14. Farmers – own account.
15. Agricultural workers.
16. Members of Armed Forces.
17. Occupations which are inadequately described.

OTHER CLASSIFICATIONS

The Registrar General's scales are often criticised for being too vague and for being too much concerned with occupations. They do not reflect divisions of status clearly enough. A librarian in Class II may have the same status as a university lecturer in Class I, possibly higher. An alternative scale was developed by J. Hall and D. Caradog Jones by asking people how they rated various occupations. The resulting Hall-Jones Scale is a seven-point scale and takes status into account as well as just occupation.

A major use for social classifications is in the market research industry. Market researchers attempt, among other things, to discover the likely demand for new products about to be put on the market and the pattern of demand for existing products. Their customers include everyone from soap powder manufacturers to political parties. As class and status play an important part in determining a person's shopping habits it is important that the researchers have a clear classification to use. The usual market research classification is shown in the right-hand column of Table 7. The link with the Registrar General's scale is only very rough. Market research organisations take many more factors into account. They would be concerned with income, house ownership, education and subjective factors like speech, and attitudes. Similar scales are used by the opinion polls which test public opinion before elections.

Social classifications such as these are used to give general indications of links between social class and education, consumption, political attitudes and so on. They do not make it possible for sociologists to make predictions about the behaviour of individuals. Their main use is to indicate general trends over an average group of people.

How do people see themselves?

We now have a fairly clear idea of how sociologists see social class. But there is one final question we must ask: does it really work out like this? If sociology is a search for reality we must consider how far the sociologists' view actually fits real life. Would the ordinary man-in-the-street decide which class he belongs to in the same way as the sociologist does? Would he reach the same answer?

In considering this we need to understand the idea of reference group, or frame of reference.

Fig. 2. *The frame of reference*

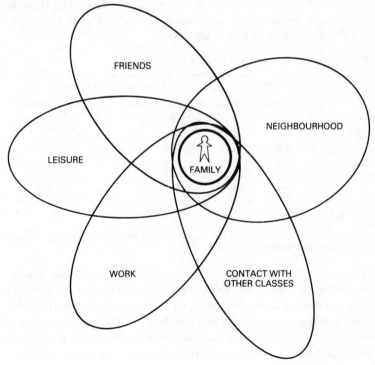

Each one of us lives in a social world. Even the hermit living in his cave cannot escape from the knowledge and ideas gained through growing up in a society. Our membership of societies shapes our attitudes and beliefs about ourselves and about the way the world is. Those individual beliefs are not unique. We share them with those around us. They are part of our social world. Our frame of reference is that community of people who are most important in shaping our ideas and beliefs. Family, friends and neighbourhood are all important. Those we work with may also have an influence and the media – television and the newspapers – may introduce us to other groups to whom we may refer.

How each individual places himself in a social scale depends on his frame of reference. Whilst to a sociologist one individual may appear to be working class he may claim to be middle class. Perhaps he wishes to keep himself at a distance from those he regards as beneath him. Perhaps he thinks he is on the way up, or his family background is middle class. A large number of things are likely to influence the individual's self-image of class and status. Butler and Stokes (Macmillan 1969, Penguin 1971) found that this 'self-assigned' class was generally related to occupational status. But there were some major exceptions. Nine per cent of the unskilled manual workers interviewed regarded themselves as middle class and one-fifth of the higher managerial group felt themselves to be working class.

Table 9. *Occupational status and social class*

	MANAGERIAL		NON-MANUAL		MANUAL	
	Higher	*Lower*	*Supervisory*	*Lower*	*Skilled*	*Unskilled*
	I	II	III	IV	V	VI
Claiming to be:	%	%	%	%	%	%
(a) *Middle class*	78	65	60	32	17	9
(b) *Working class*	22	35	40	68	83	91
	100	100	100	100	100	100

Source: Butler and Stokes 1969

(Butler and Stokes used an amended market research classification with group C1 divided into supervisory and lower non-manual.)

Obviously most people assign themselves to a social class which is close to their real position. Only 4 per cent of the Butler and Stokes sample did not see themselves in social class or status terms (including a jovial publican who said he was a member of the sporting class). In general, people are aware of inequalities in the distribution of wealth, prestige and power and through their frame of reference are able to place themselves within the class system. But not everyone sees the class system in the same terms.

Ted – us and them

In the last chapter we read about Ted, a shop steward from Banbury.

> Ted, like his father, has been a 'union man' ever since he started work. He is a Labour councillor. The class system for him is a matter of worker or not worker. He accepts his status as a worker and is proud of it, but, unlike George, he will not accept patronage from his 'betters'. 'The workers look after their own', he says. He does not accept that he has 'betters' and rejects the leadership of people like Sir William, Shaw and Grey. He supports the Labour Party. He wants to improve the lot of the workers as a class. (Stacey 1960)

Ted sees social class as a division between bosses and workers. A conflict not unlike the Marxist view we studied earlier. In Ted's mind what really matters is the way power is exercised. The workers must stand together in order to have power. Society divides into 'us' and 'them', boss and worker. A worker who crosses the line between one and the other is a traitor to his class.

CLASS AS A LADDER

The alternative view sees social class as a ladder with many rungs. If you work hard you will climb the ladder and your status will increase. What matters most is to make your own way in the world using your abilities to the full. These two views are extremes. In reality most people's ideas come somewhere between the two. But the extremes can provide models of certain types of attitude which will help us to understand the reality which lies between.

MODELS OF CLASS

We can use the terms 'Status model' and 'Power model' to describe them.

	Status model	Power model
Social class	Mainly middle class	Mainly working class
Class perspective	Individualism	Collectivism
Image of society	'Status ladder'	'Us' and 'them'
Values	Stand on your own feet, don't sponge off others	Stick with your mates, make the best of things

39

Attitudes of education	Work hard at school to get a good start in life	Get a good job with a bit of money. Learn a trade
Attitudes to work	A chance to get on in life. Earn the respect of your colleagues	It brings in money to spend when you are not working. Work is not something you enjoy
Attitudes to poverty	Hard work is the best cure for poverty. Why should we support the idle?	It can happen to anyone. We may be next. A matter of 'luck of the draw'
Attitudes to trade unions	They have too much power. They prevent individuals from using their initiative and restrict the right to work	The workers must stand together. 'United we stand, divided we fall'
Politics	The Conservatives give a man the chance to better himself	The Labour Party stands for the working man. It is out to help the underdog.

These two models represent two separate systems of thought. They are extremes but they show how the different ideas of 'power' and 'status' can fit into a system of belief and attitudes which are total, covering all aspects of an individual's view of society.

Such models could be taken even further. They could be extended to include attitudes to the family, to law and order, to religion and so on. We shall see some of these further perspectives of social class and status in later chapters.

4
Sociologists at Work

In Chapters 1 and 2 you read about the work of some sociologists. In this chapter, we will consider the methods used by sociologists in more detail. There are three things to remember before we do this. Firstly, sociologists do not always carry out their studies in the way textbooks say that they do. In real life the researcher must adapt the rule to fit particular situations. You would not expect a great artist to 'paint by numbers', nor would you expect a good sociologist to do everything as it is laid down in textbooks.

Secondly, sociologists are human. They have their own preferences and prejudices. They also make mistakes. They are on the whole honest and act in good faith when making judgements or carrying out research, but, their work needs to be looked at critically. There is an old saying 'No one is ever perfect'. It is as true for sociologists as it is for all other scientists. When you read sociological studies you must watch out for any weaknesses or any statements with which you do not agree. Remember that we all have our own view of the world which influences the way we see events. If you feel that a piece of sociology is wrong, or biased, then say so. The ability to make sensible criticism is an important part of the work of the sociologist.

Thirdly, we should always remember that investigating the social world is very different from investigating the natural world. Unlike the chemist, who works in his laboratory studying substances in test-tubes, or the physicist who probes the structure of a particular molecule, the social scientist studies something of which he is himself a member. The sociologist must never lose sight of the fact that he or she is part of that social world which is being studied. We have all grown up in it, have feelings about it and are affected by it. When we attempt to study it we cannot escape from being part of it. In a study using interviews, for example, the information we receive may be affected by whom we are, why we are doing it, how we speak or dress, or behave, to the person interviewed. A chemical in a test-tube is not going to bother about the chemist's accent, or how he dresses. A person being interviewed in a social survey may be influenced by such things, and it could affect the findings.

The sociologist as researcher

As we saw in Chapter 1 sociologists have a number of different ways of gathering information. We can sort these different research methods into four groups.

1 Research which relies on other people's evidence. We will call this a *documentary* method.
2 Research which seeks answers to particular questions from fairly large groups of people with fairly short, often very short, periods of contact. This we will call *survey* method.
3 Research which involves the sociologists working very closely among those he or she studies, often for quite long periods of time. This is an *observation* method. Sometimes the sociologists participate in the lives of those studied. This then becomes *participant observation*.
4 Research which involves carefully chosen groups of people who are placed in different situations to see what happens. This is an *experimental method*.

Very often these methods are combined to give different views of the same subject. As we saw in Chapter 1, documentary evidence on Banbury was combined with survey data and participant observation.

Whichever method, or combination of methods, is chosen the researcher must go through certain stages and apply certain basic rules. Any piece of research begins with a *creative* stage. The sociologist is faced by a problem and begins to look for explanations. He may begin with a 'why?' problem: 'Why do certain groups of people go to church?', 'Why do people cause trouble at football matches?'.

It may be a 'What if?' problem: 'What would happen to children if they were sent to different schools?', 'What would be the results of a general election next week?'. It may be a 'how' problem: 'How do the lives of people in Newcastle differ from those of people in London?'.

From the problem, and what is known about the world – including what has been learned from other sociologists – the researcher develops an hypothesis. This is a 'hunch' about what might be the answer. The hypothesis, or hunch, needs to be tested. This leads to a *technical* stage where the researcher must design an investigation, choosing the methods which are likely to lead to the best evidence. The investigation must then be carried out. Finally there is a *theoretical* stage at which all of the information must be analysed and compared to the hypothesis before any final conclusions are reached. These three stages – creative, technical and theoretical, may take anything from a few weeks to many years. Often they run into one another with each new piece of evidence producing new hypotheses, requiring new or changed methods and leading to new conclusions.

IS IT GOOD RESEARCH?

In all of this the researcher must keep certain basic questions in his mind.

1 He must decide whether he is looking for evidence which will prove his hunch to be right or evidence that could prove it to be wrong. Both methods are used. Decide for yourself which gives the better result:
   (a) the study which produces evidence in favour of the hypothesis
   (b) the study which is unable to find any evidence against the hypothesis (assuming that both studies were carried out with equal care and thoroughness).

2 He must make sure that the methods used, and the results gained are 'valid'. Has the research, in fact, measured what it was supposed to measure. A survey on crime, for example, might use police statistics as a measure of how much crime occurs. Experience has shown this not to be a valid measure. Much crime is not reported to the police and therefore does not get counted in their statistics.

3 The methods used must also be reliable. Would the same methods used by different people in different places, even at different times, give the same results. You could test this for yourself by carrying out a simple survey in a shopping street or at a bus stop, in the morning, mid-day and evening. It is unlikely that you would get the same results each time.

4 When you analyse the results of any research you must look to see how close your results are to what you might predict from your hypothesis. They will never match exactly. You must decide how close is 'close enough'. Researchers use 'tests of significance' to measure the closeness of their original hunches to what the collected evidence shows. If the prediction and the evidence do not match you must decide whether your hypothesis is wrong, the methods are at fault, or it is a chance result. Sociologists must decide how close they must be for the result to be significant.

5 In sociology it is often difficult to control the various things which might affect the result. A biologist studying the effect of light on plants can put a plant in a darkened cupboard, and leave an identical plant, treated the same in every other way, in sunlight. This second plant is the 'control'. The only difference between the two plants is

the amount of light they receive. Sociologists cannot control the various influences on their research in quite the same way. Instead they try to build in statistical controls.

6 Many sociological studies are concerned with particular groups of people – housewives, office workers, people living in Grimsby, Methodists, etc. These are quite large groups and it would be very expensive and often inconvenient to interview them all, or to send them all a questionnaire. Therefore, researchers take a *sample* from the group and base their findings on them. Sampling is considered in more detail later in this chapter. The important question which concerns us now is 'how *representative* is the sample?' Are the answers the sample gives us the answers we would get from the whole group?

We often want to apply evidence from the study of one group of people to a larger group or to other groups. It is important to know if the groups studied are typical or if they differ in important ways. Is your school or college typical of all schools or colleges? Is your class typical? How far should evidence from your class, or school, or college be used to support hypotheses about classes, schools or colleges in general?

7 Finally, the sociologist must be prepared to put his research – its hypothesis and results – to the test of review by other sociologists. It must be compared to existing theories and to previous research. The research may just fill in a gap in our existing knowledge, or it may be so revolutionary as to make us rethink all that has gone before. If that does happen, other sociologists will want to test the results, even repeat the research before deciding whether to accept it or not. Sociologists call this *replicability*.

Whenever you read a piece of sociological research ask yourself these questions:

1 Did the research actually measure what it set out to measure and would someone else have got similar results using similar methods?

2 Are the results what you would have expected on the basis of your commonsense knowledge, and from other things you have studied?

3 Could any other factors have influenced the results in ways which the researcher might not have noticed?

4 How do the results affect the way I now understand things?

Using documentary evidence

Documentary evidence is often used in sociology. When working from documents the sociologist is using evidence which has probably been collected for some other purpose – either by official agencies or by other social scientists. This will often influence how such evidence is used. The researcher must decide how *reliable* the evidence is and how *valid*. It is not enough to accept documentary evidence at face value. You must always ask yourself three questions: Why was this evidence collected? Who collected it? How was it collected?

An American sociologist, Harold Garfinkel, attempted a study of patients in a hospital out-patient clinic. His main source of information on the way patients were dealt with by the clinic came from the patients' official records which had been kept by the nurses and doctors. These documents were supposed to contain basic information about the patient – such as age, sex, occupation – and details of diagnosis and treatment. Garfinkel soon found that these 'official records' were of very little help in his research. They were in fact 'bad' records. Other researchers working with similar official files had noticed the same thing. This led Garfinkel to ask the questions: 'Why are record files like these always so bad?' and 'Why are 'bad files' normal?'. The answers, he suggests, are to be found in the way the files are written up and in the people who write them up.

When people become doctors or nurses it is not because they want to spend their time filling-in official forms. They want to get on with the job of caring for people and making them well. If the information in an official file helps them to do that job they are more likely to give it time and care. Information for which they see no value is usually less well recorded. This is often the case with information that is required for 'official' records. More effort is needed to gain certain types of information. You can tell someone's 'race' or 'sex' usually at a glance. Guesses about 'age' are fairly accurate. Most people will tell you about their religion, if they are married or where they live. Information about their health, education or occupation takes a little more effort on the part of the form-filler. As the form-fillers are usually busy people with many other things to do they must decide if the effort needed in getting the information accurately is justified by its value to them in their work. Often it isn't and the 'official document' will be a 'bad' source of information.

Garfinkel realised that collecting information for official forms in the clinic was not a matter of putting the right answers in the right places on the forms. The form filling, and the keeping of records about patients, was part of the relationship between a doctor and the patient. They were intended to be read by particular groups of people who knew the situation and understood the work of the clinic. To the doctors who used them they were probably quite good records. To the sociologist researching the organisation of the clinic they were very bad records.

45

Fig. 3. *The census districts*
(a) Enumeration District (ED)

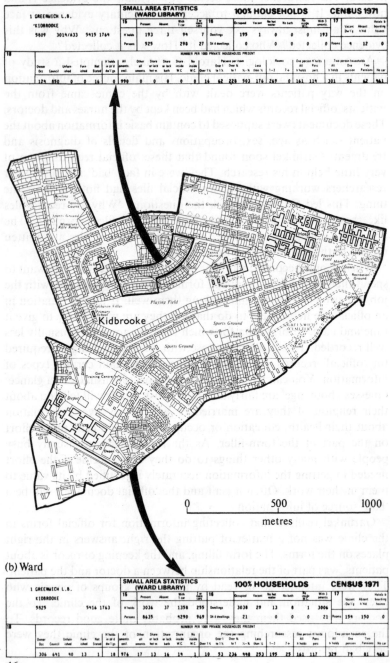

1 GREENWICH L.B. *KIDBROOKE 5809 3014/A33 5415 1764	SMALL AREA STATISTICS (WARD LIBRARY)						100% HOUSEHOLDS							CENSUS 1971		
	15	Present	Absent	With 1 car	2 or more cars	**16**	Occupied	Vacant	No hot water	No bath	No inside W.C.	With 3 amenits.	**17**	Vacant Dw'l'g	Absent h'h'ld	Hotels b boarding houses
	H'holds	193	3	94	7	Dwellings	195	1	0	0	0	193				
	Persons	925		298	27	Sh'd dwellings	0		0	0	0	0	Rooms	9	12	0

											NUMBER PER 1000 PRIVATE HOUSEHOLDS PRESENT														
18	Owner Occ	Council	Unfur ished	Furn ished	Not Stated	H'holds in sh'd dw'l'gs	All amenits. excl.	Other all amenits.	Share or lack hot w	Share or lack bath	Share inside W.C.	No inside W.C.	Over 1	Over ½ to 1½	to 1½ to 1	½–½	Less than ½	1–2	7+	All h holds	Pers pers	All h holds	One pension	Two Pensions	No car
	124	850	0	0	16	0	990	0	0	0	0	16	62	228	503	176	269	0	161	114	301	52	62	961

(b) Ward

1 GREENWICH L.B. KIDBROOKE 5825 5416 1763	SMALL AREA STATISTICS (WARD LIBRARY)						100% HOUSEHOLDS							CENSUS 1971		
	15	Present	Absent	With 1 car	2 or more cars	**16**	Occupied	Vacant	No hot water	No bath	No inside W.C.	With 3 amenits.	**17**	Vacant Dw'l'g	Absent h'h'ld	Hotels b boarding houses
	H'holds	3036	37	1358	255	Dwellings	3038	29	13	8	1	3006				
	Persons	8635		4290	969	Sh'd dwellings	21		0	0	0	21	Rooms	154	150	0

											NUMBER PER 1000 PRIVATE HOUSEHOLDS PRESENT														
18	Owner Occ	Council	Unfur ished	Furn ished	Not Stated	H'holds in sh'd dw'l'gs	All amenits. excl.	Other all amenits.	Share or lack hot w	Share or lack bath	Share inside W.C.	No inside W.C.	Over 1	Over ½ to 1½	to 1½ to 1	½–½	Less than ½	1–2	7+	All h holds	Pers pers	All h holds	One pension	Two Pensions	No car
	306	641	40	13	1	18	976	17	13	16	19	1	10	53	236	498	252	195	25	161	117	329	79	81	961

0   500   1000
metres

The example shows some of the problems we must face when using any documentary evidence. Never accept anything at its face value. Try to imagine how a number or a heading came to be on a table of figures or on a graph. Think back to the point of time when that number was an actual person doing everyday things. How did the actions of that person, and of many others come to be a statistic?

THE CENSUS

An important source of documentary evidence is The Census of Population which is carried out every ten years, and has been since 1801 (with the exception of 1941 in the middle of the Second World War). It is a unique kind of survey which aims to count every man, woman and child in the United Kingdom on one Sunday night in April. Information is also collected on their families, the dwelling in which they live, education, work and a number of other topics.

The census is planned and co-ordinated by a Government department, the Office of Population Censuses and Surveys (OPCS). The information is collected by enumerators who distribute census forms and often help people to fill them in. Each enumerator works in an enumeration district (ED) which covers an area of roughly 150 households. The information from all the households is put together into overall figures for the enumeration district which are then added to the information from other EDs to produce the figures for the ward. The ward figures are then added to the figures from other wards to produce County or Borough tables which, in turn, go towards regional and national figures. Fig. 3 shows the Kidbrooke Ward for the London Borough of Greenwich. The enumeration districts can be seen and part of the ED data for one enumeration district is shown at the top of the page. At the bottom of the page you can see the same information for the whole ward.

It is some years before the census information is finally published, though Preliminary Statistics are available within a matter of months. Apart from the sheer size of the task of co-ordinating information from 102 000 census enumerators covering over 10 million households and residential institutions the Office of Population Censuses and Surveys must also carry out checks to ensure that the information gained is as accurate as it can possibly be. Post-enumeration surveys involving 40 000 households are carried out a few weeks after the main census date and the census figures are checked against the registers of births, marriages and deaths. These checks on the census show that as a whole the census is remarkably accurate. The total population recorded in the 1961 census was within 54 000 of the expected population based on the registration of births and deaths. In a total population

47

of 52 000 000 that is a possible error in the region of 0·1 per cent.

Inaccuracies may arise within the census for a number of reasons. There is always a danger that someone may be left off the census form when it is returned to the enumerator. This is most likely to happen where there are large numbers of people living in one place, particularly in multi-occupied houses. There may be a misunderstanding of the purpose of the census which leads to under-registration. In 1971 many people objected to census questions concerning the places of birth of their parents. Immigrants feared that the answers to such questions might one day be used to return them to countries which were no longer theirs. In addition there may be people who have entered the country illegally and would not want to be identified on a census return.

Another type of problem arises when people are not sure what parts of the census form mean. In 1951, for example, the number of rooms

Fig. 4. *The census form*

1971 CENSUS — ENGLAND

H Form For Private Households

To the Head (or Acting Head) of the Household.

Please complete this form and have it ready for collection on Monday 26th April. If you need help, do not hesitate to ask the enumerator.

The enumerator may ask you any questions necessary to help him to complete or correct the form.

The information you give on the form will be treated as CONFIDENTIAL and used only for compiling statistics. No information about named individuals will be passed by the Census Office to any other Government Department or any other authority or person. If anyone in the census organisation improperly discloses information you provide, he will be liable to prosecution. Similarly you must not disclose information which anyone (for example, a visitor or boarder) gives you to enable you to complete the form.

The legal obligation to fill in the whole form rests on YOU, but each person who has to be included is required to give you the information you need. However, anyone who wishes can ask the enumerator or local Census Officer for a personal form which can be returned direct to the enumerator or local Census Officer and then you need answer only questions B1 and B5 for that person.

PLEASE TAKE NOTE

There are penalties of up to £50 for failing to comply with the requirements described above, or for giving false information.

When you have completed the form, please sign the declaration at the foot of the last page.

Office of Population Censuses and Surveys,
Titchfield,
Fareham, Hants.

MICHAEL REED
Director and
Registrar General

*A household comprises **either** one person living alone **or** a group of persons (who may or may not be related) living at the same address with common housekeeping. Persons staying temporarily with the household are included.*

To be completed by enumerator			
C.D. No.	E.D. No.	Form No.	Ref.

If sharing with another household :—

Hall, staircase, passage, etc., shared *only/not only** for entry to accommodation.

*delete whichever is inapplicable.

Number of rooms shared. ....

Name and full postal address:

....

SPECIMEN

PART A

Answer questions A1—A5 about your household's accommodation and then answer questions B1—B24 overleaf and if appropriate answer questions C1—C7.

Where boxes are provided answer by putting a tick in the box against the answer which applies. For example, if the answer is 'YES': ☑ YES ☐ NO

PLEASE WRITE IN INK OR BALLPOINT PEN

A1
How do you and your household occupy your accommodation?

1 ☐ As an owner occupier (including purchase by mortgage)
2 ☐ By renting it from a Council or New Town
3 ☐ As an unfurnished letting from a private landlord or company or Housing Association
4 ☐ As a furnished letting
5 ☐ In some other way (Please give details, including whether furnished or unfurnished)

....

Note: If the accommodation is occupied by lease originally granted for, or since extended to, more than 21 years, tick 'owner occupier'.

A2
Does your household share with anyone else the use of any room, or hall, passage, landing, or staircase?

☐ YES ☐ NO

A3
How many rooms are there in your household's accommodation? ....

Do not count
Small kitchens less than 6ft. wide,
bathrooms and toilets,
sculleries not used for cooking,
closets, pantries and storerooms,
landings, halls, lobbies or recesses,
offices or shops used solely for business purposes.

Note
A large room divided by a sliding or fixed partition should be counted as two rooms.
A room divided by curtains or portable screens should be counted as one room.

A4
How many **cars and vans** are normally available for use by you or members of your household (other than visitors)? ....

Include any provided by employers if normally available for use by you or members of your household, but exclude vans used solely for the carriage of goods.

If None, write 'NONE'.

A5
Has your household the use of the following amenities on these premises?

a **A cooker or cooking stove** with an oven
1 ☐ YES — for use only by this household
2 ☐ YES — for use also by another household
3 ☐ NO

b **A kitchen sink** permanently connected to a water supply and a waste pipe
1 ☐ YES — for use only by this household
2 ☐ YES — for use also by another household
3 ☐ NO

c **A fixed bath or shower** permanently connected to a water supply and a waste pipe
1 ☐ YES — for use only by this household
2 ☐ YES — for use also by another household
3 ☐ NO

d **A hot water** supply (to a washbasin, or kitchen sink, or bath, or shower) from a heating appliance or boiler which is connected to a piped water supply
1 ☐ YES — for use only by this household
2 ☐ YES — for use also by another household
3 ☐ NO

e **A flush toilet** (W.C.) with entrance **inside** the building
1 ☐ YES — for use only by this household
2 ☐ YES — for use also by another household
3 ☐ NO

f **A flush toilet** (W.C.) with entrance **outside** the building
1 ☐ YES — for use only by this household
2 ☐ YES — for use also by another household
3 ☐ NO

1

PLEASE TURN OVER TO PART B →

in some houses was not properly recorded. The definition asked for 'rooms used for living, eating and sleeping'. For many people this did not include unused 'spare rooms' and they were not counted. These ambiguities in the census return are usually corrected in the following census when definitions are brought up to date and new questions are included. Changes in definitions between censuses often make comparison difficult. In 1951 the census asked for 'the usual employment' of all wage-earners. Some who were unemployed put down their usual occupation and made no mention of unemployment; some who were trained in one job but were at that time doing something else wrote down what they were trained for. In 1961 this was tightened up by asking about their employment in the week before census day and in 1971 the question for the 'main employment in the week before census day'.

Other problems may arise because of administrative changes, such as changes in local government boundaries or the school-leaving age; problems in sampling when a sample census is taken; and problems of misinformation as when someone enters the wrong age. The effect of these difficulties on the whole census is usually slight. They may be more significant in particular areas or among particular groups of people. These problems are not restricted to the census: they are also found in many other types of social survey.

OTHER SOURCES OF DOCUMENTARY EVIDENCE

Social scientists use many other pieces of documentary evidence in addition to the census. Nearly every organisation in the country publishes some kind of report and many of these contain information which is useful to the sociologist. These reports which come from government departments, private and nationalised industries, trade unions and employer organisations, research associations, local councils and many other bodies contain three types of data. Firstly there are statistics which are collected in the normal work of the organisation. Your school or college will make regular returns of the number of pupils, their age, and sex; the police keep records of the number of crimes reported; the immigration officials record the numbers entering or leaving the country; employers keep records of the number of workers, hours lost through absenteeism, and so on. These data are collected and published at regular intervals.

The second type of information is also collected regularly but it involves a special survey: usually a sample of those concerned. The General Household Survey is a good example of this kind of fact-gathering. Information on housing, health, migration, education and a number of other topics is obtained from a sample of 15 000 households every year. In a similar way the Family Expenditure Survey collects

49

information on the way families spend their money. The findings are published each year.

The third type of information is collected once only for a particular purpose. Many organisations conduct investigations to help them plan for the future or discover present needs. Government inquiries or Royal Commissions often collect large amounts of information. Some, like the Robbins Report on Higher Education, produce volumes of evidence which are longer than the report itself. Many reports of this type are published every day of the week. Often they can be found in local reference libraries or can be obtained directly from the organisations which produced them.

The most important and widely-used information from many of these sources is collected together into yearbooks, or abstracts. The *Annual Abstract of Statistics* published by the Central Statistical Office is the most important collection of easily available statistics on the United Kingdom. Monthly figures are published in the *Monthly Digest of Statistics* and local data in the annual *Abstract of Regional Statistics*. *Social Trends* and *Economic Trends* are regular publications which present the information in a simpler, and more readable form. In addition many organisations publish yearbooks covering national and international events though different methods of compiling statistics in different countries can make comparison difficult.

HISTORICAL EVIDENCE

One important area of documentary evidence is historical documents. These are frequently used by social scientists. Historians take great care when using historical evidence. They ask many of the questions social scientists ask and often work in similar ways. Sometimes their evidence is very full and accurate though frequently it is incomplete and has only a limited use. Historical evidence can be of great use to the social scientist but it needs to satisfy the same tests of reliability and validity that would be applied to other social science data.

Social surveys

Surveys are carried out for many reasons and by many different groups of people. If you are stopped by someone in the High Street and asked for your views on toothpaste, insurance or the government it is likely that you are being involved in a survey being carried out by a commercial social research agency. Such agencies carry out research for their clients. One week they may be doing market research on 'soft centres' for a chocolate manufacturer and in the following week an opinion poll on attitudes towards trade unions for a national newspaper. Surveys are also carried out by academic researchers based in universities and polytechnics and by public research bodies like the Government Social Survey. Many organisations have their own research departments. Research is big business with millions of pounds being spent each year on finding out what people want, like, enjoy, do, have, and believe. Whatever the reason for the research, whoever the client may be, whatever the topic, the basic problems faced and the methods used are much the same. The basic rules for conducting a survey are similar for a classroom-based study of pocket money, as they are for a national survey of political attitudes.

Fig. 5. *A flow chart of a survey*

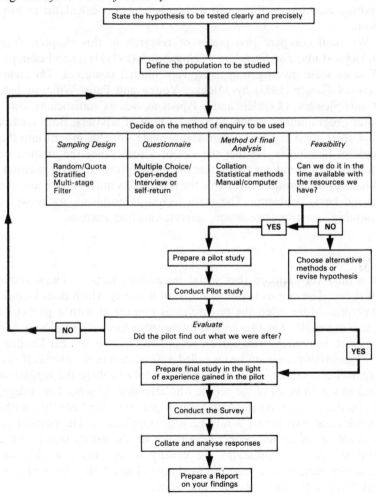

State the hypothesis to be tested clearly and precisely

Define the population to be studied

Decide on the method of enquiry to be used

Sampling Design	Questionnaire	Method of final Analysis	Feasibility
Random/Quota Stratified Multi-stage Filter	Multiple Choice/ Open-ended Interview or self-return	Collation Statistical methods Manual/computer	Can we do it in the time available with the resources we have?

YES   NO

Prepare a pilot study | Choose alternative methods or revise hypothesis

Conduct Pilot study

NO — Evaluate
Did the pilot find out what we were after?

YES

Prepare final study in the light of experience gained in the pilot

Conduct the Survey

Collate and analyse responses

Prepare a Report on your findings

PLANNING A SURVEY

Planning a survey involves both the creative and technical aspects of social research. Remember what was said at the beginning of this chapter: sociologists do not always stick to the rule-book. Every piece of research, every survey, every investigation creates new problems. A good survey is the one which adapts the rules to fit the situation. The stages in conducting a survey are shown in Fig. 5. The researcher must find a way of investigating the problem as effectively as possible within the resources of time and money at his disposal. Some surveys are able to use teams of trained interviewers, using detailed questionnaires backed up by an army of statisticians and the very latest in computer technology. Other researchers produce equally useful findings working on their own with only a pocket calculator to help them.

We shall compare two pieces of research in this chapter. Ann Oakley's study, *The Sociology of Housework* (1974) is a good example of small-scale investigation using very limited resources. *The Symmetrical Family* (1973) by Michael Young and Peter Willmott lists 60 interviewers, 14 coders and 8 typists as well as statisticians, computer programmers, supervisors and a host of advisers. Both studies have their good and bad points and provide valuable insight into the topic of family life. Neither the size of a survey nor the amount of money it can spend are guarantees that it will produce useful research. Whatever the resources available the researchers must be able to solve certain basic problems. The main technical problems are those of sampling, questionnaire design, interviewing and analysis.

SAMPLING

It is only very seldom that social researchers want to know about everyone. The census is one example of a survey which does include everyone. More often the researcher is concerned with a particular group of people. Ann Oakley was interested in housewives. Young and Willmott wanted information on people who lived in or near London. This group of people studied is called a *population* or a *universe*. If you carried out a survey on people in your school or college the *population* studied would be all of the people who attended the school or college. If you did a survey on the sixth form or part-time students then sixth-formers and part-timers would be your populations. The population is made up of all the people who make up the group that is being studied. Survey populations are usually stated very precisely, for example: 'men over 35 years old working in Luton', 'families with 2 or 3 children in South Yorkshire', and so on.

Fig. 6. *A random sample*

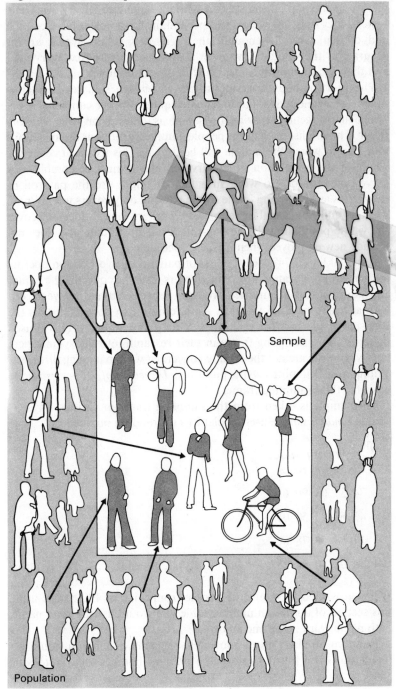

Sample

Population

Researchers have discovered, however, that they can get an accurate picture of the population studied without having to survey everyone. Instead they only interview a sample and, if the sample is large enough and chosen carefully enough, they will gets results which are as accurate as they would have been if they had interviewed everyone – and they can do it at much less cost in time and money.

The best method of sampling uses a *random* sample. In such a sample every individual has an equal chance of being sampled.

The first stage in preparing any sample is to decide on your *sampling frame*. This is a list of all of the people, families, groups or organisations found from which the sample will be drawn. This list must cover the whole of the population to be surveyed and it must be complete. A survey on attitudes to work in a factory might use the pay-roll of employees as a sampling frame. If the pay-roll only covers weekly-paid workers and not casual or temporary workers then it does not cover the whole population. If the pay-roll is not up to date and does not include new employees then it is also incomplete.

Ann Oakley (1974) used the lists of patients of two London doctors for her sampling frame. From the doctors' lists she collected the names and addresses of all married women, between 20 and 30 years old with at least one child under 5. An alternative to doctors' lists is the Register of Electors for each area. Young and Willmott (1973) used these lists as a sampling frame in their research into the symmetrical family. For the area of their study concerned with managing directors, Young and Willmott used a published *Directory of Directors* as the basis for their sampling frame.

The sample is taken from the sampling frame in various ways. A simple *random sample* uses special lists of 'random numbers'.

Table 10.

72	59	93	76	24
74	35	08	90	61
43	62	23	50	05
17	58	53	78	80
53	08	70	94	25

Source: Kendall and Smith 1939

If you wished to sample 25 people from a list of 100 names using this section of a random number table you would use the 72nd name, 59th name, 93rd name and so on.

Random numbers give a more reliable sample than you would get if you took every fourth name on the list, a method known as *systematic sampling.* Both random sampling and systematic sampling can some-times give unsatisfactory results. Small samples, for example, are less reliable than large ones. Often a researcher can only afford to use a small sample. To prevent any errors creeping in he could use a different type of sample.

Stratified samples are used where it is possible to divide the population into a number of relevant groups. Young and Willmott found, for example, that their sampling methods gave them fewer men and women between 17 and 19 than they would have expected on the information they had from the census.

Table 11. *Ages of men and women in the London region*

	Men		Women	
	Survey 1970	Census 1966	Survey 1970	Census 1966
17–19	4%	7%	3%	6%
20–24	10	10	6	9
25–29	9	9	10	8
30–39	18	18	15	16
40–49	20	18	20	16
50–59	18	19	18	18
60–64	7	7	9	8
65–69	6	5	7	6
70 or over	8	7	12	13

Source: Young and Willmott 1973

It would have been possible to have stratified their sample on the basis of the percentages in the census. They would then have sampled 7 per cent of men and 9 per cent of women aged 17–19, 10 per cent of men aged 20–24 and so on. This would have given them a more reliable sample than they actually achieved using a random method.

Young and Willmott did in fact use a *multi-stage* method of sampling.

We needed something as near as we could get to a cross-section of the adult population of the London metropolitan region. If we had simply picked a sample of individual people scattered all over the region, it would have taken far too long (and have been far too expensive) to go and interview them. We had to follow the familiar method and proceed in two stages, first selecting a sample of places in which the interviewing would be concentrated and then picking samples of people in each place. (Young and Willmott 1973)

Fig. 7. *A multi-stage sample*

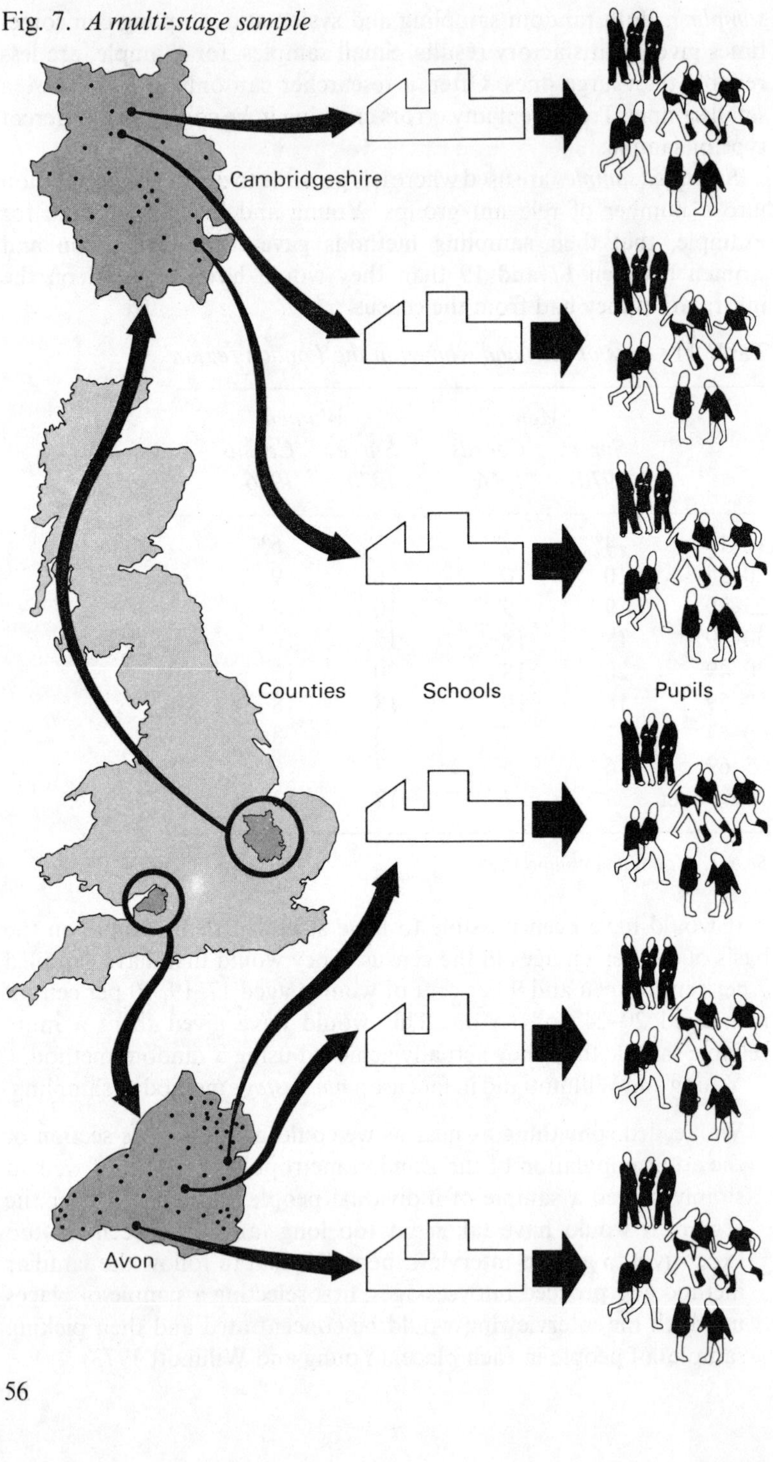

Cambridgeshire

Counties   Schools   Pupils

Avon

They used a two-stage sample (sampling the places and the people) but three- or even four-stage samples are not unusual. To get a sample of school children to interview you might first make a sample of Local Education Authorities (LEAs). From these you would sample a number of schools from which you would sample a number of children. That would be a three-stage sample (Fig. 7).

This could be combined with a *cluster sample*. Instead of sampling individual pupils from each school you might sample a number of classes. The research would then be based on *'clusters'* of children in particular classes. In this way class 4B would be 'a cluster'.

Another commonly used method is a *quota sample*. A market research interviewer may be given a quota of people to interview. This may include 10 upper middle-class families, 20 lower middle-class families and 15 working-class families. This method, however, relies on the judgement of the interviewer and not on a strict sampling process.

Very often it is not possible to locate the people you want to interview on the basis of the information which you have. Often the researcher has to filter out particular groups of people for particular aspects of a study. This involves *multi-phase* or filter sampling. Young and Willmott used their main sample as a sampling frame to obtain a sub-sample of men and women who were aged between 30 and 49 and who were married. They later used this sub-sample as a sampling frame for a further sub-sample of active sportsmen and women.

All of these different forms of sampling are used to get as accurate a result as possible.

Asking questions

If you want to find the answers you have got to ask them questions. But what questions and how do you ask them?

There are many different ways in which social researchers ask questions. The question may be printed on a form which is sent by post to all of those in the sample. They may be on a list of questions which the interviewer fills in as he or she asks the person being inter-viewed, or they may be questions which arise in the course of a fairly informal conversation.

Whichever method is used the aim is always the same – to get accurate and reliable answers about the topic being studied. The questions should be easy to understand, not using too many long words or an ambiguous turn of phrase. Very often a series of simple questions is better than one longer question. Instead of asking:

'Can you tell me the make, colour and age of your car?'

The interviewer should begin by finding out if the person being interviewed has a car. Then separate questions about make, colour and age could be asked. If the person has no car there is no point asking the further questions.

Just as they should be easy for the respondent (the person who answers) to understand, questions should be easy for the interviewer to ask. A question like this may be accurate but it is not easy to ask:

'Do you regularly eat ice-cream when you go out for the day – by regularly I mean at least four times out of five, assuming ice cream to include ice-cream products such as lollies but not iced drinks and meaning days out for leisure rather than going to work or school?'

Many interview schedules include 'filters' which lead from particular answers to further questions. These must be easy for the interviewer to follow.

When all of the questions have been asked the answers need to be 'coded'. If the questionnaire is well designed, coding is easy. Often the interviewer or even the respondent will mark the answers by ringing numbers on the form. These numbers can easily be transferred to a master sheet ready to be added to answers from other interviews.

Finally, the questionnaire must hold the attention of both interviewer and respondent. It should be as interesting as possible, and not too long.

A QUESTIONNAIRE

In Fig. 8 you can see some sections from a questionnaire used in a survey of housing conditions in the London Borough of Southwark. The survey was carried out by a private research agency. This questionnaire would be used by an interviewer who asked questions and then ticked off the answers on the questionnaire. Before the interview starts, the interviewer would mark off the boxes at the top of the first page. The questions would be read to the person being interviewed (the subject) one at a time in exactly the form shown on the sheet. This will help to ensure reliability when there are a number of different interviewers using the same questionnaire. In question 1a the interviewer wants to discover the name that the subject uses for the district lived in. Notice that the subject's name for the district is asked for first, if that does not fit with the coded list of districts the interviewer will ask 1b and show the subject a printed card with the list of districts on it. Why do you think the questions are asked in this order? Cards are often used when the interviewer wants the subject to choose between various alternatives. Question 2 is simpler and the interviewer just needs to code the answer on to the form. The coding makes it easier for the answers to be analysed later.

Questions 1 and 2 are *multiple choice* questions. Question 3 is different. The subject does not have to choose an answer. Instead the interviewer notes down the reply and may even probe to get a fuller

Fig. 8. *Southwark housing survey*

SOCIAL & COMMUNITY PLANNING RESEARCH			
16, Duncan Terrace, London N1 8BZ	Telephone: 01-278 6943		

P.362   **SOUTHWARK HOUSEHOLD SURVEY 1975**   April 1975
INTERVIEW QUESTIONNAIRE   (1–4)

(5)

Household Code ☐   (6) Card ☐ 2

(7) (8) (9)   (10) (11)
Ward/P.D. Code ☐☐☐   Serial Number ☐☐

Interview Type: Head of Household   1   Time interview started:
Household   2   WRITE IN:

		Col./Code	Skip to
1a)	What is the name of this district you live in, that is, what do you call it? WRITE IN NAME CODE IN PRECODED LIST IF POSSIBLE, OTHERWISE ASK b) IF NAME NOT ON PRE-CODED LIST ASK b) AND THEN CODE			
	SHOW CARD A b) I have on this card the names of the various parts of the Borough of Southwark; in which of these do you live?	Bermondsey The Borough Camberwell Dulwich Dulwich Village East Dulwich West Dulwich Herne Hill Honor Oak Newington Nunhead Peckham Rotherhithe Walworth	(12–13) 01 02 03 04 05 06 07 08 09 10 11 12 13 14	
2.	How long have you lived in .... (CODED DISTRICT NAME)?	Under 6 months 6–11 months 1 year, but less than 2 years 2 years, but less than 3 years 3 years, but less than 5 years 5 years, but less than 10 years 10 years, but less than 20 years 20 years or more All my life	(14) 1 2 3 4 5 6 7 8 9	

59

		Col./ Code	Skip to
3.	I would like to hear what you like and dislike about living in .... (CODED NAME OF DISTRICT).		
	First can you tell me what you like about .... (CODED NAME OF DISTRICT) as a place to live?		
	PROBE FULLY, INCLUDING "Why do you say that?" AND "What else?" UNTIL FINAL "No".	(15)	
		(16)	
4.	What do you dislike about .... (CODED NAME OF DISTRICT) as a place to live?		
	PROBE FULLY, INCLUDING "Why do you say that?" AND "What else?" UNTIL FINAL "No".	(17)	

	~~bath~~ ~~ow~~, do you ~~e wi~~ any other households?	~~Sole use~~ Shared use	1 2	
21a)	ASK ALL Apart from a sink in a kitchen, do you have a wash-hand basin with running water?	Yes No	(48) A 1	Q.22
	IF YES AT a) — CODE A b) Do you have the sole use, or do you share with any other households?	Sole use Shared use	2 3	
22a)	ASK ALL Do you have a flush toilet?	Yes No	(49) A 1	Q.23
	IF YES AT a) CODE A b) Do you have the sole use, or do you share with any other households?	Sole use Shared use	2 3	
	c) Is the entrance to it .... READ OUT		(50)	
	.... inside your accommodation outside your accommodation but inside the building or, outside the building?		1 2 3	
23a)	ASK ALL How many bedrooms do you have, including bedsitting rooms and spare bedrooms?	NUMBER OF BEDROOMS	(51)	
			(52)	
b)	Do you have the sole use of all these b~~ ~~ ~~ ~~ shared or sub-let		1	Q.24

answer. This is an *open-ended* question. Why do you think an open-ended question is used here?

What type of questions are used for 21a and 22a? If the subject answers NO for either of these two questions the interviewer has instructions to 'skip to Q.22 or Q.23' in the right-hand column. These questions will be specially for those who lack these amenities. This complete questionnaire, of which we have only seen one small part, contains 75 questions and would take up to 45 minutes to complete. If the interviewer is going to keep the subject's co-operation for all of this time he or she will need to keep their interest. This can be done by varying the questions and by making the subject feel that they are doing something which is going to be worthwhile.

Interview-type questionnaires such as this have the advantage that if the subject does not understand the question the interviewer can repeat it or in some cases explain it. This is not possible with a questionnaire that is sent through the post. Postal questionnaires have to be very clear and easy to understand. They are also generally shorter than interview questionnaires. If a postal questionnaire were too long people would not bother to complete it and this would reduce the number of questionnaires that are returned. Postal questionnaires often have a much lower response rate than interview questionnaires. There is also a danger that the subjects may be 'self-selecting'. People may only return a postal questionnaire if they are interested in the subject, or feel that it is worthwhile, or have strong views on the subject. This can bias the findings of the research. It is also more difficult to detect any false answers in postal surveys. An interviewer is more likely to be able to tell if someone is telling the truth than the researcher who just receives replies through the post.

Both types of questionnaires have their advantages and disadvantages and are used for particular kinds of research.

Observation

Observation is something we all do for most of the time. We notice things that happen around us; we store the information, fitting it into our existing knowledge; we link it to our ideas of why things happen and use it when similar events occur again. Sometimes we are just observers, for example when we are standing on the touch-line watching the game, even watching it on television. At other times we are so closely involved that we get little opportunity to observe. The sociologist has a similar experience. Observation is often closely linked to participation. At one extreme is the pure observer watching the events through a one-way mirror or a television camera lens

61

completely separated from the situation observed. At the other extreme is the participant who loses sight of his sociological task and 'goes native', joining that which he, or she, set out to study. Most participant observation research lies between these two extremes.

The evidence gained from participant observation is often very different from that provided by surveys. Surveys and questionnaires tend to produce numbers and percentages. They focus on quantity. Participant observation is more concerned with quality and produces impressions. For this reason it is sometimes called '*qualitative*' or '*impressionistic*' research.

Sociologist Howard Becker describes how he carried out a participant observation study in a medical college.

> We went to lectures with students taking their first two years of basic science and frequented the laboratories in which they spend most of their time, watching them and engaging in casual conversation as they dissected cadavers or examined pathology specimens. We followed these students to their fraternity houses and sat around while they discussed their school experiences. We accompanied students in the clinical years on rounds with attending physicians, watched them examine patients on the wards and in the clinics, sat in on discussion groups and oral exams. We ate with the students and took night calls with them. We pursued interns and residents through their crowded schedules of teaching and medical work. We stayed with one small group of students on each service for periods ranging from a week to two months, spending many full days with them. The observational situations allowed time for conversation and we took advantage of this to interview students about things that had happened and were about to happen, and about their own backgrounds and aspirations. (Becker 1958)

Becker suggests that research like this goes through four stages which overlap each other. In the first stages of the research the observer will be trying to fit together a number of separate events into a framework of ideas and concepts. At this time the researcher is deciding what is important, what it means and how it can be checked. This second stage involves checking some of the hunches that arise during the first stage. Some of these may prove to be untrue and are abandoned, others may appear to have some truth in them and will be explored further. It is also likely that new theories and ideas will appear and will need to be checked out. In the third stage the researcher tries to build the information and ideas into a theory, or model, to explain the situation studied. Finally he will present his evidence to others and show that the theory is proved.

62

Sociologists engaged in participant observation are faced with four major problems. Firstly, they have the problem of controlling bias. How sure can anyone be that the impressions they have of a given event are not influenced by their own viewpoint. This can be prevented by regular checks on the information, accurate and regular recording and sharing the work with other sociologists. The second problem concerns the extent to which the researchers become involved in what they study. Sociologists try to remain detached from the situation they study but participation sometimes makes detachment difficult. Thirdly, there is the effect the observer has on the situation he or she observes. When some sociologists tried to study a flying saucer cult which had predicted the end of the earth they found that the members of the group interpreted their interest in the group as evidence that the prophecy was true. By joining the group the researchers gave it a reason for continuing. Finally, there is always a moral problem in participant observation research. The researcher participates because he wants to do research. The people with whom he participates may not wish to be researched, and may not agree with the findings. In some cases researchers carry out '*covert*' research, not telling the subjects that research is going on. When James Patrick studied a Glasgow gang he did it in secret. If he hadn't the gang wouldn't have trusted him and might have attacked him. It could be said that covert research involves a breaking of the trust between the researcher and the researched.

Interviews

Interviews are used in research involving surveys and in participant observation. They involve two people: a researcher who presents the questions and topics for discussion and the person being interviewed who is expected to respond. An interview, therefore, is a social situation involving particular individuals who are playing particular roles. Each individual in such a situation has ideas about what is happening and what it is all about. They have their own ideas about the other person and about their role and status. All of these different things affect the way the interview goes and its value as a source of information. Some interviews may be very formal affairs with printed questionnaires and clearly defined relationships. Others may be more like extended conversations. The problems, however, are very similar.

The interviewer needs to establish a relationship with the subject who is likely to get bored, or drop out altogether, if he doesn't feel that the interview is worthwhile. To keep the subject's interest, the interviewer must appear interested in the subject and make comments which show that the subject's opinions are valued. Problems arise when the subject begins to give the interviewer the answers he thinks the interviewer wants. When this happens '*interviewer error*' makes the results less reliable. Interviewers have other problems, too. If a number of different interviewers are working on the same survey they must be consistent so that they get similar responses.

Experiments

In a science like chemistry or biology an experiment involves two situations which are identical in every way except for the one factor which is being tested. The experimental plant grows in sunlight while its 'control' is locked away in a darkened cupboard. They differ only in the amount of light they receive. Earlier in this chapter we considered some of the reasons why this kind of approach was not common in the social sciences. However, social scientists and in particular social psychologists do conduct experiments and their results may be of value in sociology.

An American psychologist, S. E. Asch (1951), conducted a series of experiments which illustrate group pressure. Groups of students were asked to help with a test of visual perception. They were shown a series of cards with lines of different length drawn on them. As each pair of cards came up, each of the group in turn was asked to say which of the three lines on one card was the same length as the one line on the other card. However, all but one of the students had secretly been told to give a wrong answer every time. The one student who was not in on the deception was placed near to the end of the row. As the lines came up and the 'planted' students kept making a wrong choice, the one real subject became more and more perplexed. In 37 out of every 100 cases the individual subject actually gave in and began agreeing with the rest of the group who were obviously wrong.

One of Asch's subjects, who did not give in and agree with the others, describes the experience: 'Despite everything there was a lurking fear that in some way I did not understand I might be wrong; fear of exposing myself as inferior in some way.' Another said: 'I felt disturbed, puzzled, separated, like an outcast from the rest. Every time I disagreed I was beginning to wonder if I wasn't beginning to look funny.' The group has a very powerful influence on our attitudes.

Another kind of experiment was used to assess the value of ITA, or the 'initial teaching alphabet', in helping children to read. 'Janet and John' readers were used in a large sample of schools. In certain schools standard readers were used while in others they had been translated into ITA. The schools were carefully matched in terms of their location, pupil-teacher ratios, social class, and size, and the pupils were matched for age, sex, social class, measured intelligence and vocabulary. In this way the experimenters tried to compare like with like, with the reading schemes as the only things that varied. This kind of control matching is common in social science experiments. The experiment seemed to show that ITA worked better than traditional methods, but how reliable were the results? A number of possible sources of error could have influenced the result. It is quite likely that there were influences present in the experiment which the researchers had not foreseen and which had not been 'matched'. The schools which used the new methods may have been so pleased at being involved in what they saw as an important piece of research that they worked harder, expecting more from the children and as a result got better results. This kind of effect is usually known as 'Hawthorne Effect' after the experiments carried out at the Hawthorne Electrical Works by Elton Mayo (see Chapter 9).

Experiments can have a value in sociology but like all other research need to be treated with caution.

Conclusion

This chapter has been concerned with social research. In the end sociology depends on the quality of the research which is carried out. The methods described and the problems they involve are part of the sociologists everyday problem of understanding social life. A chapter in a book such as this can only give a very general indication of what research is about. You can only really understand it by doing it. The books listed under Further Reading will give you some help in doing research of your own.

In 1851 the population of the United Kingdom was a little over 22 million people. By the beginning of the twentieth century it had risen to over 38 million and by 1977 reached 55 852 000. By the year 2001 the United Kingdom population will be over 57 millions.

Estimating the future population is a very difficult task with many different factors to be taken into account. It is not surprising that

Fig. 9. *The growth of the population in England and Wales*

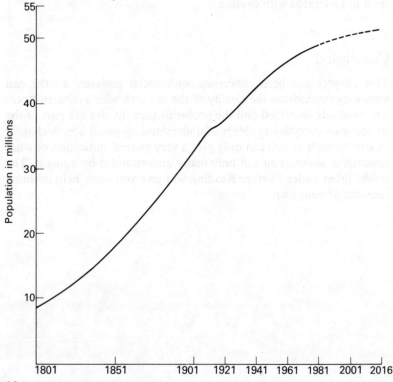

population planners often refer to their predictions as 'the best guess'.

Why has population risen in this way over the last few hundred years? There are two main influences on the level of population in any country: the numbers coming into the country and the numbers going out. It is not unlike the way the water level in your bath is determined. If you pull the plug out and leave the taps running, whether the level of the bath rises or falls will depend on the relative rates of flow of water in and out.

The main reason for the rise in population since the end of the seventeenth century has been that births have regularly outnumbered deaths. More people have come into the country than have left it. An increase in population resulting from 'natural' causes (births and deaths) is termed a *natural increase in population* in order to distinguish it from an increase (or decrease) due to migration. Throughout this period, immigrants (those coming into England from abroad) and emigrants (those going to other countries) have cancelled each other out. As many were leaving as were coming in.

The birth rate

The *birth rate* is the number of babies born in every 1 000 of the population each year. For the greater part of this century, birth rates have been falling steadily. At the end of the nineteenth century there were about 35 births for every 1 000 of the population per year, but this fell to less than half that by the 1930s. Since then the birth rate has risen, fallen, risen again, and, in the early 1970s fell again. How can we explain such changes?

The main reason for the fall in birth rate after the turn of the century was the desire of people to have smaller families. This was made possible by the increased use and availability of family planning. More and more people realised that they could improve their standard of living if they had fewer mouths to feed. With fewer children to care for they would be able to give their children a better start in life. Factory and Education Acts prevented parents from sending their children out to work and children became a burden on the family income instead of providers.

After the Second World War there was a 'bulge' in the birth rate. Soldiers returning home to their wives after a long absence started the families which had been delayed by the war. When the bulge had passed birth rates declined for a few years, but in the mid-1960s they began to rise again. This reflected an increase in the number of people who married and started families. In the depression years of the

67

Fig. 10. *Changes in the population*

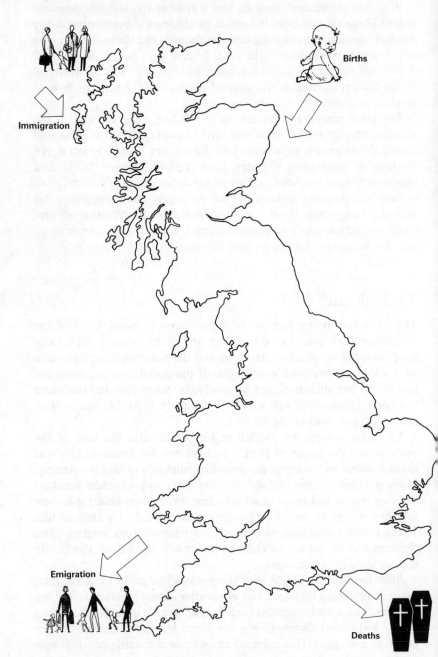

Births

Immigration

Emigration

Deaths

1930s only 42 per cent of the total population were married. By 1960 over 50 per cent were married. The size of the average family also began to rise at this time, from 2·2 children per family in the early 1950s to an average of 2·6 children per family in the late 1960s.

Table 12. *Birth rate, England and Wales (live births per 1 000 of the population)*

Annual averages or calendar years	
1871–75	35
1901	29
1911	25
1921	23
1931	16
1951	16
1961	18
1971	16
1974	13
1977	11

Source: Office of Population Censuses and Surveys

The death rate

The *death rate* is the number of deaths for every 1 000 of the population each year. Like birth rates, death rates have also been falling steadily for the past hundred years. In the early years of this century there were 16 deaths for every 1 000 of population each year, but by 1961 this was down to a rate of 12 per 1 000.

This decline in the rate of deaths per 1 000 of the population is the result of a number of factors. There has been an improvement in the overall standard of living of people in Britain. There has been no famine for over a century. We are no longer dependent on food we grow ourselves. We can import food from other countries and pay for it in exports of machinery and manufactured goods. There have been advances in medicine and in public health: cholera, typhoid and smallpox epidemics are things we read about in the newspapers, but they no longer occur in Britain. Hospital services have improved, in particular the care of expectant mothers and their babies. The *infant mortality rate* (the number of babies who die within their first year out of every 1 000 live births) is at its lowest ever.

As a result of these improvements men and women are living longer. In 1900 men, on average, could look forward to a life of just under half a century whilst women had a 'life expectancy' of just over the half century. In 1961 the average life expectancy for men was up to 68 whilst women on average could expect to live to 74.

As far as the total population is concerned the death rate has always been well below the birth rate. Each year more have been born than have died and so the population has risen (Fig. 13).

Table 13. *Death rates for men and women, England and Wales (deaths per 1 000 of population)*

	Men	Women
1930–32	20·7	16·4
1950–52	17·6	12·1
1960–62	16·4	10·4
1966	16·2	9·9
1971	15·2	9·1
1976	15·3	9·2

Source: Social Trends

Fertility

Perhaps the most important influence on the size and composition of the population is fertility. By this we mean the number of children born to women of child-bearing age. The *fertility rate* is the number of children born for every 1 000 women of child-bearing age per year. In 1933 the fertility rate was 1·79. It reached a peak in 1964 when it stood at 2·98 but has since declined to 1·75 in 1976. Explaining changes in fertility is a major problem for demographers.

The Royal Commission on Population of 1949 came at the end of a period of low fertility. The Commission produced figures linking family size to social class.

Table 14. *Estimated size (in numbers of children) of the completed family of manual and non-manual workers according to the date of marriage*

Date of marriage	Average number of children	
	Non-manual workers	Manual workers
1900–09	2·79	3·94
1910–14	2·34	3·35
1915–19	2·05	2·91
1920–24	1·89	2·72
1925–29	1·73	2·49

Source: Report of the Royal Commission on Population, 1949

If you study these figures carefully you will see that they indicate two things. Reading from top to bottom it is clear that the average size of families had fallen from 2·79 and 3·94 children to 1·73 and 2·49. Reading from left to right one can see that the average size of the families of manual workers had always been higher than the average

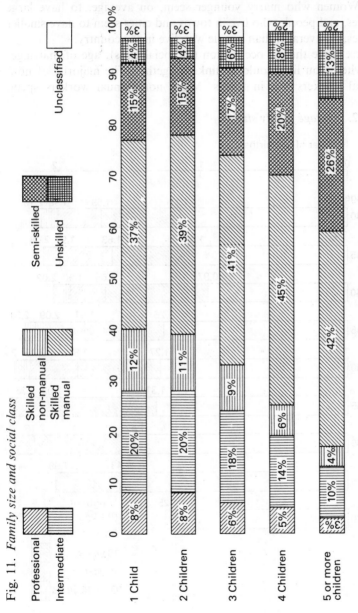

Fig. 11. *Family size and social class*

(Number of children at birth of last child by social class of husband 1976)
Source: Social Trends

71

size for families of non-manual workers, even though the later families in both groups were smaller.

From these figures we can clearly see that for some reason there has been a difference in average family size between different social classes.

There are two other noticeable features of variations in family size. Women who marry younger seem, on average, to have large families, and people who live in towns and cities seem to have smaller families, on average, than people who live in the country.

These three things: occupation (or social class); age of marriage; and where you live, could be linked together. The majority of non-manual workers live in towns. Many non-manual workers spend

Fig. 12. *Average family size*

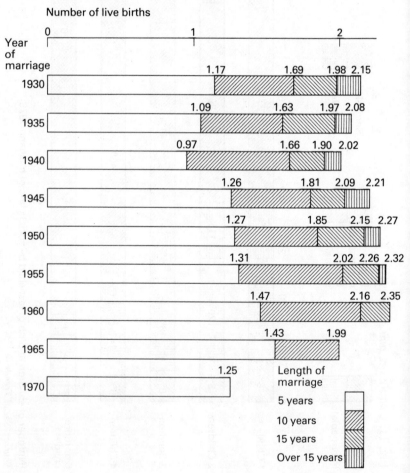

longer getting an education and therefore get married later. However, the figures for average family size for the country as a whole do show up these three influences.

As far as the second trend (a movement towards smaller families) is concerned the following figures show it more clearly:

Table 15. *Family size (mean ultimate family size for completed families)*

	Year of marriage	Family size
Actual	1861–99	6·16
	1900–09	3·30
	1920–24	2·38
	1925–29	2·17
	1930–34	2·13
	1935–39	2·07
	1940–44	2·09
	1945–49	2·22

Source: Registrar General's *Statistical Review*

At the time of the 1949 Royal Commission on Population, people were very concerned that families should not get so small that the nation's population might begin to fall. Should the number of children in each family fall below two then the population would not be able to reproduce itself. Indeed, when you take into account the number of people who remain unmarried it is obvious that all married couples must produce more than two children in order to maintain the same level of population. It is obvious from the figures of 'mean ultimate family size' that in the 1930s this danger was very real. In the event their anxiety was not justified.

THE CAUSES OF CHANGES IN FERTILITY

The decline in family size began in the second half of the nineteenth century. Between the periods 1861–69 and 1901–19 the mean, or average, family size had nearly halved. By the beginning of the Second World War it was down to nearly a third. There were many underlying causes. The trend began with the middle classes.

The fall in the value of money at the turn of the century, the growing cost of living, and the cost of educating a family, made many couples concentrate their attentions on a smaller number of children. No longer was a secure position in the Civil Service or the professions guaranteed to a well-spoken lad from a good home. Qualifications were demanded and the schools and universities which provided them were fee-paying.

In the past middle-class families had been used to living in large houses with servants to attend them. But as the conditions and wages in the factories began to improve, servants became increasingly hard to get, and increasingly expensive. The grand houses gave way to more easily manageable properties on the new suburban estates.

Gradually the trend filtered down into the other classes of society. The lower middle classes saw that with a smaller family they would be better able to ensure a good future for their offspring. They began to demand houses of their own in the suburban fringes of the cities. Such properties often lacked the space for a large family. They too could take advantage of the economies of a smaller family to send their sons and daughters to school.

Above all there were changes in people's ideas. Family planning gradually became acceptable to all classes of society. The trial of Charles Bradlaugh and Annie Besant for publishing pamphlets on birth control in 1877 gave considerable publicity to the possibility of family planning. In the years that followed, contraceptive techniques became increasingly available and better understood. The movement for women's suffrage led by Mrs Pankhurst and the Suffragettes also gave impetus to family limitation. Women increasingly questioned their roles as lifelong child-nurses and began to demand the right to choose whether or not to have children, and how many. However, you should not think of family planning as a cause of smaller families. It is simply the means which made it possible.

The whole climate of people's lives was changing. The Factory Acts and Education Acts passed during the middle years of the nineteenth century prevented children being sent to work, and later on forced them to attend school. More children began to mean more expense to the average working man, instead of more earnings. It was obviously in his best interest to keep his family to a smaller size.

All these factors encouraged people to have fewer children. At first only the middle classes were affected, but gradually the new ideas were taken up by all classes of society, with the result that family size fell rapidly.

In the middle of the 1950s the trends of family size took a different turn. In 1964 live births in England and Wales were nearly a third higher than in 1954. This sharp increase in the birth rate is the result of the greater proportion of people who are marrying, plus a rise in the illegitimate birth rate, a trend towards younger marriages, increases in average family size and higher fertility amongst immigrant groups. The mean age of marriage of spinsters in England and Wales fell from 24·58 in 1941 to 23·03 in 1962.

The baby boom did not last very long and since 1964 there has been a steady fall in fertility and in the birth rate. It is not easy to explain these changes. To predict a trend, such as changes in fertility and birth rates, it is necessary to predict how people will behave in the future. As many individuals cannot say what they will be doing in 5 years time, it is not surprising that planners find it difficult to predict. Surveys of the family-size intentions of young married couples, for example, showed that at marriage the couple anticipated a larger family than they eventually had.

In the 1950s couples were catching up on families that had been delayed by the war. During the 1960s and 70s they were delaying having families. The result was a very substantial drop in the birth rate. In 1977–78 the birth rate actually fell below the death rate, the only time that this has happened apart from the two world wars.

It is not clear what the pattern will be in the 1980s and 1990s. Will there be another period of catching up, or is there a long-term trend to smaller families? Is it possible that people are now starting their families later in their married life, after they have saved up some money and bought a house? If this is the case will their families be as big as they might have been twenty years earlier? The children born in the 'baby boom' of the 1950s were getting married in the 1970s. Even if the fertility rate remained low, birth rates could rise because of the increased proportion of women of child-bearing age. The predictions change from year to year. It is thought likely that birth rates will rise in the 1980s and 1990s, declining in the early years of the next century before they begin to rise again. The size of these trends and when they will take place cannot be predicted with any accuracy.

The balance of migration

For many hundreds of years Britain has been a place of refuge and hope for many people from other lands. Protestant Huguenot weavers escaping from religious persecution in the seventeenth century, the Irish escaping from famine in the nineteenth, Jews escaping from Hitler in the twentieth, followed by Commonwealth immigrants seeking a better future in the years since the end of the Second World War: Britain has always been a host to immigrant peoples.

It would be wrong to think of this only in terms of immigration. From the early part of the nineteenth century up to the 1930s more people were lost to Britain through migration than were gained. During that period Britain was a country of *net emigration*. This was the period of the British Empire, when young men and women left their

75

homeland to establish the Union Jack in Africa, India, Australia and New Zealand while others sought their fortunes on the American frontier. Throughout these years more people left Britain than came to Britain.

In the 1930s at the time of the Great Depression and the rise of Nazi Germany this changed.

The outward flow of young people to the Empire had dried up and was replaced by the reverse movement. The Great Depression brought many of the 'Empire builders' back home and there was also a steady trickle of refugees from Hitler's Germany. After the Second World War it seemed for a time as if a pattern of net emigration would return. This did not occur and from the 1950s a new pattern emerged. Britain once more became host to immigrants from less wealthy nations, many from the Commonwealth. They came from the West Indies, India, Pakistan, Ceylon and the African Commonwealth states, as well as from Ireland. This new inflow was not matched by an equivalent outflow. Commonwealth immigration reached its peak in 1961 with a net inflow of 172 000 people and in the following year the Commonwealth Immigrants Act became law. The net inward balance fell to 10 000 in 1963 and since then has been reversed. The United Kingdom has now a net outward flow of population which shows every sign of continuing.

When a comparison is made between those who come to Britain and those who leave we can see that, on the whole, those who come are just slightly younger than those who leave. There are equal numbers of each sex in both groups and their levels of qualification are similar.

Britain is losing slightly more skilled people than she gains, and they are slightly more experienced. In discussing the pattern of migration we should not only be concerned with the total numbers coming and going. The skills and qualifications which they either bring, or take, with them are also important.

Since the 1962 Act half of the Commonwealth immigrants entering on work vouchers have had professional qualifications such as doctors, nurses, architects, lawyers and teachers. Many have come because of a lack of suitable opportunities in their home countries or in order to gain experience which may be of use when they return. At the present time up to two-thirds of senior house doctors and over half of the registrars in British hospitals are born outside the United Kingdom and Eire. In 1968 24 per cent of all doctors entering general practice had qualifications from Asian universities.

The pattern of immigration is always changing. The expulsion of Asians from Uganda in 1974 led to a short-term increase in immigration. Britain's immigration controls are very tight and are enforced severely.

Few foreign citizens are allowed to settle permanently in Britain. The controls often cause hardship to many who feel that they have a right to settle here. Against this we must place the loss of skilled workers to America, Europe and the Middle East. It is likely that Britain will be a net exporter of population well into the twenty-first century with emigrants out-numbering immigrants. In 1966/67 'the brain drain' accounted for the loss of up to 400 doctors and as many as 1 300 'qualified specialists' in the aerospace industry. Many of these individuals were lost to Britain for ever. A large number would return at the end of their contracts, bringing back with them the skills and experience they had gained. This forms part of an international movement of skilled and unskilled workers. The growth of multi-national industries has led to an increase in short-term migration, particularly to the Arab World. Engineers, agricultural scientists, secretaries, research workers, salesmen, nurses and many other workers seek jobs overseas. Such migrant workers maintain close links with home. They return on leave regularly and often send money back as remittances for their families or as savings for their own future.

Social class; life and death

Earlier in this chapter we considered the improvements in birth and death rates which have occurred during the twentieth century. These improvements have been shared by all classes of society. But because the level of infant mortality in the lower income groups was well behind that for the middle classes at the start of the century these groups have had a lot more to catch up. On average these lower income groups have been thirty years behind the middle class. This means that the rate of infant mortality in the Registrar General's Group V is double that in Group I. So despite a national level of infant mortality which is among the lowest in the world there are still sections of the population which suffer a high rate of infant deaths.

There are many causes for this. Working-class mothers, as a group, are more likely to have premature births. This may be because they are younger. John and Elizabeth Newson's study of 500 mothers and young children in Nottingham showed that over half of the Class V mothers were 21 or younger when their first child was born. This was twice the proportion found in Classes I and II combined. They are also more likely to stay at work longer into the pregnancy. Working-class families are more likely to have a number of children fairly close together, regarding family planning as a way of stopping any more

77

children rather than as a way of planning a family. As a result the mother often has to cope with a new-born baby and a toddler at the same time. One child is hardly out of nappies before the next arrives. This places extra strain upon the young mother.

Ante-natal care is often less good. This does not mean that working-class mothers do not care for their babies, they obviously do, but if the mother is tired, living in poor housing, on low pay, standards of care are bound to suffer. Attitudes to child-care are often outdated. Old wives' tales are often preferred to sound advice from the welfare clinic or the health visitor. The greatest risks occur in the first few weeks but the young child remains vulnerable throughout the first year. Bronchitis, gastro-enteritis, and pneumonia are killer diseases at this time and it is the child in the large family, in overcrowded conditions, with a poor diet, that is in the greatest danger. We can get some idea of the extent of the problem from the following tables.

Table 16. *Age of mothers (average age of mother at birth of first child)*

Social class of husband	Average age of mother (years)
I	26·3
II	25·8
III Non-manual	24·9
III Manual	23·4
IV	22·9
V	21·9
Not classified	22·8
All classes	24·0

Source : Social Trends, Official Population Census and Surveys

Table 17. *Birth and social class 1973 (Scotland)*

Social class of mother	Stillbirth per 1 000 births	Perinatal death* per 1 000 births	Average birthweight (grams)
I	7·4	15·3	3 359
II	8·5	17·1	3 346
III	11·2	21·5	3 273
IV	13·5	23·5	3 244
V	16·2	31·5	3 163
All classes	11·6	22·5	3 262

(*Stillbirth and deaths within one week of birth)
Source: Social Trends

One reason for this continuing high rate of infant mortality in low-income families is the carryover of general health and development from one generation to another. The birth weight of children is in general related to the birth weight of the mother. Poor diet and ill health in one generation are passed on to the next.

The child of the unmarried mother is also more vulnerable. As the illegitimacy rate is now approaching 9 per cent of all live births, and more 'lone mothers' are choosing to keep their babies, this will become an increasingly urgent problem. Evidence suggests that these children have even less chance of a secure future than any other group. Their health is often less satisfactory, their educational progress is slower and they are without the security which two parents can bring. Their disadvantages are in sharp contrast to the benefits gained by adopted children, who tend to do even better, on average, than children born into a normal home. The single-parent family is faced by many extra burdens.

The structure of the population

So far in this chapter we have looked at population from the point-of-view of the *total* population. We have viewed 'the population' as one

Fig. 13. *Population changes*

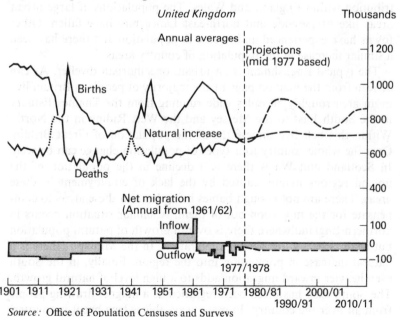

Source: Office of Population Censuses and Surveys

79

large mass of people. If we want to understand changes in population more clearly we need to break the 'mass' down into its various parts. We can do this in four ways.

1. Where do people live and how do they move about the country?
2. How do people earn their living?
3. What is their sex?
4. How old are they?

The regional distribution

Table 18. *The population of England and Wales by type of region at the last 3 full censuses (in millions)*

Region	1951	1961	1971 (provisional)
Conurbations	16·79	16·74	15·93
Other urban areas	18·77	20·41	22·10
Rural districts	8·19	8·95	10·57

Source: Census 1971, Preliminary Report

From these figures we can see the major trend of population distribution within England and Wales. The populations of large urban areas like Merseyside and north-east Lancashire have fallen. Other towns have experienced an increase in population and there has been a similar increase in the population of country areas.

The typical Englishman is an urban, or suburban dweller. As can be seen from the map on page 81 the majority of people in Britain live in an area roughly 50 miles wide running from the Thames Estuary in the South East to the Mersey and the West Riding in the North. Within this belt live three-fifths of the population of Great Britain. Over the whole country four types of population change can be seen. In Scotland and Wales there is a decline in the population of the upland regions mainly caused by the lack of employment in these areas. There are not enough babies being born in these areas to compensate for the migration out of them. A similar situation occurs in northern England where there is overall growth of natural population but again a heavy loss through migration. In the Midlands there is a natural increase in population into the region. Finally, in the South even heavier inward migration adds to a high level of natural growth. The South East has often been regarded as a magnet drawing people from all over the country. In many ways this is true but it is counter-

balanced by an equivalent movement of population out of the area.
London, of course, is at the centre of all population movements in
the South East. The population of Greater London has in fact fallen
by 800 000 since 1951.

Fig. 14. *Population density*

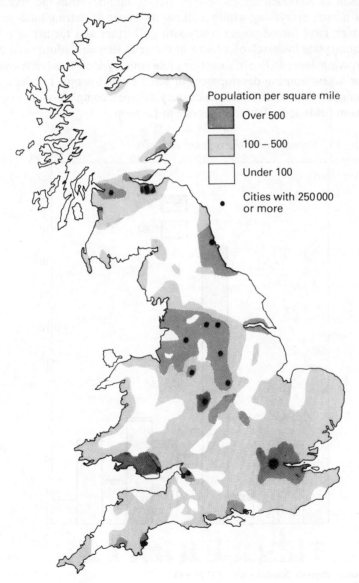

Population per square mile

Over 500

100 – 500

Under 100

• Cities with 250 000 or more

The result of these trends has been to pack people even more tightly into the already overpopulated strip of land running from the Thames to the Mersey. Within this area a process of 'urban dispersal' has been taking place. Fewer people are choosing to live in the centres of the big cities and are moving out to the suburbs and further. This is the result of increased car ownership, freeing families from the necessity of having everything within walking distance; of soaring land prices which have forced young couples to go further and further into the countryside in search of a home at the price they can afford; and of a growing desire to live in something like countryside. An advertisement for a new housing development in Kent enticed people to 'share the delights of a latter-twentieth-century village', complete with woods, green fields and a fast train service to London.

Fig. 15. *Population in the regions 1961–76*

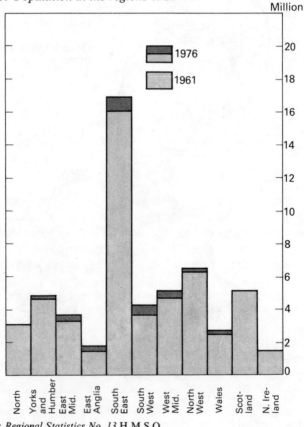

Source: Regional Statistics No. 13 H.M.S.O.

Fig. 16. *Population in the regions 1971–76 (% change)*

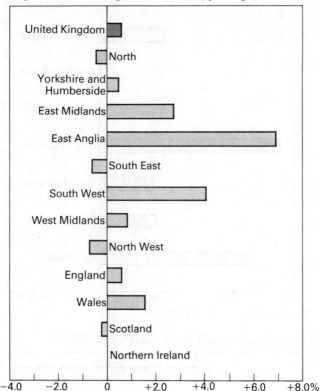

Source: *Regional Statistics No. 13* H.M.S.O.

Urban dispersal has also had the effect of reducing the amount of green countryside which is available for all to enjoy. In the late 1960s 11·6 per cent of the area of England and Wales had been built on, by the year 2000 15·2 per cent will be under concrete. A vast new city of Milton Keynes is being built on farming land in north Buckinghamshire.

This movement out of the city centres has also been influenced by the job situation and birth rates. When many older industries were established, cities grew up around them. As these industries declined people moved away to look for new jobs. New industries were more likely to be established in New Towns or in the suburbs. Young people were more likely to move to find jobs leaving only the old. This led to a declining birth rate which worsened the situation in the older cities.

There can be no doubt that the British people are moving house more often. From the 1966 Sample Census we can see that 10·7 per

83

Fig. 17. *The decline of the cities 1971–76*

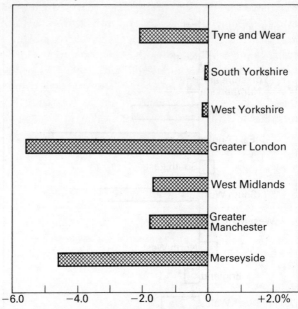

Source: *Regional Statistics No. 13* H.M.S.O.

Fig. 18. *Population changes in the countryside 1971–76*

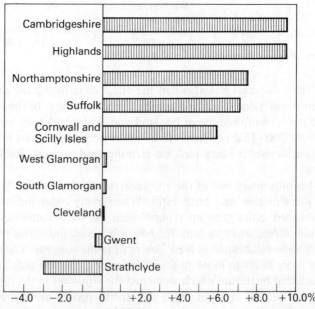

Source: *Regional Statistics No. 13* H.M.S.O.

cent of the population had moved house within the previous year and a third had moved within the previous five years. Much of the movement is over fairly short distances. Margaret Stacey's study of Banbury showed that nearly 15 per cent of the workers who came into the town came from within a 25-mile radius. Not quite as many (13·7 per cent) came from the surrounding industrial Midlands, 12·1 per cent from Lancashire, Cheshire and Yorkshire, 11·6 per cent from Greater London, and only 3 per cent from as far as Scotland. Population movements tend to have a 'ripple' effect moving in slowly towards the centre.

Moving house does not affect all classes in the same way as Table 19 shows.

Table 19. *Number of moves in the previous 5 years (1972)*

Socio-economic groups	Percentage of households which moved	
	No moves	*2·4 moves*
Professional	·53	16
Employers	62	11
Intermediate	56	16
Junior non-manual	64	11
Skilled manual	66	10
Semi-skilled manual	67	9
Unskilled manual	70	9
Average number of moves for all groups	64	10

Source: General Household Survey

GOVERNMENT ACTION

Central and local government authorities are well aware of the problems created for the country as a whole by these movements of population. Incentives in the form of grants to industry and provision of industrial training have been given to the worst hit areas. Tight controls have been placed on industrial and commercial building in Central London and a number of government departments have moved away from the South East to areas of high unemployment. Local authorities have engaged in vast rebuilding programmes which have transformed city centres. Birmingham, Glasgow and London are only three of the towns which have undertaken a programme of urban renewal. New Towns have been built to provide work and homes away from the cities. Since 1944 half-a-million people have moved to New Towns and by the beginning of the twenty-first century they will provide homes for two-and-a-half million people.

The earliest government action came in the 1920s and since then there have been a succession of policies for regional development. These have involved subsidies to firms to enable them to build factories or to keep them going, subsidies towards the cost of labour in particular areas, training programmes and industrial developments and a range of legal controls. Such measures have had little overall effect and in some cases have increased problems.

The Home Office funded Community Development Projects studied a number of areas affected by the decline of particular industries. They felt that the regional policies had had a limited success but at a considerable cost.

> But what about the costs of this limited success? The Exchequer has spent enormous amounts. In the ten years up to 1973 nearly £500m (at constant 1970–71 prices) was spent on regional development incentives in the northern region alone, excluding loans, factory buildings and so on. Assuming that the figure of 50 000 additional jobs created is correct, each extra job in the north costs roughly £10 000 to create and maintain over this period. It would be truly remarkable if such an expenditure of public money had not succeeded in luring a number of firms to the Development Areas in the name of regional policy.
>
> Leaving aside the question of cost, doubts have also been growing about the type of jobs brought to the regions by regional incentives. For a long time, many people felt that any job was welcome in those areas, but slowly it dawned on them that perhaps a perfume factory, for example, was not the answer to the run-down of a coal mine.
> (Community Development Project 1977)

The occupational structure

In 1881 one in every eight workers was employed in a primary industry such as mining, fishing or agriculture. By 1951 only one in twenty worked in these industries. At the turn of the century 47 per cent of the population were engaged in manufacturing with 44 per cent working in service industries, such as banking or distribution. In 1978 little more than 3 per cent of the population worked in the primary sector, over 40 per cent were in manufacturing industries and nearly 57 per cent provided services. This is evidence of a major change in the economic basis of life in Britain. Manufacturing industry has lost its position as the major employer of labour in Britain and its place has been taken by service industries.

This change can be seen even more clearly in the kind of jobs people do. In 1911 manual workers made up nearly three-quarters of the working population. By 1961 they were less than three-fifths and whereas clerks accounted for little more than 4 per cent of all workers at the turn of the century, by 1961 they amounted to 12·7 per cent.

It is clear, therefore, that Britain has experienced change not only in the types of industry within which people work but also in the kind of jobs that they do. The majority of people in Britain today work in service industries at non-manual jobs.

Fig. 19. *The jobs people do. Occupational distribution, 1978 (U.K.)*

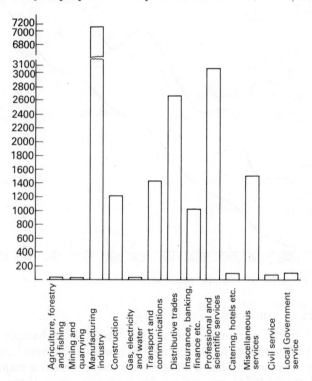

Source: Central Statistical Office, *Monthly Digest of Statistics, No. 398*

There are a number of reasons for these changes. The twentieth century has seen a decline in manufacturing industry in Britain. Increased competition from overseas and insufficient investment at home have both had an effect. The industries which have taken their place have often been highly mechanised, often automated, and have required fewer workers. This is seen clearly in Fig. 20.

The proportion of men and women employed in 'white-collar' jobs has risen steadily since the end of the Second World War.

Fig. 20. *White-collar workers in manufacturing industry.*
Administrative, technical and clerical staff as a percentage of all workers in the industry

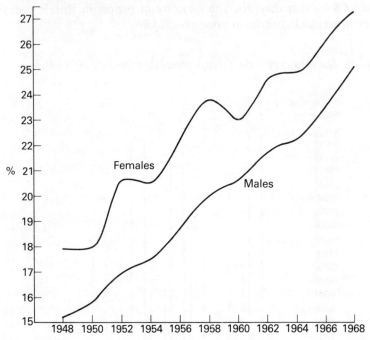

Source: *British Labour Statistics: Historical Abstracts 1886–1968*

BALANCE OF THE SEXES

A third factor in changing population trends is the balance of the sexes at different levels. For much of this century there have been more women than men at almost all ages. At present there is a majority of men in the under 15 group, and this is likely to grow between now and the end of the century. In the 15–64 age range there are at present more women than men but by 2001 this may have been reversed. For every 1 000 women in 1931 there were only 920 men. By 1965 there were 940 men and by the end of the century there are likely to be 970 men to every 1 000 women.

For most of this century more boys have been born than girls. In recent years roughly 106 boys have been born for every 100 girls, but this is not a constant rate and there seems to be no biological
88

Table 20. *Sex ratio 1901–2001 (the number of males to every 100 females) (United Kingdom)*

	1901	1921	1941	1961	1981 (estimates)	2001
Under 16 years	99·8	101·4	102·8	104·5	105·9	106·2
16–44 years	92·4	87·9	97·4	101·1	103·5	104·8
45 years and over	86·6	87·7	81·9	81·1	81·5	84·1
All ages	93·7	91·5	93·3	94·1	95·2	96·9

Source: Social Trends 1979

reason why it should be. The boys' early advantage is not maintained. Males seem to be less sturdy on the whole than females and the balance eventually shifts in the women's favour. It can be argued that men are generally in more vulnerable occupations. They do most of the dangerous jobs and are more likely to experience stress. They also suffer greater risks in war time. The dramatic decline in the ratio of men to women aged 16–44 following the First World War can be clearly seen in Table 20.

Improvement in medicine, a greater concern for industrial health and safety and the absence of war do seem to be enabling men to hold their own for a longer period of life. It is also likely that as women gain greater equality, particularly at work, they will be prone to the same stresses and risks which have in the past affected men. However, it still seems likely that women will continue to live longer than men. The life expectancy of women at birth is about 74 years compared with 68 for men.

Age

The final division of the population is based on age. The main trends can be seen in Fig. 21. Britain has an ageing population. In 1901 6·2 per cent of the total population were over 65; by 2001 it is likely that 16·6 per cent will be in this age group. Improved standards of living and early retirement have meant that men and women are now living longer than ever before.

The size of younger age groups show the greatest variations. At the beginning of the century nearly one-third of the population was under 16. This dropped to one-in-five in the 1940s and, as a result of the bulge in birth rates in the late 1950s, rose to one-in-four in the early 1970s. It is likely that this group will remain at about 22 per cent with

Fig. 21. *The age structure of the population*

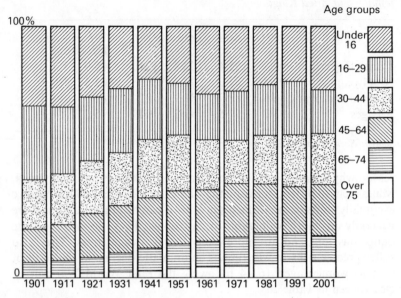

Source: Adapted from *Social Trends*

the possibility of a rise early in the next century. As these different proportions move through the age groups it is possible to see some of the effects they will have on the country as a whole.

Future populations are to some extent influenced by the size of the 16–44 age group as this is the period when people are starting families.

The percentage of the total population in this age-group was greatest in the first half of the century. From the 1950s it declined rapidly until the 1980s when the 1950s bulge worked its way through and seems likely to decline again in the next century.

Another important group is that from 45–64. These are people who are at the top of their careers. In 1901 only 13 per cent were in this age group. By the 1960s it was 22 per cent. This could mean that there are more people chasing a limited number of senior jobs. This has been the effect of the growth of managerial jobs described earlier in this chapter.

The most important age division is based on economic activity. Those under 16 and over 65 are generally non-productive members of the society. They are either too young, or too old to work. They depend upon the work population which is mainly in the 16–44 age group. Table 21 shows the changes in the economically active and dependent groups.

Table 21. *Economically active and dependent age groups percentage, United Kingdom*

	1901	1921	1941	1961	1981	2001
Under 16	32·5	27·9	20·9	24·7	22·0	23·3
16–64	61·3	64·0	67·3	60·7	60·3	60·1
65 and over	6·2	8·1	11·8	14·6	17·7	16·6
Total	100	100	100	100	100	100

Source: Social Trends

Since the middle of this century the size of the main 'productive' age group has settled down to roughly three-fifths of the total. At its peak in the early 1940s it was 67 per cent and it fell in 1971 to 58 per cent. However, these figures do not give the whole picture. They only show those who could work. Throughout this century there has been a trend towards a later start to the working life – because of the need for longer periods of education and training – and an earlier finish – because of early retirement. The clear result has been that the 'burden of dependency' has fallen upon a smaller working population.

In addition, whereas in 1901 only one-in-six of the dependent population was over 65, in 1981 it will be one-in-three. Old people cost the nation more than young people. Though they have contributed to the nation's wealth throughout their lives they require a greater amount of the nation's resources when they retire. Retirement pensions, for example, make up over half of all social security payments. The older people get the greater are their demands upon the health service and welfare departments. This change in the balance of young and old in the dependent population adds to the 'burden of dependency'.

The future

How will population change in the future and what will be the consequences of these changes be? We have already discussed in this chapter the problems of predicting population growth. Official estimates of the size of the population in Great Britain in the year 2051 vary between 60 million and 116 million. The gap between highest and lowest estimates made in 1971 for the 1991 population was 4 million. If such estimates are so unreliable why do people still bother with them?

The real answer is that government and industry must have some

91

basis on which to plan ahead. Even unreliable predictions are better than no prediction at all. The size and structure of the population is so important in every area of planning – housing, schools, hospitals, jobs, etc. – that some idea of future trends is essential.

In the past the greatest concern has been that population growth will get out of control. An eighteenth-century clergyman, Thomas Malthus, wrote one of the first books on population.

In his *Essay on the Principles of Population* Malthus wrote that while food supplies would grow in arithmetical progression, population would increase geometrically, and that soon population growth would outpace the available food supply. Then, he claimed, 'vice, misery and poverty' would cause the population to fall back to a reasonable level. Malthus urged 'moral restraint' as a means of holding back the population and so preventing misery and starvation. His fears seemed to be unfounded. The Industrial Revolution, development of new sources of food in Canada, Australia and Argentina, improved agricultural methods at home, all made possible an increase in population far greater than Malthus could have considered possible.

An alternative theory of population, the optimum theory, sees the total population of a country in terms of the number of workers needed to produce goods for the market and the number of people who are needed to buy them. The 'optimum' level of population is that which allows the economy of the country to function most effectively. The role of the government is to enforce measures which keep the population at its optimum level. There may be some justification for this in conditions of full employment but population levels cannot be controlled 'on demand' like the output of electricity. Attempts to relate the growth of the economy to a population policy since the Second World War have not met with much success.

The difficulty is that industrial and economic changes take place much more quickly than changes in the population. It will take seventy years or more for the 1950s bulge in the birth rate to work its way through the system. In that time men have stepped on the moon, computers will have taken over many jobs and the new technology of the silicon chip will have entered every area of life. To add to the problems no one really knows what causes changes in fertility patterns and birth rates which have a major effect on future populations. The sociologist, therefore, must do the best that is possible with the information that is available and should approach any prediction with a certain amount of caution.

6
The Family

Any study of society must include society's basic components. Jus⁺ as the scientist in the laboratory studies the atoms and molecules that make up matter so the sociologist must study the basic groups which make up society. The most important of these is the family. In almost all societies children are born into families and as they grow older it is the family which introduces them to wider human society. In time they will start families of their own and the cycle will repeat itself once more.

The family is a basic form of social grouping. Every society has some such group which introduces new human beings into full membership of the society. As each individual grows from infant, to child, to adolescent, to adult so he or she moves away from the close community of the family into the looser (associational) groups of school, work, government and the law.

What is the family?

Different people have different ideas about what 'a family' actually is. A good rule for sociologists is 'define your terms'. If you asked every-one in your class to define 'family' you would probably get a wide range of definitions. If you asked them all to write down a list of the people who they regarded as 'their' family you would get a number of different ideas too.

In ancient times the family was made up of all the people in the household, including slaves. Even in Victorian England people regarded their servants as part of the family. In Llanfihangel hired labourers lived in the farmhouse as 'one of the family'. A reasonably precise definition of the family would be:

'A group of people' – united by ties of blood, marriage or adoption;
     – who form a single household;
     – in which they perform their respective roles of

husband and wife, son and daughter, mother
and father, brother and sister;
– creating a common culture.

Under a definition like this servants cannot be members of the
family because they are not 'united by ties of blood, marriage or adoption'. Similarly the wife's sister who lives 'just around the corner' is
not a member of the family either. She is related by blood but is not
part of the 'common household'. But many people do regard 'close kin'
as members of their family.

Fig. 22. *Family patterns*

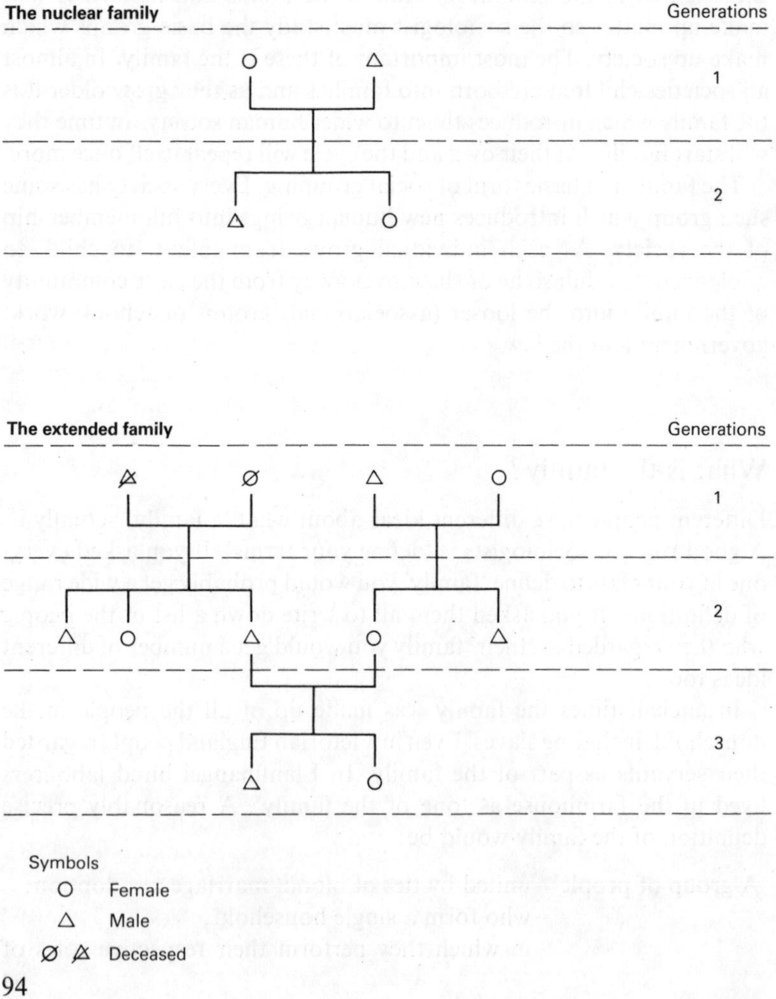

The nuclear family   Generations

The extended family   Generations

Symbols

O   Female

△   Male

Ø △   Deceased

94

To get over this problem of definition sociologists in Britain have got into the habit of using two terms to describe the family. The definition we have just seen describes 'the nuclear family' – just parents and children. The large group including aunts, uncles, grandparents and others is called 'the extended family'. The differences are clearer if we use the sort of family diagrams which a social anthropologist would use when studying kinship (see Fig. 22).

We can see now that the extended family is made up of a series of nuclear families linked by ties of 'blood, marriage or adoption'. If we are going to be really particular about the use of words we must say that the extended family is not really a family at all. It is 'an extended kinship group'. However, most writers do refer to it as 'an extended family'. From these family and kinship diagrams you can see that whereas the nuclear family contains only two generations (parents and children), the extended family contains three (grandparents, parents and children). For this reason they are sometimes called two- or three-generation families.

Patterns of family life

Family life in simple societies is often very different from family life in societies like ours. Were it not for the basic fundamentals of childbirth and caring for the young and old many of these families would be unrecognisable to us. In Samoa, for example, older children take over the task of caring for young children as soon as they can feed themselves. In the Negev desert the young Bedouin will not be so interested in whom he marries. He leaves the choice of his bride to his parents, knowing that if he is not happy with their choice he can persuade his father to arrange an exchange marriage. If he were a wealthy Bedouin he might even contemplate having a number of wives. Because life in 'small-scale' societies is so much simpler than life in our society they have been closely studied by social anthropologists. The knowledge that has been gained is especially useful when we try to get an idea of what the terms 'family' and 'marriage' really mean.

Marriage in Britain is based on *monogamy*. No one is allowed by law to have more than one husband or wife at a time. In some societies *polygamy* (more than one marriage partner) is common. The most common form of polygamy is called *polygyny* and occurs when one man has a number of wives. Amongst the Bedouin of the Negev it is important that a sheik has many sons. Infant mortality is so high that a wise sheik would have a number of wives in order to ensure him plenty of sons. Many wives would also give a sheik important political links with other sections of his tribe.

The other form of polygamy is *polyandry*. Polyandry involves two or more men, often brothers, sharing a wife. It is not very common. Young men of the Lele tribe in Central Africa practise polyandry because the older men have the right to have more than one wife and do not leave enough marriageable girls for the rest of the tribe.

THE LINE OF DESCENT

Apart from differences in the number of marriage partners which a society finds acceptable there are also differences in the way in which societies reckon descent. In England descent has always been through the male line; from father to the first-born son. Traditionally the eldest son would inherit the main share of the father's fortune, and his title, if he were a member of the aristocracy. Today most people simply inherit their father's surname. This system is termed *patrilineal* and is also found in the Bible. In the first chapter of St Matthew's Gospel the writer gives a list of 'the house and lineage of David' which attempts to show that Jesus Christ was descended, eldest son to eldest son, from King David and from Abraham. Jewish society has always been patrilineal.

The Trobriand Islands in the south-west Pacific Ocean have a *matrilineal* society. They reckon descent through the mother. Instead of passing possessions and titles from father to son they are passed from the mother's brother to her son. From uncle to nephew through the mother. The Trobrianders do not recognise the blood relationship between father and son. They believe that the child is placed in the mother's womb by the spirits of her ancestors and that it is the duty of her brother to care for her and her child because they are his ancestors too.

So far we have seen that marriage in our society is monogamous and our family is patrilineal. There are also rules concerning whom a person may marry. At the very back of the Book of Common Prayer used in the Church of England are 'Tables of Kindred and Affinity' which lay down the 'kin' whom you may not marry. If you look at this list you will notice that all those included are your near relatives. Because our society lays down that people must choose a marriage partner from *outside* of a particular group of people it is said to be *exogamous*. In some societies there are rules which ensure that people marry *inside* a social group. They are *endogamous*. As we saw in Chapter 3, in Indian Hindu society a high caste Vaishya could never marry a lower caste Sudras. He can only marry into his own caste.

Our society has no rules concerning where a married couple may live. In some parts of England they may rely on the bride's mother to 'speak for them' to the landlord and as a result may end up living near her, but this is as much chance as anything. The mother-in-law would be thought an interfering old busybody if she insisted that her daughter lived around the corner. Some societies do have such rules. Among the Manus tribe of New Guinea the newly-weds are expected to live in the husband's village, whereas the children of the Nayar tribe of coastal India would be brought up in their mother's home. The Manus are *patrilocal* and the Nayars *matrilocal*.

Like any social group families have patterns of authority. Where the mother, or the grandmother is recognised as having the greatest say in making decisions we would say that the family is *matriarchal*. When the father, or grandfather, is in command it is a *patriarchy*.

Families, therefore, can be analysed in a number of ways. There are five questions we can ask.

Firstly – who do you count as 'kin', who are your family?

Secondly – how many marriage partners are permitted in any society?

Thirdly – how is inheritance organised?

Fourthly – with whom does the family live?

Fifthly – who is in authority?

Marriage

It is often very difficult to separate ideas about the family from ideas about marriage. They are very closely linked in our everyday experience and in the way we think. However, they need not be linked in real life. It is quite usual for people to marry but not to have a family and it is becoming more acceptable to have a family without being married.

In our society a wedding is an important social and legal event. It is socially important because it states in public, in a ritual fashion, that two individuals have accepted certain social conventions and obligations. It is important legally because the law, at marriage, recognises certain rights and duties. Once legally married the status of the marriage partners changes. They cannot become *un-married* without the agreement of the law. The marriage partners also have certain rights in law. Increasingly, however, many of the rights, and the obligations, involved in civil marriage are being applied to those who have the appearance of marriage without the legal certificate. Couples are often said to be 'living together', or in official words are 'cohabiting'. Frequently the relationships of these couples are as strong and binding as those found in so-called 'proper' marriages. Often they are even stronger. Such marriages are termed *common-law marriages* and may be recognised by the law where it can be proved that they are well

97

Fig. 23. *One-parent families*

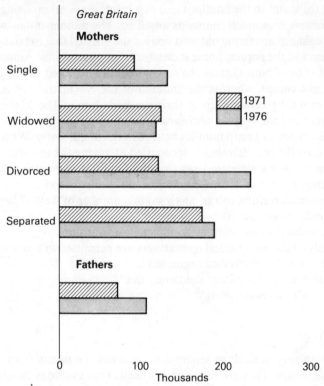

Great Britain

Mothers

Single

Widowed

Divorced

Separated

1971
1976

Fathers

0   100   200   300
Thousands

Source: Office of Population Censuses and Surveys

established. Many couples with common-law marriages have families and are quite indistinguishable from other families in society. Bringing up a family may not involve marriage at all. Single-parent families exist where one person takes responsibility for their children. This may occur when one parent – mother or father – may not wish, or be able to live with, or marry, the other. Sometimes this occurs through divorce or widowhood but often through a deliberate choice. Roughly nine out of every 100 households are 'one parent households'.

It is important, therefore, to keep these two ideas, marriage and family, quite separate in our minds. We will consider this in more detail when we discuss changes in divorce at the end of this chapter.

The functions of the family

Among sociologists today there is debate on the value of examining society in terms of 'function'. It does, however, help us to understand family life if we consider the functions of the family within modern society.

Families in all societies have four basic functions: reproduction, maintenance, socialisation and placement. They may have other functions: religious, political, economic, educational and so on. None of these functions is carried out only by the family. Other institutions in society also carry out similar functions.

REPRODUCTION

A fundamental function of the family in all societies is reproduction. In fact we do not recognise that 'a family' has begun until a married couple have children. To say that someone is 'in the family way' means that reproduction is taking place. Having children is recognised as a central purpose of marriage. In some societies the marriage itself is not recognised until children have been born. Within our society there are strong pressures to keep childbirth within the family. In the past illegitimacy has been frowned on and illegitimate children have not been treated as equal to legitimate children. This stigma attached to illegitimacy has largely disappeared, and all children have equal rights irrespective of their parents' relationship. Social controls against sexual intercourse outside marriage are weaker and it is now more acceptable for a single girl to have children. Many people would regard it as irresponsible, but the level of illegitimate births is rising and more single girls are choosing to keep their children. If the trend continues it is likely that nearly one out of every ten babies will be born outside a legally recognised marriage. Society will have to face up to the needs of the one-parent family.

MAINTENANCE

A major problem for the 'lone mother' is that of bringing up her children – the problem of maintenance. We have already seen in Chapter 5 that the infant mortality rate among illegitimate children is double that for the legitimate. This is an indication of the problems of childcare faced by the unmarried mother. Parents are expected to care for these children, to maintain them. In the last hundred years the period of time during which parents needed to maintain their children has lengthened. Changes in the school-leaving age and increased voluntary staying-on have meant that young people have needed the support of their parents for far longer. Against this we should remember that family size has decreased and resources have therefore been concentrated on fewer children.

The family does not face the problem of maintenance alone. The state and local authorities assist the family in many ways. Welfare clinics, family doctors and hospital services are available to help and advise mothers. Welfare foods are provided as well as free school milk and dinners for those who are in medical need or come from large families. Cash grants and tax relief are paid to the parents of young children. Voluntary organisations like the National Society for the Prevention of Cruelty to Children are on guard lest children should be neglected and local authorities have the power to take children into care should the parents fail to maintain them adequately.

In the Israeli kibbutz this function of maintenance has, to a large extent, been taken over by the community. Children are cared for by trained nurses, only seeing their parents in the evening when they return from work. The family, however, provides other things than just food, warmth and clothing.

SOCIALISATION

A newborn baby is helpless. It cannot feed itself, or move itself about; it has great difficulty in communicating with others. As the baby grows into the child so it needs to exercise its muscles and to coordinate its movements. The baby also begins to discover that certain actions, such as smiling, produce pleasant results, whereas other actions produce painful results. When a baby is hungry it cries. The cries bring someone who will feed it; once fed the baby stops crying. The baby has begun to learn that it must communicate with others to get what it wants. Language develops and the child will learn that it is better to ask for things, to say 'please' and 'thank you', rather than lie on the floor screaming. At the earlier stage the baby is only concerned with itself, with its own needs. As the child grows it becomes more aware of others and begins to learn to adjust its behaviour to allow for others. Social behaviour begins to develop. The child is learning how to live in society. This process is known as 'socialisation'. It involves the learning of right and wrong, good and bad, value and worthlessness. Socialisation is an essential part of the process of learning, and it continues throughout our lives.

As the child grows he or she is gradually socialised into the roles that are expected by society. Roles of son and daughter, brother and sister, friend, playmate, have all to be learned. Each role involves certain expectations of behaviour. Very little of human behaviour is instinctive. Unlike many animals little of our behaviour is passed on from parents to children genetically, that is, through the genes and chromosomes which pass from parents to children at conception. Most human behaviour has to be learned. Each individual needs to learn the behaviour which is appropriate to each role in any situation. As each child gets older he or she enters into more complex situations involving new learning. Going to school, for example, means that the child has to learn the role of pupil. The family plays a vital part in socialisation. It is within the family that the basic personality, attitudes, values and moral ideas are laid down. It is upon this foundation that adult socialisation will be built.

PLACEMENT

In a caste system each individual's position in life is determined at birth. He is born into a caste. The family in Hindu caste society has an important social placement function. Similarly in Chapter 1 we saw how some people were born into particular roles and statuses in Banbury. There were others who had achieved a different level of status from that into which they were born. We must ask ourselves how far the family in modern Britain actually has a placement function. In Chapter 7 we read that social placement is one of the purposes of education. Could it be that this is a function which has been taken over by the schools? It must, at least, be a function which is shared by family and school. However, if we consider the effect of social class on an individual's progress through the educational system we shall see that family does play an important basic part in social placement. While British society is nowhere near so rigid as a caste system it would seem that most people end their lives in a social position not far from the one they began in.

We mentioned earlier that families have other functions: religious, economic and political, etc. These functions are not so essential to the family as reproduction, maintenance, placement and socialisation. To a large extent they have been taken over by other institutions in society. Families in general are not expected to carry out religious duties. This might not be true for Roman Catholic, Jewish or Mormon families which have family religious obligations. For most people in this country religion and family are not bound up closely together. In a similar way the family's political function is slight; nor do families involve themselves in economic activities. There are economic aspects of family life. Fathers go out to work to earn money to keep the family. But this is a part of the maintenance function. In domestic industry in the eighteenth century the whole family worked on the woollen cloth. The children would prepare the wool; the mother would spin and the father would weave. In that way the family itself became an economic unit. Such families are the exception today. Health and medical welfare is no longer a basic function of the family in modern society, nor are recreation or education. Professor McIver has argued that the modern family concentrates its efforts on the basic 'essential' functions and has handed over the other 'non-essential' functions. In this way the family

101

is able to devote itself to doing those things which it can do better than anyone else.

Changing attitudes

CHILDREN

One very important change which we have mentioned concerns the position of children in the family. Within the modern family there has been a tremendous change in relationships. Conjugal relationships (those between husband and wife), relationships between generations, and relationships between siblings, have all changed in some way. Families today are better off. The 'breadwinner' is able to keep his family and if, for some reason, he cannot then the state will help out. This increased affluence has benefited children to a tremendous extent. Parents have more time to devote to their children. Fathers want their sons to 'have a better start in life' than they had. The children are seen as the means by which the family can progress. They are also the recipients of considerable attention, aimed at nurturing their development. The ideas of Sigmund Freud earlier this century emphasised the importance of childhood and the relationship with parents. Authors like Benjamin Spock provided the knowledge which parents sought after in a readable form. Families became increasingly 'child-centred'.

A Nottingham mother gave her views to some research workers who were inquiring into the way she brought up her children:
'People nowadays think more about what's good for the children, from the children's point of view. Everything I do with him, I try to do the best for him, I'm thinking about him all the time. I'm careful about his food, and I hold him on my lap after his bottle so he won't have a tummy-ache, he's inoculated so he won't catch diseases, later on I take them to the dentist so they won't get toothache: I'm thinking in advance of their comfort all of the time. I know there's some people leave their children and go to work now never mind what happens to the children so long as you get the money, but that's just a few – most people think more of the children's good. It used to be just the higher classes that did that, but now I think that . . . thinking . . . has spread right through the general classes.

'Nowadays, if they don't turn out all right you wonder where you've gone wrong, don't you? It used to be they made you do this and do that and you did it, and if things went wrong it was the child's fault, not the parents', they could never be wrong. I think that we're not so happy about ourselves these days, we blame ourselves, not the child. I do not know. I wish I didn't sometimes.' (Newson and Newson 1971)

WIVES AND MOTHERS

The woman's position in the modern family has changed too. In 1869 John Stuart Mill wrote 'There remain no legal slaves except the mistress of the house'; and the mid-Victorian husband could declare: 'My wife and I are of one mind – and that mind is mine.' The legal status of women in England little over a century ago was the same as children and lunatics.

Much has changed. Women have legal equality with men: they can own property and sue for divorce; they have political equality: the right to vote was gained after years of struggle; they have equal rights to education; and they are able to take on careers in their own right. Within the family the changes we have already studied: smaller family, more child-centred, limited functions etc., have made the life of today's mother radically different from that of her Victorian sister. The average married woman a century ago was faced with a life which stretched

Fig. 24. *Changes in the pattern of women's lives*

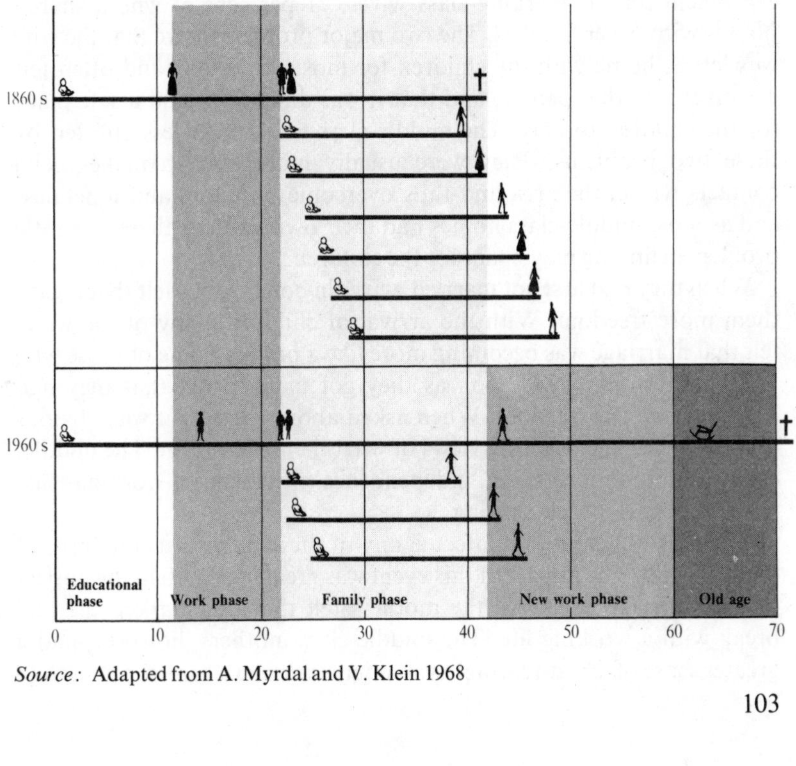

Source: Adapted from A. Myrdal and V. Klein 1968

103

from marriage to an early grave. Each year brought an almost inevitable extra child, many died before the next was born; by the time she was thirty she had given birth to nine or ten children and was faced with ten or more years of caring for them.

In the mid-twentieth century a woman's period of child-bearing is well out of the way by the time she is 30 and she has only two or three children to care for. When they are five the state takes charge of them for much of the day. By the time the mother is 45 her children are able to look after themselves and she has twenty or thirty years of active life ahead of her.

The captive wife

It would be wrong to think that smaller families and emancipation put an end to *all* the problems of married women. Hannah Gavron (1970) conducted a survey in the early 1960s into the ordinary lives of 96 mothers with young children living in North London.

There were equal numbers of middle-class and working-class wives in the group studied. They were asked questions on a number of topics: the home, marriage, equality in the marriage, children, the organisation of family life, leisure, social contacts, and work. Housing was especially a problem for the working-class wives, 71 per cent of whom shared houses with other families. The two major problems were that the wife was left at home with the children for most of the day and often felt cut-off from other people, and that it was difficult to find a safe place for the children to play. The middle-class wives were less affected by these two problems. They were usually more able to make social contacts within the area and thus overcome boredom and loneliness and as most middle-class homes had their own gardens there was little problem in finding play-space for the children.

When they had first got married, wives in both groups felt that it gave them more freedom. With the arrival of children many of the wives felt that marriage was becoming more like a prison. Some of those who had children almost as soon as they got married felt that they had hardly tasted the freedom. When asked about equality it was obvious that the wives had differing views of what the word meant. The middle-class wives took it to mean 'independence', whereas the working-class wives understood it as 'sharing'.

The greatest event that affected any of the families was the birth of the first child. The impact of this event was greater even than the impact of the marriage itself. All the mothers felt that this marked the real break with a working life. The middle-class mothers, however, had a greater sense of 'child-rearing' as an interruption in a career, rather than the end of the career. In nearly all cases husband and wife shared in the task of running the home; for some this amounted to a sharing in decisions as well as sharing the jobs of the home, such as washing up and putting the baby to bed. Leisure was a problem for many families. The working-class wives were not keen to have baby-sitters whom they did not know well, which usually meant that they relied on relatives. Often husband and wife had to take their leisure separately. One would stay in whilst the other went down to the pub or to the pictures. Very often the middle-class wives were more aware of the danger of becoming 'house-bound' and took steps to prevent it. They joined clubs and classes and made more of an effort to get out and meet people. Whereas the middle-class wives had friends, the working-class wives had relatives.

Social contact was seen as a reason for getting a job by the middle-class wives. It was not the only reason. 'Something to do' and 'extra money' were both important, but they were more important to the working-class wives.

In the conclusion to her study Hannah Gavron described the urban mother at the centre of a conflict between the demands of motherhood, a career, and a useful life. Social changes in recent years have increased this conflict and there is a need for rethinking of the educational opportunities for girls, the demands of employers upon married women, and the social role of the young mother.

The family in the community

Hannah Gavron called her report *The Captive Wife*. She was concerned about the mothers with young children who were 'captive' in their own homes; having no friends or relatives nearby whom they could talk to, or visit. One of the causes of such a state of affairs has been the transition from extended families, or kinship systems, to mainly nuclear families. Rehousing, improved standards of living, better education, and better jobs have all helped to weaken or destroy many closely knit communities. It is less common today for a son or daughter to marry and set up house within a mile or two of 'Mum'. Instead they are moving away, to new towns or to housing estates on the edge of the city. Fewer and fewer people are living out their entire lives within the bounds of a single community.

Much has been written about the types of community in which the three-generation family is common. They are usually found in older areas near the centre of cities, or in villages, either in the depth of the countryside or near a coalmine. In these old traditional communities many of the men will work in the same job, they will drink in the same pub, they probably went to the same school. In the past there has been little to encourage the young to seek education or jobs outside the community. In such places two or three generations of the same family will live out their lives in the same cluster of streets.

Michael Young and Peter Willmott have studied extended families in Bethnal Green in East London. Here they describe the lives of Mr and Mrs Banton.

Mr and Mrs Banton and their two young children live at present (1955) in a four-roomed house in Minton Street. These houses were built in the 1870s of brick which has become a uniform smoke-eaten grey. They are nearly all alike in plan; on the first floor two bedrooms, and on the ground floor a living room, a kitchen, a small scullery opening on to a yard which has a lavatory at the end of it and a patch of earth down one side.

On the warm sunny evening of the interview, children were playing hop-scotch or 'he' in the roadway while their parents, when not watching the television, were at their open windows. Some of the older people were sitting at upright chairs on the pavement, just in front of their doors, or in the passages leading to the sculleries, chatting with each other or watching the children at play.

Mr Banton was a small, downright man in shirtsleeves and braces; he looked (though he was not) much younger than his wife, who at thirty-five was beginning to fill out into the figure of a Bethnal Green 'mum'.

They told us they were married in the last year of the war. When her husband was demobbed they took over the two small rooms at the top of her parents' house. Though they were glad to have somewhere to live they were not happy: they did all of their cooking on two gas rings and had to come downstairs into their parents' part of the house for water, sink and w.c. They had to stay there for four years.

When Mrs Banton's widowed grandfather moved out of the house he had been occupying in the next street (into an Old People's Home), her mother spoke to the rent collector and he allowed them to take over the grandfather's tenancy; and there they still are.

She still goes round every day to see her mother and get shopping for her; her mother, although getting on in years is not so active as she was but is still able to look after the grandchildren whenever the need arises. (Young and Willmott 1957)

CHANGE AND THE EXTENDED FAMILY

At one time communities like Bethnal Green were stronger and more in evidence than they are today. Their strength rested on the continuation of tradition, on the stability which comes when generation after generation inhabit the same few hundred yards of street, or block of terraced houses.

But progress demands movement: new houses, new jobs, more learning, new ideas, as a result many traditional and close-knit working-class communities have been weakened. People today are more mobile; they are on the move from place to place, from job to job. Their mobility is geographical, educational, occupational and social.

Many of these old communities were settled in areas of old housing. The people needed better homes and the old slums had to make way for modern blocks of flats. The old neighbourhood groups were broken up and the common street life was lost among the lifts and landings of the tower flats. Some families chose to move out of the area altogether: to the suburbs and the expanding new towns out in the country. Here, too, the old community spirit was lost and new patterns of family life developed to make up for the loss of the family network.

Peter Willmott and Michael Young followed some of their Bethnal Green families out into the suburbs; to Woodford in Essex. They wrote about the changes which they found.

> In one way Woodford has turned out to be much as we expected it. Kinship ties there are much looser than in Bethnal Green. When a couple marry they set up a genuinely independent household; relatives' homes are more often connected by occasional missions, not by the continuous back and forth which makes two homes into one in Bethnal Green. Kinship matters less – friendship more. That is no surprise. (Willmott and Young 1960)

Improved education has also encouraged the break-up of the extended family. As long as young people were content to leave school early and find a job near home there was little chance of them leaving the local community. A young man would probably meet a local girl, get married, and, after living with the in-laws for a while, find a place in the area in which to set up house. With the spread of greater educational opportunities more young people are leaving home to go to college or university. They meet someone from another part of the country and when they do get married they are likely to live at a distance from either group of kin. A better education would also open to them a wider range of jobs than would be found 'back home'. Their 'job market' would probably cover the country and often promotion meant moving house yet again. They would very quickly be cut off from the community in which they grew up.

Improved education also leads to greater social mobility. Young men and women who have been away to college, or have made a success of their careers often see themselves as members of a different social class from their parents. They would have acquired different attitudes and new styles of life. They would not have been happy returning to the community in which they had been born.

The symmetrical family

In Chapter 2 we considered some of the methods used in Young and Willmott's *The Symmetrical Family* (1973) and in Oakley's *Sociology of Housework* (1974). It will be useful here to consider some of their conclusions. Young and Willmott traced family life through three stages. Stage 1 can be seen in Britain before the Industrial Revolution. At this stage the family is the unit of production. In an agricultural society all of the family must work together to make a living. The second stage is the 'stage of disruption' when the unity of the family is broken. The husband becomes a wage-earner, the wife runs the house, or works elsewhere, the children go to school. This stage comes in with the Industrial Revolution. Stage 3 begins early in the twentieth century. These families are 'home-centred'; they share much of their lives; they are more 'nuclear' than 'extended'; roles have become similar but separate; and, above all, they depend upon technology.

> Gas light and electric light were inventions as crucial as piped water; at least husbands could see the faces of their wives after dark without too great an expense. The miniature electric motor was another key invention, powering home laundries, home ice-makers, tiny cold stores, floor cleaners and cooking aids. The average housewife has been given 'about the same amount of mechanical assistance (about two horsepower) as was used by the average industrial worker around 1914'. These inventions have, perhaps, done more for the wife than the husband. But he has been just as absorbed by the machines which have brought entertainment into the home, starting with the gramophone and ending (so far), with colour television, and more so than she by the new style of do-it-yourself handicraft production with its power tools and extension ladders and stick-on tiles and emulsion paint. (Young and Willmott 1973)

At stage 3 we can see the appearance of the symmetrical family. These three stages follow from one another but also overlap so that within modern Britain families at each of the stages exist side-by-side. Young and Willmott's slightly rosy view of family life in modern Britain has not gone unchallenged. Ann Oakley in her study *The Sociology of Housework* questions the whole idea of a 'symmetrical family'. Her evidence suggests that in a number of very important areas of family life roles are far from equal. Women's lives were firmly based in the home carrying out domestic tasks and looking after children. The involvement of the husbands in these activities varied considerably.

Table 21. *Husband's participation in housework and child-care.*

Husband's participation in housework	working class %	middle class %
low	85	35
medium	5	45
high	10	20
	100	100
Husband's participation in child care		
low	50	40
medium	40	20
high	10	40
	100	100

Source: Oakley 1974

Ann Oakley comes to the conclusion that:
1. Only a minority of husbands give the kind of help that is evidence of real equality in modern marriage.
2. The pattern of husband's participation differs between social classes.
3. Men are more likely to take part in child-rearing than in housework.
It is very difficult to speak generally about family life in Britain. Every family is different and the common patterns are not always clear. Ann Oakley also reminds us that most sociologists are men and this may influence the way in which they look at changes in the family.

Divorce

Before 1857 it was only possible to get a divorce by Act of Parliament. After the Matrimonial Causes Act of that year it was still only the husband who could petition for divorce, and then only on the grounds of his wife's adultery. A further Act of 1878 gave the wife the right to apply to the courts for a separation order on the grounds of her husband's cruelty but it was not until 1923 that husband and wife could sue for divorce on equal terms. In 1937 the grounds for which a

109

divorce could be granted were extended to cover desertion and insanity as well as adultery and cruelty. In 1943 the first Divorce Court outside London was established.

CHANGES IN THE LAW

Immediately after the Second World War the demand for divorces rose rapidly. So great was the rise that special arrangements had to be made to revise Divorce Court procedure and clear the backlog of cases. This took place in 1946 and 1947. The Matrimonial Causes Act of 1950 gathered all of the previous legislation under one Act of Parliament, and in the previous year, 1949, the Legal Aid and Advice Act had allowed the cost of divorce to be borne by the state under Legal Aid. By 1950 a divorce could be obtained anywhere in the country, by men and women of all classes on equal terms.

Fig. 25. *Divorce*

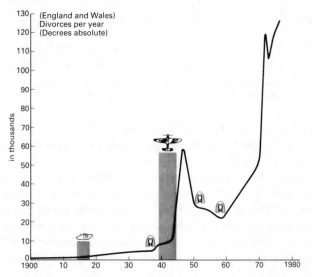

During the 1960s however, there was increasing concern about 'the grounds for divorce'. It was felt that if a marriage had obviously 'broken down', and there was no hope of a fresh start being made, a divorce should be granted whether or not adultery, cruelty, desertion or insanity were involved. This led eventually to the 1969 Divorce Law Reform Bill which gave 'irretrievable breakdown' as the only reason for granting a divorce.

This occurs when the couple have lived apart for at least two years and both agree to a divorce, or five years apart if only one partner wants

110

a divorce, in which case the court has to ensure that a divorced wife is adequately provided for. If the respondent has deserted the petitioner, without cause, for two years before the petition, or if, as the result of some action on the part of the respondent (including adultery), the petitioner can no longer be expected to continue living with the respondent, then a divorce would be granted. The courts are required to make every effort to get the husband and wife back together before granting a divorce. Courts are also able to ensure that proper arrangements are made for the care of any children of the marriage. As we can see from Fig. 25 the rise in divorces has not been smooth. A high level of divorces was reached at the end of the Second World War and it did not reach that figure again until the mid-1970s. A divorce trend such as this does not support the view that marriage as a whole is breaking down. Divorce rates are more closely tied to changes in the law, social upheavals and changed attitudes to divorce itself. When the Divorce Law is changed it is because society has changed its view of how unsatisfactory a marriage must become before the partners are allowed to part.

Marriage is, however, more popular than ever. People are marrying younger and more are choosing to get married. Combined with increased expectancy of life this means that there is more 'marriage' going on today than ever before. People expect more of their marriages today. Films, television, books, and magazines increasingly tell people what they should expect from their marriage. Mass media provides a yardstick against which couples can measure the success of their marriage. It is not surprising that more decide that they have made a wrong choice.

Fig. 26. *Divorce by length of marriage 1976 (percentage)*

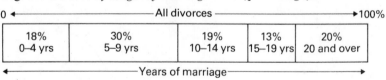

0 ◄─────────────────── All divorces ───────────────────► 100%				
18% 0–4 yrs	30% 5–9 yrs	19% 10–14 yrs	13% 15–19 yrs	20% 20 and over
◄────────────────── Years of marriage ──────────────────►				

Source: Social Trends

Very often the increase in the number of divorces is used as evidence of the breakdown of family life in Britain. Such statements need to be looked at carefully: firstly very few divorced couples remain unmarried for very long. Re-marriages, after divorce or widowhood made up nearly one-third of all marriages in 1976 and, as Fig. 28 shows, the proportion is rising. Divorce tells us more about a person's desire to have a good marriage than about any wish not to be married at all.

Fig. 27. *Children and divorce 1976*

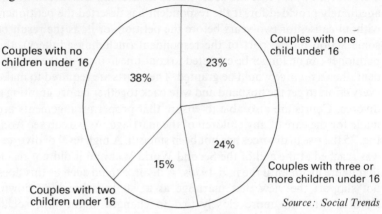

Couples with no
children under 16

38%

Couples with one
child under 16

23%

24%

15%

Couples with three or
more children under 16

Couples with two
children under 16

Source: Social Trends

Secondly, though most divorces do involve children, two out of every five do not involve children under the age of 16.

The greatest risk of divorce is within the first ten years of marriage and people who marry while they are still in their teens are especially at risk. In 1977 12 per cent of all women married ten years earlier had divorced but for women who were married before their twentieth birthday it was closer to 19 per cent.

An increase in divorce rates indicates the greater strain put upon marriage today and people's desire to have a happy marriage even if it means a second or a third attempt.

Fig. 28. *Re-marriage (either divorced or widowed, as a percentage of all marriages)*

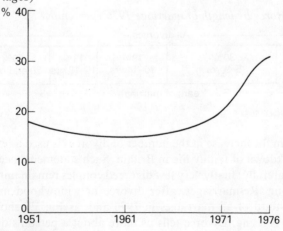

Source: Social Trends

7

Schooling

Schools are a feature of all industrialised societies. They are not nearly so important in peasant societies or in small-scale tribal societies. Why is this? Why do industrial societies need schools? Of course there were schools in Britain long before industrialisation.

Education in England

The first schools in Britain were founded by the monks, but many of them disappeared at the dissolution of the monasteries under Henry VIII. The schools which replaced them were the result of demands by the citizens of each small town to have a place where their sons could get a grounding in 'grammar'. Many of these old grammar schools still remain. While the wealthy paid for their sons to be educated, there were always endowed scholarships for the sons of the poor. In 1541 Archbishop Cranmer wrote: 'If the gentleman's son be apt for learning, let him be admitted; if not apt let the poor man's child that is apt enter in his place.'

In the centuries which followed many of these schools fell into decline. Some disappeared altogether for lack of pupils and many survived in name only. Gentlemen had private tutors for their sons and governesses for their daughters. A prospering tradesman might send his son to a small private 'academy' or to a country parson, for instruction. A poor man might be fortunate enough to send his children to a dame's school, or to a ragged school, possibly even to a Sunday school. More likely than not the children of the lower classes received no education at all, for as Britain moved into the period of history known as the Industrial Revolution, children were increasingly expected to earn their own living.

THE EARLY NINETEENTH CENTURY

The nineteenth century saw a new pattern of education emerging in response to two major forces in society. First, the nation was moving away from an emphasis on agriculture towards a reliance on industry; secondly, as the benefits of industrialisation seeped down through all classes of society more and more people began to see education as a right. Education became an important part of the growing democracy of the nineteenth century.

An agricultural society had no great need for an elaborate system of education. The skills of farming were passed on from father to son; the skills of the farm kitchen from mother to daughter. Young men had no need to pass examinations in order to prove their skill. Their positions in that society were ascribed. Similarly a merchant in a nearby town had no great need to find a school which would teach his son a trade. Schools there were, but booklearning was not thought to be as valuable as learning a skill. A young lad would be indentured to a craftsman or to another merchant. He would live with the 'master' and his family as an apprentice. Not only would he learn the job but he would also be expected to learn morals and good Christian behaviour.

Industry made different demands, presented different kinds of problems, which a system of education based on the family could not cope with. New skills arose, skills which fathers could no longer teach to their sons. Families moved from the countryside into the towns, not to work at traditional crafts but in new factories. There was also a demand for qualifications: some indication that a person could do a job he claimed he could.

TWO NATIONS

The wealthier classes still had the old grammar schools, some of which were now acquiring the name of 'public schools'. These schools, under men like Dr Arnold at Rugby and Samuel Butler at Shrewsbury, came into a new period of their history. In them the status of the old landed aristocracy rubbed shoulders with the wealth of the new industrialists, fusing the two elements into a new ruling class.

But the task of educating the mass of the nation's children was left to the voluntary societies: the National Society for the Church of England and the British and Foreign Society for the Free Churches. The schools run by these bodies provided an elementary education for the poorer classes.

THE 1870 ACT

The year 1870 marks a turning point in English education. Under the Education Act of that year the state ceased leaving education to the churches and began to allow, then to encourage, education provided by local school boards. Such boards were, at first, to fill the gaps in the voluntary system. They soon, however, became the leading partner in

114

what was described as a dual system – involving state and church together. From 1870 onwards the state was fully involved in the education of the nation's children. Industry and commerce demanded more and more skilled workers, more and more people who could read and write, and were 'good with figures'. More people got the vote, and so demanded the right to know what was going on, the right to be educated. It was not enough just to have more voters, they had to be educated voters, able to make the decisions which voting entailed. As a nineteenth-century member of Parliament told the House of Commons in 1870: 'Educate your masters'. These pressures gradually shaped the pattern of education in the country and led the state to devote an increasing proportion of the nation's wealth to education.

Table 22. *Percentage of young people of various ages receiving full-time education, Great Britain, 1870–1962*

Age	1870 %	1902 %	1938 %	1962 %
10-year-olds	40	100	100	100
14-year-olds	2	9	38	100
17-year-olds	1	2	4	15
19-year-olds	1	1	2	7

Source: Robbins Report 1963 Table 1

SECONDARY EDUCATION FOR ALL

In 1902 the 1870 school boards were incorporated into local councils, setting up a pattern which exists to this day. The next great step forward came with the Education Act of 1944. This Act laid down that schools should be provided for children on the basis of 'age, aptitude and ability'. Under this system children should first go to a primary school. Starting at five in an infants' school or infants' department and going on to the junior school at the age of eight. At eleven each child would sit an examination, the eleven-plus, after which a choice would be made, transferring the child on the basis of 'aptitude and ability', to one of three types of school. For children whose interests and ability suited them for book-learning, for an 'academic' education, there were the 'secondary grammar schools'. Able children whose interests lay in a more practical area went to the 'secondary technical school' and the remainder went to a 'secondary modern school'. Some schools chose to remain outside the state system and remained as 'independent' schools; others elected to receive a grant direct from the government while retaining their independence and some fee-paying pupils in return for taking some local authority pupils. These were known as 'direct grant' schools. The schools provided by the churches lost much of their independence but gained a place on the edge of the state system, with the church having some control over the curriculum.

This system of secondary education made up of grammar, technical and 'modern' schools became known as the tripartite system. It was based on the idea that it was possible to decide at the age of eleven the type of job, or career, a child would be suited to. This was the principle of selection.

THE PRIVATE SECTOR

Outside the state system was the 'private sector', made up of those schools which charged fees for the education they provided. The foremost of these were the great public schools: Eton, Winchester, and Harrow; there were also a large number of minor public schools and 'independent' fee-paying schools.

Schools in the private sector take their pupils at different ages to those laid down for state schools under the 1944 Education Act. After a spell in a nursery or pre-preparatory school a child would go, at the age of eight to a preparatory school which would prepare him, or her, for a place at a public or independent school, after taking a Common Entrance Examination at the age of thirteen. Most of such schools are residential. The majority of their pupils are boarders and day-pupils are in the minority.

This long process of change in the pattern of education did not come to an end in 1944. Since then Britain's system of education has changed still more, reflecting those aspects which society as a whole thinks are important. The Education Acts of 1870 and 1944 reflected the social pressures of the years before them. Those pressures are still with us.

The comprehensive debate

Not everyone viewed the 1944 Education Act with approval. Some education authorities regarded the tripartite system as unsuitable for both practical and educational reasons and devised alternative schemes for their areas. Anglesey, for example, lacked both resources and children to provide three different types of secondary school, and instead introduced a system based on one 'comprehensive' school.

London, on different grounds, also rejected the tripartite system and produced a long-term plan for 'All-through' (11–18) schools. Leicestershire in 1957 introduced a further alternative form of 'comprehensive education': children went from the primary school, at eleven plus, to a high school, with the option of transferring to a grammar school if they wished at fourteen.

These alternative approaches to the problem of providing a secondary education suited to each child's age, aptitude and ability grew out of criticisms of the principles of the 1944 Act and the experience and evidence which was built up by sociologists and educators in the 1950s and 1960s. This resulted in the continuing debate about the best structure for secondary education. On one side were those who advocated 'comprehensive schools' and on the other were those who pressed the claims of the grammar schools. Because education is a matter for the state, involving large sums of government money and centralised administration by a government department, affecting the whole future development of British society, this debate has become an important issue for each of the main political parties.

The Conservative Party, on the whole, favours the arguments of those who wish to see grammar schools remain alongside other types of secondary school. The Labour Party, on the other hand, feels that it is wrong to divide children in this way and that the needs of society are best met by having one school, providing equal opportunities for all children of the same age.

The argument over the best way to organise schooling is a long and bitter one. The great majority of children today are educated in comprehensive schools of one type or another but a number of local education authorities still maintain their grammar schools.

Those who favour comprehensive schools point to the lack of precision in the process of eleven-plus selection. There is considerable disagreement among psychologists about the true meaning of 'intelligence', and as a result doubt arises whether it is possible to measure it. Similarly there is some doubt whether success or failure at eleven-plus has any bearing on how a child will develop. Many comprehensive schools can point to 'so-called' eleven-plus failures who did well at school and even went on to college or university, some to get first class honours degrees.

A third criticism concerns the unequal chances of children in different areas of the country. A survey by J. W. B. Douglas showed that one out of every three to four children living in Wales had the chance of a grammar school place compared to one in eight in southern England. There has also been criticism of the social effects of an education system which deliberately divides pupils.

On the other side those who wish to see grammar schools retained point to the academic record of such schools which they fear would be lost if they were merged into new 'non-selective' comprehensives, to the need for the nation to educate the really able to be its leaders and innovators, to allow parents an element of choice in sending their children to school, and to allow local authorities to decide on the type of schooling best suited to the area without pressure from central government. The argument in favour of grammar schools is, at heart, an argument in support of tradition and the pursuit of excellence, both thought to be features of the grammar school system.

Why education?

In advanced industrial societies there are many highly specialised roles which need to be learnt before an individual can 'fit in' to the society. Apart from social roles, learnt through socialisation (see Chapter 6) individuals need to learn how to earn a living, how to find a place to live, even how to use money. Children have to learn how to read and write, how to count and use ideas of number. Living in an advanced industrial society requires many skills which must be learnt. School is the place where we learn them. In a later section of this chapter we shall see how our educational system has grown as a result of the growth in the number and variety of things to be learnt.

THE PURPOSES OF EDUCATION IN OUR SOCIETY

If you had a quick survey in your class to see how people answered the question 'Why do you go to school?' you would get a number of answers. The simple answer may be 'because you have to'. But if you think about it a little more carefully, you would probably get answers like 'to get a better job', or 'to learn how to do a job when I leave'. School often only seems to have point to it when we think about its value in the future. This is one very important purpose of education.

Skills

At school people learn the skills they will need in order to get a job. These may be the very ordinary skills like reading and writing and arithmetic (the so-called 'three Rs'), or they may be specifically related to the job you are going to do. In many schools people learn things like motor engineering, catering or typing, which will give them a start when they go out to work. Either way the things you learn in school will have some effect on the kind of job you do.

Qualifications

One way in which school subjects may affect your career could be through the examinations you take and the qualifications you get. Schools provide people with qualifications which are generally
118

recognised and give employers and other educational institutions some idea of what can be expected from applicants. Secondary schools prepare people to take examinations for the General Certificate of Education at both 'ordinary' ('O') and 'advanced' ('A') levels and for the Certificate of Secondary Education. These two basic qualifications – G.C.E. and C.S.E. – may be merged into one new basic qualification. At colleges there are other qualifications which can be taken. Employers look for qualifications and it is usually up to schools to provide young people with the opportunity to study for them.

Socialisation

But schools do more than just provide training and qualifications for jobs. They help people learn how to fit into society. In this they continue the socialisation process which begins in the family. Schools are often said to provide 'secondary socialisation' to distinguish it from the 'primary socialisation' of the home. This is a matter of fitting into a more complicated society, of learning new roles and how to adapt to new positions of status and prestige. Schools, are after all, organisations, they are larger and more involved than family and neighbourhood, they introduce children to the roles and positions common in society at large.

Placement

Part of this initiation into a wider society takes the form of social placement. We read earlier that positions in advanced industrial societies are achieved and not ascribed (Chapter 2), and that families have a 'placement' function (Chapter 6). Your education has a great influence on how you spend the rest of you life. In our study of Banbury we met Mr Brown. He was born into a miner's family. Through education at school and university he was able to move into a different social class. He achieved his place in society through his education. Many parents are well aware of this function of education and seek to 'buy' their children into a particular 'style of life' by sending them to fee-paying public schools and other private schools.

Social control

We should always remember that adults control the schools. One very important purpose is to pass on to children those things which past generations (of adults) have thought important. These things are many and varied. We have discussed some of them already. The adults who control the schools often feel that it is important that the schools should pass on to children ideas of 'standards' and 'correct behaviour' and 'right and wrong'. Schools are expected to pass on those aspects of

119

our national culture which will lead to stability and order in society. This is natural, and very important. Many things which were once part of the family's duty to its offspring have now been passed over to the schools. Religious education is still taught in schools by law: it is the only subject which is. Yet each year fewer and fewer people attend churches or take part in organised religion. Religious education is seen by many to be a way in which schools pass on some sort of 'traditional morality', some sort of 'right behaviour' to the children. In all these ways, and many more, the school is acting as an 'agency of social control', passing on aspects of a traditional culture.

Views of schooling

These various purposes which schools provide can be understood in different ways. There are different viewpoints on what schooling is about and what it does.

One view sees schooling as having a technical function to provide the right number of workers with the right qualifications at the right time. Schools are seen as part of the economy serving the needs of industry and commerce. As the needs of industry change so must schools change what they teach. Success in a career in this view depends on having learned the right skills at school. Underlying this kind of approach is the belief that the best jobs go to those who are best suited to fill them, and that schools provide the training that is required.

Against this 'technical function' approach there is a view which sees schooling as part of the conflict between groups within society. Schools, in this view, are used firstly, to control entry to positions of status and power, and secondly, to convince everyone else that such a situation is 'natural'.

This 'conflict' view sees society as a series of 'status groups' each with its own culture and values. Schools strengthen and maintain the position of these groups. The existence of these different groups within society and their different life chances are seen as a natural part of life. A teacher in a secondary modern school described it in this way:

> There must be hewers of wood and drawers of water. This is an inescapable fact and people tend to look down on the lad, 'Well, of course, he's gone on the milk round'. But you think of your own milkman. Is he doing a good job in the community? Is he a pleasant fellow? Does he give good service? . . . Most of our milkmen are blooming, charming blokes. Little Jimmy's as thick as two short planks but he'd make a marvellous milkman or breadman (Paul Willis 1978)

120

These two views of schooling (the technical function view and the conflict view), introduce us to the idea of 'ideology'. An ideology is a set of beliefs which support the interests of particular groups, or social classes, within society.

The view that education enables each individual to gain their 'natural' position in society is an ideological view. Ideology may also be seen as a 'mask' which hides the real character of education. The technical function view of education and the 'conflict' view may be seen as 'ideological' because they represent the interests of particular classes and because they may 'mask' some of the ways in which education functions.

Equality of opportunity in education

This debate over the best pattern of organisation of education is only one aspect of a far larger debate concerning the equality of opportunity within the educational system.

In brief, the problem of equality of opportunity is how to provide every child in the country with an equal chance of going as far as his ability allows. In theory the 1944 Education Act provided an education suited to 'aptitude and ability' in which any child who had the ability could get to the top. Within ten years doubts were growing about the accuracy of this idea. The *Early Leaving Report* of 1954 showed that when working-class children were placed in the top ability group at grammar school they ended up doing, on average, less well than their middle-class classmates. They tended either to leave before their exams or to do less well than would have been expected from knowledge of their abilities. In addition it was found that the higher up the education ladder a working-class child went the more were the odds stacked against him.

Interest centred on the relationship between social class and the education system, the extent to which 'education' is a middle-class activity and the way working-class children are 'alienated' from the aims of education. In an advanced industrial society achievement is the key to the positions of highest status and reward. Michael Young describes the system as a 'meritocracy' with the highest positions going to those who have the greatest 'merit' or academic success.

An American sociologist, Ralph H. Turner, pictures the English system of education as a sort of private club. Those who are in positions of power in the club (Turner calls them an 'elite') choose those people who will be invited to join. Each new candidate needs to be *sponsored* and to possess the personal qualities which the 'elite' think new

121

members ought to have. Turner compares this system to the American education system which is more like a race. Everyone starts off from the same point and runs until he can get no further. Those who have stayed in until the end are the winners. There may be rules of 'fair play' in the race but winning is open to all on the basis of ability and achievement. In the race or '*contest* system' everyone knows the rules and the 'prize' is obtained by the contestant's own efforts. No one can hand out success in life. It has to be won. In the 'sponsored system' Turner believes that certain groups have the power to hand out success to people who possess certain qualities not connected with ability or achievement. Some support is given to Turner's picture of a 'sponsored

Fig. 29. *Education and social class*

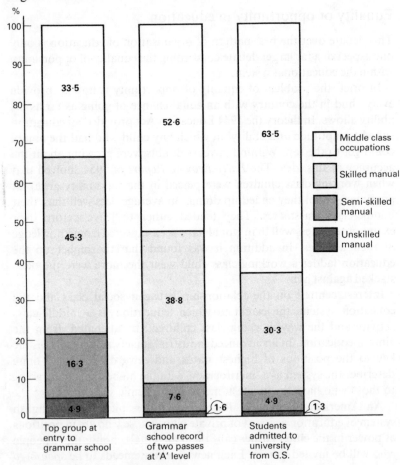

Source: Taken from R. K. Kelsall 1957

system' by the fact that 32 per cent of Conservative Cabinet ministers between 1916 and 1955 had been to one school – Eton. The idea of the 'old school tie' as a means of 'getting on in life' is still very much alive.

Turner's 'contest' and 'sponsored' systems are no more than 'ideal types', pictures created in order to explain something which, in reality, can only be seen in a less clear form. Turner does not say that the English educational system *is* like that, only it *could be* viewed that way.

Other sociologists have been concerned to investigate the reality of English education, to find some evidence of the link between educational success and social class.

Three approaches to the study of education

Sociologists have approached this problem in differing ways. Three examples of the ways in which sociologists have studied education can be seen in the books of J. W. B. Douglas, particularly those entitled *The Home and the School* (1964), and *All our Future* (1968); Brian Jackson and Dennis Marsden, *Education and the Working Class* (1962); and David Hargreaves, *Social Relations in a Secondary School* (1967).

Douglas looked at education on a very broad canvas: his concern was with quite large numbers of children throughout the country; Jackson and Marsden took a narrower view, concentrating on one town and a small group of children; David Hargreaves looked at one school and the pattern of relationships which had built up within it.

THE HOME AND THE SCHOOL

The Douglas study was based on over 5 000 children born in one week of March 1946. The children were followed through from birth and information was collected from health visitors, teachers and parents, and from the children themselves. The children were given intelligence tests at the ages of eight and eleven.

Douglas begins by pointing to the strain placed on children by the eleven-plus examination. Though the process of selection for secondary school was not *meant* to be competitive it very soon became so: those who were awarded places at grammar schools had 'passed' the exam whilst the rest had 'failed'. The secondary modern school became the school for 'the failures'. Parents naturally wished for their children to get to the grammar school which, in their eyes, provided a gateway to a good career. Of those parents who wanted their children to go to grammar school two-thirds were disappointed. Similarly only two-thirds of those children thought by their teachers to deserve a grammar school place actually got one, and of those parents whose children did get to grammar school one-third expected their children to leave at the earliest moment the law allowed, before they could take any qualifying examinations.

Geographical factors

When Douglas looked at the distribution of grammar school places across the country he discovered further inequalities. Children in Wales and the South West had twice as much chance of a grammar school education as did children in the south of England; there were simply more grammar schools in relation to the number of children in each area. When it came to the effects of housing Douglas discovered that children who lived in unsatisfactory housing conditions did worse on his tests than those from good housing, and, even when a child from a slum area did do well he soon began to slip back, whereas the middle-class child of similar ability continued to progress.

The role of parents

The help and encouragement given by parents was also found to be important. The children from manual working homes were doubly handicapped. Not only did their scores at the tests tend to get worse instead of better between eight and eleven, but they also had less chance of a grammar school place than a middle-class child of the same level of ability. A child's progress and achievement was seen to be directly related to the encouragement given by the parents and their ambitions for their child. Family size was also observed to be important, as was the child's position in the family. The eldest child in a large family tended to do better than either of the younger children in the family, or an only child. This can be explained in two ways. The eldest child has the stimulus of the younger children who put pressure on him to succeed whereas the younger children might easily receive less of the parents' attention just because there are more of them.

Teacher expectations

So far all of the influences discussed have been outside of the school. Douglas does not leave his investigation there. He takes his survey right into the schools and seeks to examine those factors in the schools which might affect a child's chances of getting to grammar school. Boys and girls, for example, got fairly similar results at the tests at eight and eleven. But their teachers expected the girls to do much better. Obviously the teacher's expectations must have some effect on the way a child works in school. If the teacher encourages you and gives the impression that you can really do well you are more likely to try than

124

Fig. 30. *Regional differences in grammar school places*

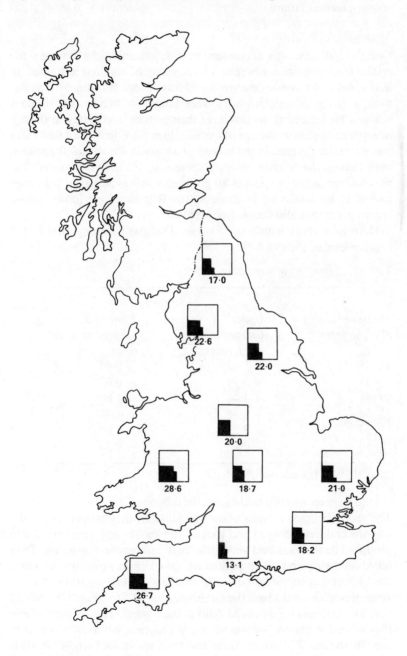

you are if the teacher makes it quite plain to you that he thinks you are an out-and-out failure.

Streaming

Douglas looked at this in connection with streaming. Streaming is the system used in schools whereby a large group of children is divided up into classes of more-or-less similar ability. From his sample Douglas took a group of children who were taught in two-stream primary schools. He looked at the results of their tests of intelligence at the age of eight and again at the age of eleven. He noticed first of all that there was no real difference in the spread of ability in the A and B streams, even though the teachers thought there was. He then discovered that the children in the A streams all got higher scores at eleven than they had at eight, whilst all of those in the B streams got lower scores, regardless of the child's measured ability.

Here is a chart which summarises Douglas's findings (50 is the average level of ability).

Table 23. *The effect of streaming*

	Stream	
Measured ability at eight years	*Upper (A)* Change in score 8–11 years	*Lower (B)* Change in score 8–11 years
41–45	+ 5·67	− 0·95
46–48	+ 3·70	− 0·62
49–51	+ 4·44	− 1·60
52–54	+ 0·71	− 1·46
55–57	+ 2·23	− 1·94
58–60	+ 0·86	− 6·34

Source: J. W. B. Douglas 1964

Douglas explains this evidence in the following way:
The teachers made a guess about the children they taught. From the way the children behaved and looked and spoke they were sorted into groups. The teachers had very little 'real' information to go on. They relied on their own skill at 'predicting' how a child would get on. Once the children were 'streamed' the teachers looked on them as 'A' streamers who would pass the eleven-plus or 'B' streamers who would not. The teachers were proved right in their guess. The children whom they placed in the 'A' stream all made progress, while all of those in the 'B' stream got worse. Were the teachers in fact 'right' in their judgement of the children, or did the children make progress or not as

a result of the teachers' predictions and the teachers' expectations? Certainly it had very little to do with the *actual* measured ability of the children in those classes. Douglas calls this a 'self-fulfilling prophecy'.

Conclusion

Douglas begins the final chapter of his book *The Home and the School* with these words:

> The evidence set out in this book gives strong reasons for believing that much potential ability is wasted during the primary school years and misdirected at the point of secondary selection.

He concludes the chapter as follows:

> The pool of talent found at the end of the secondary school period is likely to be only a portion of that which would be found if it were possible to draw fully on [the] potential. . . Over a period of three years in the primary schools, there is a substantial loss of ability in the manual working-class children which could be prevented.

J. W. B. Douglas was concerned with the development of a large number of children, chosen at random, and studied in great depth as they grew up. This next study does not claim any such 'objectivity'. It is a personal study by two sociologists looking at something they themselves have experienced.

EDUCATION AND THE WORKING CLASS

Brian Jackson and Dennis Marsden were born in Huddersfield. They both came from working-class homes, won places at grammar school and scholarships to Cambridge University. In *Education and the Working Class* (1962) they attempt to trace the lives of some of the other Huddersfield children, from similar homes, who also went to grammar school. They gathered a sample of ninety working-class children. Two of the names on that list were Brian Jackson and Dennis Marsden, so their report is concerned with the other eighty-eight. Ten middle-class children were also interviewed to provide a comparison.

Despite a higher proportion of manual workers in the city there were indications that, as a group, manual workers were not as well represented in the city's grammar schools as might have been expected. Between the years 1949 and 1952 64 per cent of the pupils passing the Higher School Certificate or the General Certificate of Education at advanced level came from the homes of non-manual workers. Only 36 per cent of these awards went to children from the homes of manual workers. Thus though three-quarters of the city's workers had manual

127

jobs their children gained little more than one-third of the higher qualifications.

This state of affairs was not confined to Huddersfield, nor was it something which disappeared as the education system developed after the 1944 Education Act. Jackson and Marsden's findings agree with those of the *Early Leaving Report* (1954); the Crowther Report (1959); the Robbins Report (1963) and other Government and independent surveys. They are well summarised in the Schools Council's 'Enquiry One' on *Young School Leavers* (1968) when it states: 'As the expected leaving age rose the proportions of fathers in professional and managerial and in clerical occupations increased while those in skilled and semi- or unskilled manual work decreased.'

The children

The starting point of *Education and the Working Class* was the group of ten middle-class children. These children came from families which, in many cases, had a long tradition of secondary education. The system of education and these middle-class families fitted together. They talked the same language, shared the same hopes and values. The home supported school and likewise school supported the home. When difficulties did arise teachers and parents were able to cooperate to gain the best for the child.

This picture contrasted sharply with the situation of the average working-class child who had won a place at grammar school. For one thing, the working-class child at grammar school was in the minority. The whole life of the school emphasised things that were often foreign to him. An example of this was the grammar school's attitude to sport. One of the 88 working-class children made this comment about 'team spirit':

What about the old team spirit, eh? Ask me about the old team spirit – that's all you get at that school. Team games, football, cricket, all kinds of games they make up, but always team games. Load of crap the whole lot! By jove, chaps, the team needs you; by jove chaps, well played... The kind of games you can play yourself, they don't count. It's no good going on to Marburton College if you're a dabhand at snooker, Christ no! Too tough, that snooker doesn't count, cricket counts. Team spirit, by jove chaps! (Jackson and Marsden 1962)

Many of the working-class children who went to grammar schools were faced with a choice. They had either to accept grammar school and all that it involved, often to go with the tide; or to root their ideals firmly in their neighbourhood, which meant rejecting school and all that it stood for. Those who chose school found that this created new

conflicts at home, an increasing separation from home and parents.
Grammar school introduced the boy or girl to new ideas and new skills
which were outside the experience of the parents. Many parents felt
that their children were growing away from them, despite their attempts
to keep up.

When he started at the college I was very interested indeed, especially
in these mathematics. He'd bring these problems home and I'd really
look at them with him, and I'd get fair excited. The first year I really
enjoyed it, looking at his sums and trying to do his homework with
him. And then the next year came a lot of this algebra, a bit tricky if
you've never had it before, but you can get the hang of it. I liked that
year too; but afterwards the problems got a bit harder and our lad
couldn't be bothered to show them to me. I'd have liked to do a bit
more with him, but no, he wouldn't let me. We couldn't keep up in
the same kind of way. (Jackson and Marsden 1962)

The vast majority of the eighty-eight children studied chose to go the
way of the school and their parents could often do no more than watch
them go from certificate to certificate.

The working-class families

The families of these children did have many things in common. The
majority came from small families; a third from one-child families.
Their fathers were all manual workers, but the families often had some
connection with the middle class.

The remainder of the families included in the sample may not have
had direct links with the middle class, but they certainly shared certain
values and aspirations. Like the later findings of the Douglas survey,
Jackson and Marsden found that the children who got to grammar
school were those who had the most support from their parents.

After studying the children and their families 'in the past' through
school records and memories of schooldays, Jackson and Marsden
went on to make contact with 'their children' as adults. All 88 were
tracked down and interviewed. Only 27 of them still lived in Huddersfield; the other 61 were scattered over the rest of the country, some in
Yorkshire, but quite a large proportion in industrial Lancashire, the
Midlands or the South East. Their jobs were very different from those
held by their parents. Over half of them had become teachers – the
majority of these were women; the remainder were all in other professional jobs: draughtsmen, civil servants, management, medicine.
Grammar school had been an 'avenue of social mobility' for all of them,
providing a route out of the working class.

Not only their jobs but also their homes were different to those of

129

their parents. In general they lived in pleasant suburban semi-detached houses well away from the industrial back streets of their childhood. It would have been difficult to tell them from their middle-class neighbours. The researchers noticed some differences in their attitudes; they were perhaps less confident, a little less contented than their neighbours but by and large they had all developed into well-adjusted middle-class adults, well satisfied with the system of education which put them where they were.

SOCIAL RELATIONS IN A SECONDARY SCHOOL

Lumley School is the fictitious name given by David Hargreaves to a boys' secondary modern school somewhere in an industrial area in the North of England. The majority of the boys who go there are the sons of manual workers and most live in the cluster of drab streets which make up that part of the city. In time the whole area will be redeveloped and the school with it, but for the present, both school and neighbourhood remain.

At the time of Hargreaves's survey, the school contained some 450 boys taught by twenty-six teachers. Each year's intake was divided into five streams on the basis of the boys' results in the eleven-plus examination. Each stream contained boys of roughly the same level of ability. The lowest stream, known as E – contained boys who were so backward that specialised remedial help was needed. Hargreaves concentrated his study on the boys in the fourth year of the school, but as boys in 4E were separated from the rest of the year his findings were based on 4A, 4B, 4C and 4D, each of these forms containing roughly thirty boys.

Most of the boys left school at the end of the fourth year, but some stayed on into the fifth year so that they could take the Certificate of Secondary Education (C.S.E.), examination. All the boys who wished to stay on for the extra year were put into form 4A. Thus the school had a formal structure which was made up of four 'years'; with five 'forms' in each year, boys being streamed into each form on the results of the eleven-plus examination. In the fourth-year form 4A were those who would, in time, go on to a fifth year and take the C.S.E. examination. This was the formal structure of the school. Most organisations have some sort of formal structure like this. They also have an 'informal structure' and it was this informal structure which Hargreaves investigated. While the formal structure is made up of 'years' and 'forms' and 'streams', the informal structure comprises groups of friends who choose their own leaders. To a stranger coming into a school it is not easy to see the informal structure; even some people who have positions in the school, some teachers, for example, may not be able to plot it at all accurately. Unlike the formal structure it is never written down, and

130

it is seldom fixed for very long at a time. The informal structure of a school has its own way of doing things, its own ideas of what is good or bad, right or wrong, what is acceptable or unacceptable to the rest of the group, and its own way of making its members conform. In some cases there may be little difference between the formal and the informal structures, but often they are very far apart. The head boy of Lumley was called Adrian. He was also recognised as leader by a fair number of the other boys in class 4A of which he was a member. Clint, however, was in form 4C, held no formal position of authority, but to the vast majority of the boys in all years was the 'top'. He was the best fighter in the school and though there were many rivals none had, so far, managed to take over his position. Whereas Adrian held a position of 'formal' leadership, it was Clint who was the 'informal' leader.

In the formal structure it was Adrian who had the highest status, but in informal terms highest status went to Clint. In addition to having different views of status these formal and informal structures also had different norms (accepted ways of behaving in any situation) and different values (ideas of right and wrong, good and bad).

Methods of study

Hargreaves used a number of different methods of studying these formal and informal structures of the school. He asked the boys in the four fourth-year forms who they thought the best leaders were, who they disliked, who their particular friends were. He also asked them to complete a number of sentences which began with things like 'All schoolboys should . . .' or 'Teachers think of me as . . .' In these open-ended questions the boys could write anything they wished. The answers gave some indication of where the boy stood in the informal groups. Another type of question was made up of a list of statements and the boys had to say whether they 'agreed', 'disagreed' or 'didn't mind either way'. This also gave an indication of how each boy felt about school, their mates and their own position. They provided some insight into the norms and values of the groups in the school.

From the answers to the question: 'Who are the boys you go around with most while you are in school?' Hargreaves was able to draw a plan of the informal friendship groups which existed. 4B's chart is shown in Fig. 31.

Notice how the form divides into three clear groups. Clint and Chris form a pair, only linked into the others in group A by Clem, who is the focus of the choices of the boys numbered 62, 64, 73 and 70. Group B is a fairly closely knit little gang with 81 on the outside wanting to come in but not being wanted. Group C is made up of three smaller groups linked by choices that have not been returned. When David Hargreaves came to measure the informal status level of each of these three groups, he found that both A and B groups of 4C had fairly high informal status. They were popular and respected by other boys in the fourth year. Group C, however, had a very low informal status level. Generally these boys were not very popular with their classmates. But these boys in Group C of Form 4C had a fairly high academic average. They were boys who got on with their work and got results even though they were not popular with the others.

Two subcultures

Lumley School contained 'two subcultures' each with its own status leader, its own norms of behaviour, and its own values. By conforming to the academic norms and values, a boy would be deviating from the norms and values of the anti-academic group and vice versa. In 4A the academic subculture is predominant. Boys who mess about are regarded as deviants. In 4D it is the anti-academic subculture which sets the tone of the class and anyone who 'swots' is regarded as deviant by the rest of the class.

In his analysis David Hargreaves observes that the higher the stream the greater is likely to be commitment to the formal school values. Boys in 4A did not tend to 'mess about'. They respected their teachers and

Fig. 31. *A sociogram for 4B*

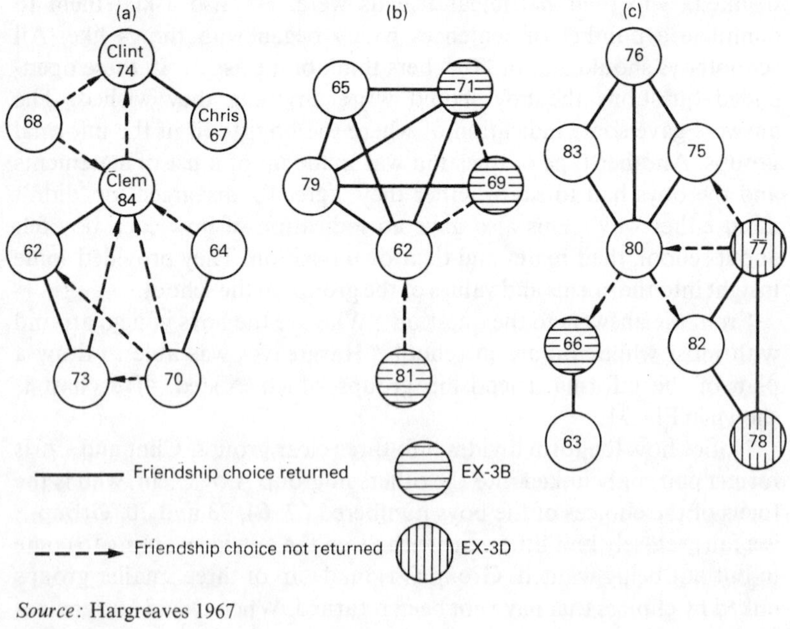
(a)
(b)
(c)
Clint 74
68
Chris 67
Clem 84
62
64
73
70
65
71
79
69
62
81
76
83
75
80
77
66
82
63
78
Friendship choice returned
Friendship choice not returned
EX-3B
EX-3D

Source: Hargreaves 1967

sought to earn the praise of the teachers through their hard work. They looked down upon the 'messers' and 'the roughs' in the lower forms. Because the school's values were basically middle class those boys in the 'academic' subculture were the boys who accepted a middle-class view of life. They were probably those boys who were encouraged by the teachers and gained some measure of status or reward in the formal school system. In the opposite way the boys in 4D did 'mess about'. It was the normal thing for them to do. They saw no reason to 'swot' or to do what the teachers expected. Throughout their school lives they had been deprived of status. Not only has their low achievement at the eleven-plus examination told them that they were failures, but it had been rubbed in when they were put into the bottom form at secondary school. Hargreaves suggests that the 'anti-academic' subculture develops in its own way of giving status and reward because it members have been given neither by the school. Being a good fighter, getting into trouble with the police, playing a good game of snooker, become the marks of achievement. Not success at school, passing exams or being made a prefect. These boys have rejected education because it has rejected them. Instead they have created their own form of society, making themselves independent of the pressures of the school.

Whereas Douglas and Jackson and Marsden looked at schools from a distance, Hargreaves took a very close look. The focus of the earlier studies was to see education as one part of a larger system and to try to understand why it was not working properly. Hargreaves instead focused on the relationships between the various groups which made up the schools and the ways in which school was seen by each of them. The teachers, the 'academic' pupils and the 'anti-school' each had their own views of what school was about and how they should behave.

The problem of knowledge

Knowledge and schooling are often tied together in our minds. If anyone asked you what school was for you, you would probably say something about 'knowing things' or 'getting knowledge'. But what is the knowledge we get at school, what use is it and who decides it should be there?

The world is full of knowledge and it grows more every month and every year. The Encyclopaedias in a library are packed full of knowledge and there is even more knowledge which cannot be squeezed into them. In universities there are even bigger libraries with even more books packed full of even more knowledge. If you went to school for every day of your life you could never hope to learn everything that there is to

133

Fig. 32. *A school curriculum*

	0–5	5–10	10–14	14–18	18–22	22–26	26–30	30–32	32–34	34
A 3 classes	English	Mathematics	French or German or History	Physics or Biology or Economics	Chemistry or Geography or Biology	Art or Metalwork or Home Economics or Sociology	Latin or Chemistry or Music	Tutorial Period	Religious Education	Games and PE
B 3 classes	English	Mathematics	French or History or Social Studies	Science or Business Studies or Technical Drawing	Geography or Commerce or Rural Studies	Art or Metalwork or Home Economics	Woodwork or Needlework			
C 2 classes	English	Mathematics	Social Education	Office Skills or Rural Studies or Catering	General Science or Art	Woodwork or Metalwork or Home Economics	History or Geography			

know. The knowledge you get at school is a selection from that vast stock of knowledge in the world. School knowledge is not only selected, it is also organised. Encyclopaedias have a way of organising knowledge. They do it alphabetically, starting at 'A' and going through to 'Z'. In schools knowledge is organised into subjects. This organisation of subjects in a school is known as 'the curriculum'. Fig. 32 shows you a typical fourth year curriculum in a secondary school.

In school the organisation of knowledge can be seen in the school timetable. The timetable gives a certain amount of time to each subject. If you look at the timetable you will see three things: Firstly, it does not include every possible subject. Few schools would include pharmacology or archaeology on their timetables though bits of them may be squeezed into other subjects. Secondly, different subjects do not receive equal amounts of time in the week. For example, English and mathematics usually receive more time than music and history. Thirdly, some subjects are taken by everybody, and are therefore compulsory, while others are only taken by some. This selection of who-takes-what may involve choice on the part of the student or it may involve decisions by those who run the school.

Your school timetable may also show some areas where subjects are not kept apart, where the boundaries between subjects are blurred. Integrated studies or Humanities are examples of the breaking down of subject boundaries. You may also notice that the amount of choice and compulsion, the type of subjects taken and the amount of time spent on certain subjects differs between different groups.

Some of these differences can be seen in Fig. 32 which shows a secondary school curriculum. This is not a timetable. It only shows the subjects available and the amount of time given to them. It does not show when pupils will study these subjects during the week. This school's fourth year is arranged in three blocks. The cleverest children are in block A. The slowest in block C. Each block has certain subjects of its own. Only block A has German, Latin or physics, block B has business studies and commerce and block C has social education. The block A subjects are more 'academic' and have clearer boundaries whereas block B and C have 'practical' subjects and more integration. In general terms block A has more of the 'high-status' subjects – French and German, Latin, physics and chemistry and biology – while block C gets 'low-status' subjects. For example block C has 'office skills' where block A has 'economics' and 'general science' instead of separate physics, chemistry and biology. Fig. 32 gives us a very simplified picture of the school curriculum. Your school may use a far more complicated pattern. The main features of Fig. 32 are likely to be found in many schools.

1. School subjects can be divided into high- and low-status subjects. High-status subjects are:
   (a) more specialised
   (b) more academic or theoretical
   (c) more traditional

   Low-status subjects are likely to be:
   (a) more general
   (b) more practical
   (c) vocational, or 'job-centred'.
2. There is a wider choice and less compulsion in the more able 'blocks'.
3. Pupils placed in particular blocks are directed towards certain careers or occupations.

To get an even better view of school knowledge you can look at the syllabuses for particular subjects. For example you could compare G.C.E. sociology syllabuses with C.S.E. social studies. How far are the differences between them based on differences in their difficulty rather than differences in the kind of knowledge they contain?

It should by now be clear that we cannot consider the selection of knowledge to be taught in schools separate from matters of status and power in schools. School curricula and syllabuses are the result of decisions made by individuals who have the power to make such decisions. They are also decisions which affect the way others learn and in the end, affect how they see themselves and the world. We have already seen that such views can be termed ideological because they support particular groups who have power. Decisions about school knowledge are, in the last resort, political decisions.

THE POLITICS OF SCHOOL KNOWLEDGE

Who decides about school knowledge and what influences their decision. Obviously teachers are involved. Although the teachers plan what happens in the lessons it would be wrong to assume that they have complete control. Schools have a number of levels of authority – heads of department, faculty-heads, curriculum co-ordinators, head teachers and their deputies – each having some influence over areas of the school's work. Beyond them are the local inspectors or advisers, the school governors, the Education Officer and the local Education Committee. In addition there are the civil servants at the Department of Education and Science in London and Her Majesty's Inspectors (H.M.Is.) As well as this network of authority there are examination boards, teachers' unions, parents and employers, newspapers, and television each influencing what goes on in school in some way.

Fig. 33. *What parents and headmasters think is important at school*

(a)

Parents of Boy 15 year old leavers

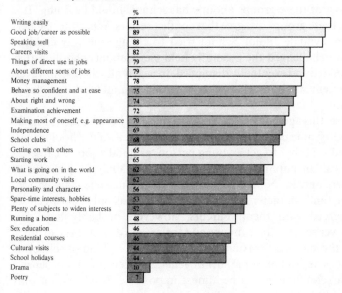

	%
Writing easily	91
Good job/career as possible	89
Speaking well	88
Careers visits	82
Things of direct use in jobs	79
About different sorts of jobs	79
Money management	78
Behave so confident and at ease	75
About right and wrong	74
Examination achievement	72
Making most of oneself, e.g. appearance	70
Independence	69
School clubs	68
Getting on with others	65
Starting work	65
What is going on in the world	62
Local community visits	62
Personality and character	56
Spare-time interests, hobbies	53
Plenty of subjects to widen interests	52
Running a home	48
Sex education	46
Residential courses	46
Cultural visits	44
School holidays	44
Drama	10
Poetry	7

(b)

Headmasters

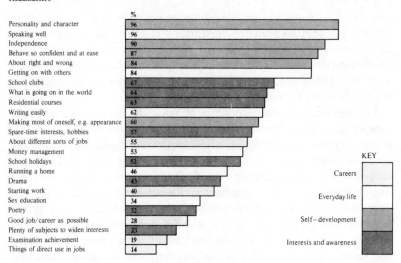

	%
Personality and character	96
Speaking well	96
Independence	90
Behave so confident and at ease	87
About right and wrong	84
Getting on with others	84
School clubs	67
What is going on in the world	64
Residential courses	63
Writing easily	62
Making most of oneself, e.g. appearance	60
Spare-time interests, hobbies	57
About different sorts of jobs	55
Money management	53
School holidays	52
Running a home	46
Drama	43
Starting work	40
Sex education	34
Poetry	32
Good job/career as possible	28
Plenty of subjects to widen interests	23
Examination achievement	19
Things of direct use in jobs	14

KEY

Careers

Everyday life

Self-development

Interests and awareness

Source: Schools Council Enquiry One: *The Young School Leaver* (H.M.S.O. 1968)

137

The question 'who decides what and why?' is therefore difficult to answer. The teacher or the headmaster who is at the centre of all of these influences has to decide, but the decision is likely to be affected in some way by wider social pressures. In society there is general agreement among most of these groups about what school should be doing. It is only when these groups disagree that conflict results. When the teachers at William Tyndale Junior School tried to change the way children learned and challenged the generally held views about schooling they were suspended and eventually dismissed. In nearly all schools, however, there is agreement about what schools should do and what knowledge is important.

Of course, this agreement is not always shared by everyone, as Fig. 33 shows. Eighty-nine per cent of the parents of 16-year-old school leavers interviewed said that to get a young person 'as good a job or career as possible' was an important aim for the school. Only 28 per cent of headmasters agreed. Ninety-six per cent of headmasters claimed that 'personality and character' were important whereas only 56 per cent of parents agreed with them. Parents, however, probably have less influence over schools than anyone and their views do not carry so much weight as those of headmasters and inspectors. The kind of schooling we have does depend on some sort of general agreement, or consensus. Without it schooling would be almost impossible. It affects not only what is taught but how it is taught and it provides reasons for 'why it is taught'. However, even though there is agreement amongst those who have the power to influence what happens in school, it does not answer our basic question of why certain things are taught in certain ways. Why is it that certain types of knowledge are more highly valued than others? The reasons are partly historical. The basis of the present day education system was laid over a hundred years ago at a time when English society was very different. The 'high-status' subjects of today are those which were found in the universities and public schools of the late nineteenth century.

The differences in the curriculum of blocks A, B and C in Fig. 32 are very close to the differences between the education provided for the aristocracy, for the merchants and industrialists; and for the factory workers a century ago. Ideas about what schooling ought to be like are very firmly rooted in people's minds. Schools have a habit of reproducing themselves in each generation. Remember that today's teachers were yesterday's pupils. This does not mean that schools do not change but that they change very slowly. But it is not enough just to say that schools teach the things they do teach because they have always done the same. That is not the whole answer. Schools teach particular subjects in particular ways because that is what society at large expects.

138

School knowledge is the knowledge that people in society have come to expect schools to be handing on.

Education for girls

We can see how schools reflect the ideas and values of the wider society if we look at the education of girls. On the surface girls are educated in much the same way as boys. They go to the same, or similar, schools, have the same teachers and much the same choice of lessons. Their measured intelligence is very similar yet out of these basic similarities important differences appear.

Fig. 34. *'A' Levels in the sixth form of single-sex schools 1970–71*

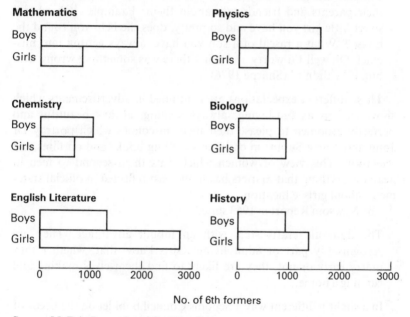

No. of 6th formers

Source: I.L.E.A. Research and Statistics Group

Girls take different subjects from boys. They do less well at things like maths or science. They go into different jobs. In 1970 42.3 per cent of boys took apprenticeships leading to skilled jobs. Only 7.1 per cent of girls did the same and most of these went into basically female-oriented occupations like hairdressing and tailoring.

Women were also less likely to make a career in any of the professions except for jobs like teaching and nursing which are thought to be women's jobs.

139

Table 25. *Women in the professions*

	% *of all in profession.*
Architects (1973)	5.8
Chartered accountants (1976)	2.3
Solicitors (1975)	5.2
Professional engineers	0.5
University professors	1.7

Girls are, throughout their lives, expected to behave differently to boys. A fourteen-year-old girl described it in the following way in a social studies lesson:

Children learn how they are different from one another by the way their parents and friends talk about them: Example – 'Oh what a sweet little girl you have and so pretty, does she help you round the house? 'What a rascal of a son you have, always getting into mischief. Oh well I'd worry and think there was something wrong with him if he didn't.' (Sharpe 1976)

These different expectations are continued in advertisements which show women as fun-loving, always smiling, always beautiful and perfectly groomed to please their men; in comics which portray Dr John and Nurse Susan; in children's reading books and on films and television. This view of women which puts them second to men in nearly everything that matters has in the past reflected in official statements about girls' education.

The Newsom Report in 1963 stated:

The domestic crafts start with an inbuilt advantage. They are recognisably part of adult living. Girls know that, whether they marry early or not, they are likely to find themselves making and running a home.

In a slightly different way a Schools Council booklet on the needs of disadvantaged children suggests that self confidence can be developed:

when older secondary school girls (and why not sometimes boys?) are involved in the care of pre-school children. (Schools Council 1970)

Statements like these can be supported in two ways. The first argument stresses the biological differences between males and females. Differences in achievement between boys and girls and differences in the education they receive are, it is claimed, caused by innate differences between the sexes. This point of view sees girls as being in some way limited by their sex. Rarely is it suggested that it might be the boys who
140

Fig. 35. *Learning to read*

20

Here we are at home,
        says Daddy.

Peter helps Daddy with
    the car, and Jane helps
    Mummy get the tea.

Good girl, says Mummy
        to Jane.

You are a good girl to
    help me like this.

Good   good   girl

are limited. The argument breaks down when differences between girls as a group and boys as a group are compared to differences between individual boys or girls. The differences of ability between different boys and between different girls are far greater than differences between the sexes. If differences are 'biological' then we would expect them to be shared by all females of the human species throughout the world – and they are not. In other countries women do all of the jobs that men do in Britain. This is not to say that males and females are not biologically different but the differences are not important when it comes to education or jobs.

The second argument stresses differences in the life styles and careers of girls. Differences in what women do at home and at work now are used as reasons for continuing to educate girls to do those jobs in the future. This point of view fails to recognise the need for women's roles to change. These two points of view lead to a pattern of schooling which either sees girls as (a) lacking something that boys have got and therefore in need of special treatment to make them more equal or (b) a different kind of human being in need of a different kind of education. A third approach to the education of girls is to see boys and girls as having similar needs, similar hopes and aspirations and similar opportunities.

The problem for the sociologist is to discover how far this third alternative is being achieved. There are some signs that girls are catching up. In school subjects like mathematics, physics, chemistry and economics where boys have been the majority of G.C.E. 'O' level candidates, the increase in the number of girls gaining passes has been greater than the increase of boys. But important differences still remain and though most schools recognise the need for equal opportunities there is still a strongly held belief that girls need to be educated differently. Such a belief is not confined to the schools. It is often shared by employers, parents and the girls themselves. When boys leave school they expect to have a good job or a career to go into. When girls were asked about their careers they replied,

'It's a bit hard to combine a career and marriage'.

'A person who does full time . . . I don't think should have children anyway as it would interfere with her career'.

'Career girls are girls who don't want to get married'.

'I think men should have careers. If girls want to they can but I think it suits men really'. (Sharpe 1976)

The problem of changing the way girls are educated is not just a problem for the school. The way girls are educated reflects the dominant attitudes towards women in the wider society. In considering the

142

question—Why do schools do what they do?—we cannot separate schooling from the attitudes and beliefs of society as a whole.

8

Work and Industry

Nearly half of the men, women and children in Great Britain go to work: a total of over 25 million people. Half the women of working age have jobs and of these women nearly half are married. The average man works a 45½-hour week. A man's working life may begin at sixteen and continue until 65 or later, or earlier. Work is an important part of the life of every individual in society. Those who do not work are mostly either too young or too old. Some are students, some are housewives, some are unable to work because of poor health or disablement. There are some men who would like to work but cannot find jobs and some who are changing from one job to another.

The size of the working population depends in the first place on the number of jobs available, a result of the level of prosperity in the nation as a whole. The jobs must also be near where the workers live, and the workers must have the right skills and qualifications. A shortage of punch-card operators in London does nothing for unemployed miners in County Durham. Similarly there is no point in turning out large numbers of sociology graduates from universities when industry needs chemists, physicists and engineers. Secondly, the size of the labour force depends on 'demographic' or population trends. The age distribution of the population, the trend for staying on at school or retiring early, or late, each have an effect on the number of people who could be working.

The pattern of industry

These 25 million workers are divided amongst 40 000 different occupations as classified in the Census figures by the Registrar General. In mining and quarrying, there are jobs like 'dragger down', 'back stripper', 'hitcher up', 'joy loader'; in metal manufacturing there are 'plier minders', 'second benders', 'pump doctors' and 'bogeymen'; in the building trades there are forty different types of bricklayer from

144

'boiler fixer' to 'tuck pointer'.

This working population is spread over twenty different industries, or groups of industries, covering firms which range in size from giant combines like I.C.I. and the British Steel Corporation down to self-employed men and small family businesses. The average firm tends to be fairly small. In 1959 there were 40 000 factories employing less than 100 people and only 3 000 which employed more than 500. Despite mergers and takeovers the average man or woman still works in a fairly small productive unit.

The pattern of industry has changed in the past hundred or so years. The great majority of people are now engaged in 'making things' instead of 'growing things' or 'mining things'. In 1851 22 per cent of the labour force was in agriculture; today it is less than 4 per cent. Employment in manufacturing grew by 150 per cent in the first half of this century, while employment in mining and quarrying fell by 20 per cent. In part, these are the results of changes in the methods of production, more machines and less men, but they also reflect changes in the pattern of industry over the country as a whole.

Many of the older industries have faced decline. Their products have been replaced by new, improved, materials. The wool industry has had to compete with new 'man-made' fibres, such as Orlon and Tricel, made, not in mills in Bradford or Bolton, but in vast chemical factories in Harrogate. Other industries have lost their overseas markets in time of war, or, like coal, have seen their supplies of raw materials gradually running out.

These older industries often depended on coal, on imported raw materials, or on the water of Pennine streams. As a result they became rooted in the North of England, South Wales or the Scottish Lowlands. The newer industries – chemicals, cars, electronics, aerospace – had no need to be so tied to one area. They chose to be near to their markets, near to big centres of population which provided consumers and workers. While coal was found in the North, imported oil was in the South, brought in by great tankers from the Persian Gulf. The social consequences of these changes were considerable. As we saw in Chapter 5 workers were drawn towards the South East. The old industrial centres became 'grey areas' lacking new industry and with rising unemployment. The newer industries needed different skills, new trades. The older men found it difficult to adapt. Many of the jobs were women's jobs. In this situation the Government provided incentives to get firms to move into the 'grey areas', they imposed strict controls on new industrial building in the South East and industrial training was expanded to cope with the needs of these workers. Despite these measures and the large sums of money pushed into Development Areas,

145

as they were called, their levels of unemployment are still above the national average.

In the early stages of industrialisation, when firms were small, the bosses worked alongside the workers. Contact was close and there was no need for anyone to be totally concerned with the administrative side of the business. As firms grew and their organisation became more complicated, managers and supervisors were needed to undertake the routine administration of the business. At first such people were few in number. In 1907 only 8 per cent of the labour force were in office jobs, but by the mid-1960s nearly one in every four workers was a 'white-collar' worker. We shall consider 'the managerial revolution' and 'the blackcoated worker' in more detail later in this chapter.

The organisation of industry

There are many ways of making things. In modern industry machines are very important. But machines have different uses and the way they are used has an effect upon the worker, on how he regards his job and on his social contact with other workers.

CRAFT INDUSTRY

The earliest stage of industrialisation was 'craft industry'. We can use the same term to describe a form of production which is still important today. In 'craft industry' each worker is responsible for a complete product. No two jobs are exactly the same and the craftsman is expected to make his own decisions on how to carry out each particular job, he sees each job through from beginning to end. Printing is an example of a modern craft. The master printer is a skilled, highly trained craftsman who sets up his press to turn out a perfect piece of work. Printers are proud of their trade and form strong unions to protect their rights. They have a sense of solidarity which binds them together as a group.

MACHINE PRODUCTION

At one time all furniture was made by craftsmen. Each man was able to choose his wood, cut it, join it and create a chair, or a table. Unlike printing the job of making chairs and tables could be broken into stages. One machine could be set up to cut hundreds of chair legs to the right size. Another machine would cut all the joints. Other machines could shape, glue, smooth and polish. The worker became a machine minder. Carrying out one task, without any need to make decisions, possibly not even knowing how his little piece fitted into the finished product. One skilled man could set up dozens of machines, and leave them in the charge of unskilled 'minders'.

Workmen in this situation have no sense of satisfaction in seeing a job through, nor do they have the opportunity to have much social contact with other workers. As their pay depends on their output they try to compensate for the boredom of the job by getting as much in their pay packet as they can.

MASS PRODUCTION

In mass production industries the use of machines has been taken a stage further. The machines are laid out along a conveyor belt along which the product travels. As it proceeds through each stage workers carry out small tasks so that when it reaches the end of the line it is complete. As a method of production it is as well suited to mince pies and chocolates as it is to motor cars. In this situation the worker has no control over his work. He performs one or two simple tasks, often boring, always repetitive, at a speed dictated by the moving belt along which the car or mince pie or 'almond whirl' travels. Each worker's task is so small that although he may see the finished product he gets no sense of having shared in it. The pressures of 'the belt' often prevent any real social contact developing. Money becomes the only compensation. The worker becomes 'alienated'. He sees no purpose in what he is doing and becomes dissatisfied and unhappy. Strikes and absenteeism are likely to increase in such a situation. Most of the evidence on 'assembly line' working is based on the motor car industry where it has been the standard system since the days of the Model T Ford. There is some evidence that the experience in other assembly line industries may not be the same and that even in the British motor industry there may be ways of overcoming the tension and boredom of 'the line'. The assembly line has often been seen as man's greatest slavery to the machine. It may be that with good management, more varied jobs and more teamwork, car workers could find greater personal satisfaction in the job.

PROCESS PRODUCTION

Another method of production is that which involves some form of continuous process. Raw materials are fed in at one end and the finished product appears at the other – 'untouched by human hand'. This system is common in the petroleum and chemical industries but is also used in making glass, steel, beer and an increasing number of other products. Process production creates a need for two types of worker: those who have control and those who maintain. Both have a certain

147

amount of control over their own work routine and operate in often pleasant surroundings with opportunity for social contact. Their situation is more similar to craftwork than to either the machine minder or the assembly line worker.

AUTOMATION

An important part of process production is the idea of automation. Automation is more than just letting machines do jobs men once did. It goes beyond simple mechanisation in three different ways.

Linked machines

At its simplest it can take the form of devices which link machines together so that a continuous process can be created; a form of automatic production line. In a bottling plant a machine would lift the bottles from a crate, load them into a washer from which they would be fed automatically into a filling machine, which also fixed the tops before passing them along a belt to a labelling machine, and then back into the crate from which they came. Such a system is fairly simple to create and removes the need for unskilled workmen who previously spent their time loading and carrying.

Checking and controlling

A more advanced form of automation occurs when machines are given the job of checking or controlling production. On the bottle line there might be an optical device for detecting cracked or chipped bottles. In an egg packing plant there might be a device for automatically grading and sorting the eggs. Such devices are able to take simple decisions and act to correct or alter the production flow in some way. The type of automation removes the need for the semi-skilled workers previously employed to carry out these simple tasks.

Advanced technology

The most advanced forms of automation require very elaborate electronic machines: computers which are able to perform complicated tasks at great speed, to land men on the moon or to navigate supersonic airliners. Such machines make the 'push-button' factory a reality. They are expensive, and can only be justified when the workers they replace cost more than the computers. Despite people's fears computers are not likely to bring vast unemployment. Some groups of workers may be replaced, usually those who do the simpler, more boring jobs; but other workers will be in greater demand. Engineers will be needed to service the machines, technicians, programmers, punch card operators and system analysts to operate them.

Automation will no doubt have a great effect on industry and work. The more repetitive jobs are likely to disappear. Unskilled and semi-skilled workers may not be needed. New skills will be needed and training will have to be provided. Work situations should be improved, creating better working conditions, less stress and better opportunities for social contact. The management structure of the firm may change. The new 'computer personnel' may be better placed to make decisions or advise the management. Firms will need to be more aware of the factors which influence their operations, information on the firm's working will be more readily available for management's decisions.

The blackcoated worker

In 1851, the year of the Great Exhibition, 'blackcoated' or 'office' workers made up only eight of every thousand workers in Great Britain. A century later, at the time of the Festival of Britain, one out of every ten workers was in an office job. This tremendous shift of labour from manual, factory based work to non-manual, office based work has been an important change in work and industry in the twentieth century.

Even more important have been the changes in office work itself, and in the everyday lives of office workers. The counting house of the mid-nineteenth century was very different from the modern office of today.

Charles Dickens describes counting-house life in *A Christmas Carol*:

The door of Scrooge's counting-house was open, that he might keep his eye upon his clerk, who in a dismal little cell beyond, a sort of tank, was copying letters. Scrooge had a very small fire, but the clerk's fire was so very much smaller that it looked like one coal. But he couldn't replenish it, for Scrooge kept the coal-box in his own room; and so surely as the clerk came in with the shovel, the master predicted that it would be necessary for them to part. Wherefore the clerk put on his white comforter, and tried to warm himself at the candle; in which effort, not being a man of strong imagination, he failed.

The typical nineteenth-century office was small. The main activity of the office centred around 'the ledger', a book, or books, in which were entered the daily income and expenditure of the firm. Maintaining the ledger, filing, undertaking correspondence, book-keeping and accounting were all the duties of the clerk. Within the counting house there would be a certain division of labour. At the top would be the 'partners',

149

in whose hands all power and responsibility lay. Beneath them would be a chief clerk, or cashier, who organised the day-to-day running of the office. And, on the lowest rung would be the clerk, carrying out all of the routine, often tedious, jobs. An ambitious clerk might hope one day to rise to the position of senior clerk, or chief clerk, perhaps even to a partnership, should his employers so recognise his hard work and loyalty that they chose to reward his services in such a way.

THE COUNTING HOUSE

The counting house was organised so that all levels came together in a fairly close relationship. Factory work cut a man off from his bosses and made him congregate with his equals. A clerk, on the other hand, knew his bosses and they knew him, he often shared their secrets, and his skills were essential to them. Loyalty, confidence, trust, hard work and respectability were the marks of a good clerk. He may have earned little more than a manual worker, but his education, clean clothes and middle-class style of life set him apart. He saw himself as a member of the middle classes, and modelled himself on them. But in many ways he was only just middle class; his income was often little higher than his working-class neighbour. He lived with his family in a working-class neighbourhood. The clerk stood at the frontier between the middle and working classes. He looked in one direction towards greater participation in middle-class life and in the other towards submersion by the working class. He knew that he must struggle to keep his family moving ahead.

The nineteenth-century clerk depended heavily on his employer. He had no qualification or skills he could offer in the labour market should he fall on hard times. He would have learned the job in one office and that learning would not transfer easily to any other. His hope for the future was to remain steadfast and hope that he would in time attain a high position in his firm. Vacancies arose on death or retirement and each clerk would hope and pray that he might be preferred for the position.

There were, of course, many variations to this general pattern. Between the highly paid banking and insurance clerks and the poorly paid railway clerks were many intermediate levels of clerkdom.

CHANGES IN THE COUNTING HOUSE

Change did not come overnight. There was no sudden revolution which transformed the lives of millions of clerical workers. The changes were spread over much of a century. Machines were part of the cause. The typewriter replaced copying by hand. It was followed by adding

machines, duplicators, and eventually by computers and data pro-
cessing. Social changes also played their part. Better education was
turning out more people qualified to do clerical work, rising costs of
living forced many girls who would previously have stayed home into
office work. In 1851 only 1 office worker in a 1 000 was female, at the
turn of the century it was 13 in every 100, but by 1951 it had risen to
nearly 6 out of every 10: the phrase 'blackcoated worker' should be
replaced by 'whitebloused' worker. The Factory Acts and trade union
pressure gradually improved the conditions and wages of manual
workers. By 1951 the small, close counting house atmosphere was
disappearing fast as offices and firms grew in size.

THE MODERN OFFICE

How did such changes affect the life and work of the clerk? David
Lockwood, in *The Blackcoated Worker* (1958) describes three areas
in which the clerk's situation changed: his position on the labour
market; his work situation and his status.

The clerk's average income kept pace with the factory worker until
about the 1930s. The Second World War and postwar prosperity gave
the manual worker a chance to catch up. In 1914 the ordinary clerk
earned as much as a skilled manual worker, but by 1956 his earnings
were only at the level of the average manual worker. In general the
manual worker had been improving his position whilst the clerk had
had to try hard to keep up. Many of the privileges which once set the
clerk apart from the worker are now accepted as everyone's right.
Holidays with pay, a pension scheme, sick pay and social facilities, are
no longer for clerks alone. One of the attractions of the counting house
was its openings for promotion into management. Fewer people today
work themselves up from tea-boy to managing director. Firms prefer
to take on trainees with qualifications, who can be 'groomed' for the
board room. Professional 'head hunters' are employed to find the
right person for a particular position and then to persuade him to take
it. More often than not 'the right man for the job' is tempted away from
another firm, over the heads of long-standing employees.

As we have seen earlier in this chapter the factory worker is separated
from his employers and management. His time is spent amongst his
equals. The pace and routine of his work is dominated by the machine.

The clerk's working life has also changed but not in the same degree.
The spirit of the counting house still lingers in many modern offices.
Many offices are still fairly small. Often a large factory only needs a
small office. Even in a firm employing large numbers of office workers
the structure of the business divides them up into fairly small units,
departments which bring different grades of worker closely together.

151

The large offices do exist. Typing pools, punch-card rooms and accounting departments employing hundreds in one vast space are often more like factories than offices. There are, however, limits to such developments. The very nature of clerical work prevents it from being organised into large impersonal units or being taken over by machines.

THE STATUS OF THE CLERK

During the earlier part of this century the clerk had a certain standing in society. The status went with the job. As we have seen already office work has changed. Most employees now are women. Wider educational opportunities have opened up office work to a wider section of society.

It has seemed to some people that white-collar workers have seen a decline in their status when compared to the position of the manual worker. Newspaper reports about the high wages of dockers or construction workers have led people to believe that office salaries in general have been overtaken by manual workers' wages. The evidence does not bear this out. In almost every respect the white-collar worker is still better off than the manual worker. Salaries have, on the whole, risen faster than wages; office workers have better holiday arrangements; better sick-pay facilities; better pension schemes and so on. Looked at over the whole of the worker's life there can be no doubt that the office worker still holds a leading position.

However, the clerk's status in society, on the frontier between working class and middle class, is not so sharply drawn as it was. It is on this frontier that the clerk stands. We would say that his status is ambiguous (see Chapter 3). On one hand clerks themselves are not agreed about their position in society. Recent surveys in different parts of the country found that 72, 65, 71, 49 and 51 per cent of clerks questioned said that they were middle class. Other groups may have doubts about the clerk's position. Manual workers, for example, may not have a very high regard for 'chaps who sit on their backsides pushing pens all day'; they may not accept that such people have any reason to claim higher status than they have.

Because of this 'status ambiguity' clerks have been slow to organise themselves into trade unions for unions have been seen as 'working class'. When white-collar unions did develop it was because the clerk was placed in a situation similar to the manual worker. Clerical unions began in larger offices where there was a clear division between clerical worker and management, where the chances of moving from one to the other were limited either because the management recruited workers from outside the firm or because the number of management openings was so small that only a minority of clerks had any chance of internal

152

promotion. Clerical unions have been slow to develop in small offices where there is close contact with the 'bosses' and some chance of internal promotion. Trade unions develop when the clerical workers see themselves as a class separate from the employers. This realisation of 'class' on the part of many non-manual workers has been an important change in the recent history of the blackcoated worker.

The managerial revolution

An important theme in any discussion of changes in the pattern of big business is the idea of a managerial revolution. The earliest firms grew out of the energies of one man, or a family, or even a partnership. Many firms still bear the name of their founder: Pilkingtons, the glass makers, can be traced back to a family wine business; Wedgwoods, makers of fine china, go back to Josiah Wedgwood, an eighteenth-century potter.

As firms grew it became more and more difficult for one man or a family group to keep control in a few hands. They often needed to sell shares in the firm on the Stock Exchange to raise money for expansion. The new shareholders demanded a say in how the firm was run by electing directors on to the board of the company. Control of the business was spread amongst many people, shareholders, directors and also managers. Control was so widely spread that some people felt that those who owned the firm, that is the shareholders, ceased to have any say in how the firm was run. There was a divorce of ownership and control. Firms came to be controlled by their top managers, men who were often employed by the firm and paid a salary. The old division into employer and employee has ceased to be true. All are now employees. Their only claim to power is that they have authority over those beneath them. They no longer own the firm.

P. S. Florence (1961), who studied 98 of Britain's largest companies, found that the proportion of shares held by the largest shareholders had fallen. In 1936 the leading 20 shareholders in each company held 30 per cent of all the shares. By 1951 the average shareholding of the top 20 shareholders had fallen to 19 per cent. In addition the proportion of voting shares and the number of directors among the top 20 shareholders also fell. All of which supports the idea that control is becoming separated from ownership. In a later study of 300 large companies Florence concluded that two-thirds of companies were not owner-controlled.

These conclusions have been questioned by M. Barratt-Brown (*Universities and Left Review* 1958–59). A wider spread of shareholding

153

may, in fact, increase the power of certain shareholders on the Board of Directors. Not every shareholder chooses to vote at the annual general meeting of the company. I.C.I. would have difficulty finding a place to hold their A.G.M. if all the shareholders turned up. Even Wembley Stadium would be too small. Luckily for them a very small proportion actually attend. Barratt-Brown argues that ownership of 10 per cent of the shares is enough to give an individual control. As very large amounts of shares are held by insurance companies, pension funds and unit trusts which seldom involve themselves in the day-to-day affairs of the company, the chances of control with a minority shareholding could be increased. Perhaps even more important is the 'interlocking directorate' when one individual is a member of the boards of a number of companies. Sometimes these are holding companies, which control subsidiaries through certain directors who sit on both boards. Barratt-Brown points out that 58 per cent of the seventy

Fig. 36. *Levels of authority in management*

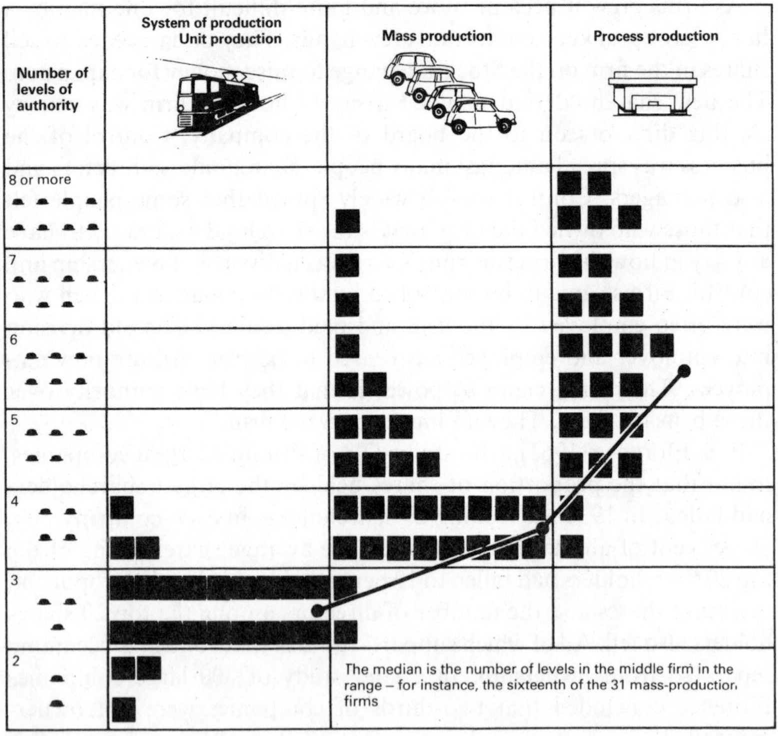

Number of levels of authority	System of production Unit production	Mass production	Process production
8 or more			
7			
6			
5			
4			
3		The median is the number of levels in the middle firm in the range – for instance, the sixteenth of the 31 mass-production firms	
2			

■ 1 firm   ● Median

Source: Woodward 1968

largest companies have bankers on the board of directors and it is these companies which are most likely to be manager-controlled. Either way the control of industry is concentrated in fewer hands, even though those in control may own less shares.

Marx, writing in the nineteenth century, claimed that power in industry would pass from the capitalist owner to the worker. In fact it would seem that power has passed from the capitalists to the managers.

Organisation

Work in our society needs to be organised. That is, after all, why there are managers and supervisors in industry. They are responsible for the organisation of the firm. Of course firms are not the only organisations. What we shall be reading about in this section could also apply to schools, churches, hospitals or any other body which is set up to achieve certain set aims and which has some form of continuity over a period of time. Firms are an important type of organisation because so many people spend such a large amount of time at work.

The way a firm is organised depends very much on the nature of the business carried out. A car hire firm will be organised in a different way from a steel works. The kind of production methods used will also have some influence on the firm's organisation; continuous flow, or 'process' production will require a different pattern of organisation to assembly line mass production. Woodward's study (1968) of 100 firms in south-east Essex showed that the number of levels in the organisation was closely related to the method of production used.

Each of the hats in Fig. 36 represents one level in the organisation. Each of these levels would have its own area of responsibility, its own aims and methods of communicating with other levels. At some point in the firm's pyramid would be a group of individuals who would have the job of planning and controlling the activities of the organisation. They would also have the power to remove workers who were not working well, to promote others and generally to ensure that the firm is achieving its aims.

BUREAUCRACY

Max Weber called such organisations 'bureaucracies'. This had nothing to do with how efficient firms were or the amount of 'red tape'. Weber describes bureaucracy as an 'ideal type', a perfect example of a type of organisation. Weber's bureaucracy is made up of a series of officials whose position and power is written down in a contract or book of rules. These officials are arranged in a pyramid – one above the other – and each has responsibility for those below. Within the bureaucracy is a set of rules, or procedures which cover all things that are likely to affect the running of the organisation. Writing things down is important for a bureaucracy and documents are stored in a safe place – every office needs a filing cabinet. Business and personal matters are kept separate. There are often rules about making personal telephone calls in office time. Jobs in a bureaucracy are awarded to the most able, best qualified applicant, and the terms of employment are written into a contract. In such organisations, individuals are obeyed because of 'what they are', because of the positions they hold. The rules state who can issue commands and also who must obey them.

Weber's idea of bureaucracy is very 'mechanical'. Like a machine. Everyone has his place, his function to perform, and if all follow the rules the firm ticks over nicely. In practice organisations may not work quite as efficiently as this. In an employment exchange the desk clerks were told to treat people who came into the office in a formal way, just getting on with the job and not wasting time trying to get to know them. Certain clerks disliked this approach. They liked to chat to the people and treat them as individuals. This made the desk clerks more satisfied with their job and worked well for the clients they got on with. However, those clients they did not get on with received unsatisfactory attention and all of the clerks had to go back to obeying the rules. In this situation, the 'rule book' performed a valuable function. Bureaucratic methods were better suited to the task in hand. We would say that bureaucracy in this case was 'functional'.

However, bureaucracy involves obeying rules. A good bureaucrat needs to be trained to accept rules and get on with the job. It is not satisfactory when there is a need for change. Such an organisation cannot easily adapt to new situations. In this case we would say bureaucracy is 'dysfunctional'. It limits the effectiveness of the organisation to achieve its aims.

AN 'ORGANIC MODEL'

An alternative to this picture of organisations as 'machines' is to view them as 'organisms'. In an organic type of organisation new situations would be continually arising. The management would need to adapt itself to each new problem. Just as a tree adapts itself to its surroundings, putting out a root here, a branch there, so an organic type of organisation will be able to adapt itself to changing situations. Designing a block of flats requires a number of different skills to come together. In addition to the architect, there will probably be a structural engineer, a cost accountant, and a quantity surveyor, each with his own contribution to make, and the finished flats will be the result of a team effort. A similar organisation might be found in the planning of an advertising campaign.

A pyramid represents the way people communicate in a mechanistic type of organisation. The boss is at the top and instructions travel down to those at the base. As we saw in Fig. 36 different firms have different numbers of layers to their organisation pyramid.

Fig. 37. *The pyramid of organisation (mechanistic)*

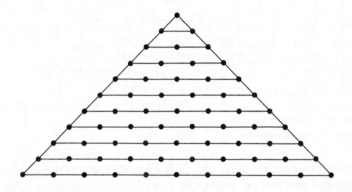

Fig. 38. *The network organisation (organic)*

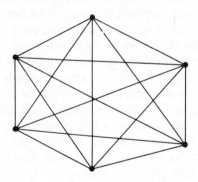

An organic type of organisation is more like a network. There are no set lines of communication and most people are on, or close to, the same level.

Between these two extremes of 'mechanistic' and 'organic' types of

157

organisation are many organisations which combine features of both. A real-life 'pyramid' might look something like this.

Fig. 39. *The organisation structure of a small plastics factory*

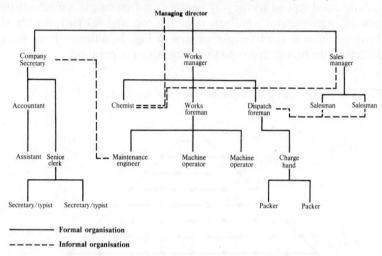

——————— Formal organisation

– – – – – – Informal organisation

Twenty people work for this firm. 'The Guvnor' is the managing director, under him are section heads each responsible for a different area of operations. The company secretary manages the financial and legal affairs of the company. He has a staff of five under him. The works manager has a staff of 9 including the firm's chemist and a maintenance man. The sales manager has 2 salesmen to help him. According to the formal, or 'bureaucratic', structure of the firm communications between sections should go through the section head. The salesman deals with the accountant through the sales manager and the company secretary. The managing director deals with the chemist through the works manager. In fact this 'formal' organisation is often by-passed. Informal contacts enable people to get things done quicker by going direct. The managing director, for example, is a qualified scientist. He spends a lot of time discussing new developments with the chemist. He does not bother the works manager who is busy in the machine shop. The sales manager has contacts with the firm's customers and passes on requests and information on products directly to the chemist. In similar ways there are informal links – between the company secretary and the maintenance engineer, the salesmen and dispatch, and many others not shown in the diagram.

This informal organisation is 'organic', whilst the formal organisation is 'mechanistic'. Informal links between individuals have grown up over many years and serve to make the firm not only more efficient but also happier. People are able to move out of their restricted bureaucratic position and develop wider patterns of communication. The informal organisation is functional. It helps the firm to achieve its aims more effectively.

Why do people work?

People go to work to earn a living. To get money to buy things with. This is certainly one answer to the question 'Why work?' – but it cannot be the whole of the answer. What about the nurse who works for long hours at a very responsible job, involving long training, when she could earn as much working in a factory for only half the time? Surely she is not only concerned with cash? What about the milkman who wins the pools but still gets up at four o'clock to do his milk round? What is he getting out of work?

One answer is that work gives a man a status. 'What do you do?' is a regular question to ask when you meet someone for the first time. By knowing what a man does you are able to place him in society. By working you are able to feel that in some way you are valued by society, that you are making a contribution to the community. The wife of an unemployed man wrote: 'You were giving something to society; you weren't shoved on the scrapheap, rendered useless, never to be worth anything again – well you might as well be dead.'

WORK IS A SOCIAL ACTIVITY

For most people work is a social activity. Few work completely alone. Many people prefer 'a good set of mates' to a bigger pay packet or better conditions. In a slaughterhouse a group of women had the job of sorting out the innards from the animals. The job was not pleasant and neither was the cellar-room in which they worked. However, these six women enjoyed themselves at work, laughing and singing as they got on with the job. A new medical officer was appointed to the factory. When he saw the room and smelt the reek of blood and intestines he decided to move the women to clean jobs in other parts of the factory and put men into the cellar to do the sorting. There was an immediate protest from the women: 'Why were they being picked on? If the firm wasn't satisfied then they should say so.' This group had worked together for years. Their supervisor let them get on with the job and praised them regularly. They formed a happy working unit. Elsewhere in the same factory were girls with nice clean jobs, and bright airy comfortable offices, yet all of the time hating it. Social contacts are very important if work is to be satisfying.

159

There are other reasons for working. For some people it provides them with power or authority over others. A craftsman derives pleasure from using his skill to create something. A toolmaker describes the satisfaction he got as he completed his apprenticeship:

> Later the ability to produce, largely by myself, a rather complex tool which then passed the inspector's experienced eye gave me a sense of satisfaction which later achievements could not rival. It gave me the instinct for creative work, and the realisation that in work alone some personal fulfilment can be found. (Fraser 1969)

To some people work provides an opportunity to help others. Nurses, doctors and social workers often choose their careers with such a thought in the back of their minds.

For some it is hard to tell work from leisure. The Press photographer whose hobby is photography; the footballer who watches 'Match of the Day' on television; the carpenter who makes toys for his grandchildren: all these people lack a clear dividing line between work and leisure. Work gives people far more than just money. It provides status, social contacts, and satisfaction in many different ways.

The study of work

The study of people at work is the job of psychologists and social psychologists. Very often they are known as 'time and motion' or 'organisation and methods' experts, or 'industrial psychologists'. They are interested in people's behaviour at work and in particular in how to get workers to work better. One of the earliest experts in time and motion study was an American, F. W. Taylor, commonly known as 'Speedy Taylor'. His greatest achievements were the invention of the overhand throw in baseball and getting a Dutch steel worker to shovel $47\frac{1}{2}$ tons of pig-iron in one day, nearly four times the previous average. Taylor worked on three principles: first, find the best men for the job then teach them to do the job efficiently and with the most economical movements; and finally, give high wages as an incentive to the best workers. Standing beside the worker, timing him with his stopwatch, noting every movement, changing the layout of the factory, all earned Taylor the title 'most hated man in America'. Workers hated the thought of 'Speedy Taylor' and his methods. 'Time and motion' was seen as a method to oppress the workers.

THE HUMAN RELATIONS APPROACH

Later psychologists took the view that a man worked best when he was most comfortable. They sought for the 'correct' temperature, or level of lighting, for the worker, experimenting by altering conditions and then measuring changes in productivity. Each man was viewed almost as a machine only needing the right working conditions to function properly. Such ideas were overthrown by the work of Elton Mayo and his research at the Hawthorne Works of the Western Electric Company in Chicago between 1924 and 1927. The Company, which provided generous sick pay, pension schemes and recreational facilities, called in Mayo to investigate a general feeling of discontent amongst its 30 000 employees.

The team of research workers began by experimenting with the levels of lighting in two similar workshops. They assumed that there must be something wrong with the working conditions in the factory. Too little light, or too cold, perhaps too hot or too nosiy. They started with the lights. In one workshop lighting levels were increased. In the other they remained the same, as a control group. Observers noted the changes in attitudes and output in each group. As expected, the work output increased with each new rise in the level of lighting in the experimental workshop. The problem seemed to have been solved. But, in the other workshop, where the lighting remained the same, output also rose. And when the lighting in the first workshop was reduced, output did not fall, it rose. When lighting in both workshops was reduced, output rose yet again. In the end, lighting in both workshops was back to its original level and output had doubled. The level of light was not in this case linked to the efficiency of the workers.

A second experiment was set up. Six girls were selected to work at assembling telephone relays. The finished relay was dropped into a chute at the end of the bench and could easily be counted. The girls set to work, and their daily output was recorded. In the first week each girl produced 2 400 relays. Sitting with them at the bench for the five years of the experiment was an observer who noted what went on, answered the girls' questions and listened to their complaints. Every few weeks a change was made in the girls' working conditions and the changes in output were recorded. Extra rest breaks were introduced and then taken away. Free meals were provided, they clocked off at 4.30 p.m. instead of 5 p.m. Piece work was introduced. They were sent home at 4 p.m. instead of 4.30 p.m. Eventually the girls were put back to the working conditions they had had at the start. At every change the girls' output had risen until at the end the girls each produced 3 000 relays a week under the same conditions as when they produced 2 400.

How were such results to be explained? Elton Mayo came to the conclusion that the main influence on the girl's output was the attention being given to them. The girls felt important because they had been chosen for the experiment. They appreciated having someone who would keep them informed about what they were doing, who would listen to their complaints. As a result they worked harder. The girls felt that they were valued members of the firm and no longer cogs in a machine. The very fact that they were being studied led to changes in their behaviour. Social scientists still refer to the 'Hawthorne effect' when describing how the very activity of investigation has an effect on the subject investigated.

Elton Mayo's research at the Hawthorne Works led to a revolution in the study of work. When workers were treated as individuals who needed to feel appreciated instead of just 'cogs in a machine' to work, and get paid, they responded by working better.

AN ALTERNATIVE VIEW

This view of attitudes to work derived from the studies of Elton Mayo has been called 'the human relations' approach. Earlier in this chapter we considered another approach when we discussed the effect that a particular method of production might have on attitudes to work. Under this 'technological' approach it has been thought that workers who were either in craft occupations or in advanced 'process' productions would be happier in their work than those who worked at machines or on assembly lines. Recent studies carried out by a team of sociologists led by John Goldthorpe and David Lockwood (1968) suggest that neither the 'human relations' nor the 'technological' approaches provide the complete answer to job satisfaction. Studying a sample of 229 workers in Luton in the 1960s they found that the workers who were most satisfied were the machine setters, who were well ahead of both craftsmen toolmakers and process workers. These setters were men who, though still only semi-skilled, had worked their way up from machine-minding. Because they had come up from the machine-floor and could look back to the times when they stood all day 'minding' they were inclined to look favourably on their new job. Job satisfaction was influenced by the attitudes these men took with them to the job. In any study of human society we must be aware of beliefs, values and ideas held by those we are studying.

The way the individual worker, whether in a factory or an office, experiences work is of great interest to the sociologist. We cannot, however, separate the individual's experience of work from the wider social life of the worker. Work roles have to be learned. Workers become socialised into roles with all the attitudes and beliefs that go with them. But these roles are not just roles you learn at work. They are closely linked to other parts of life and begin to be learnt long before you start work.

162

Learning to labour

In Chapter 7 we considered the idea that schools reproduce certain relationships and ways of behaving. Handing on particular skills, attitudes and values from one generation to the next. One of the most important tasks of the school is to keep producing workers. Fig. 33 showed how aware parents were of this need. Industry needs workers able to do all kinds of jobs. Some jobs require long training and considerable skill, others need no training because they need no skill. Schools prepare young people for all levels of work – skilled and unskilled. Schooling must prepare people to be brain surgeons, car mechanics and labourers. It prepares them not only with skills but also with attitudes. We can begin to see the attitudes of people at school. Paul Willis examined this through a group of boys who, in the school's terms, were failures. They were all due to leave school without qualifications as soon as they possibly could. To the school they were the trouble-makers and were all likely to go into unskilled jobs. The attitudes these boys had towards school and towards work were picked up from their fathers and uncles. Whereas the schools saw work in terms of an interesting, worthwhile career requiring qualifications, attitudes and behaviour, which the school could give to a boy, the boys saw work as unpleasant, boring and hard and it was only endured because it gave them money. To make work more endurable the boys looked for 'laughs', diversions to slacken the load, and ways of showing their own power and manhood. Willis suggests that the boys anti-school attitudes were closely linked to the attitudes they would require to survive at work.

Another group of boys in Willis' study took an opposite view. They were 'conformists' who accepted the school's values. Their attitudes prepared them for a different kind of work, as one of the boys described:

> I expect work to follow on really, you know, if you enjoy things all your life, just keep on getting on, but if you don't enjoy school, you don't intend to work. I think it just follows on into work, you won't do enough . . . work is like going to school, after you've left school, say, I'm going to get an apprenticeship, you've got your apprenticeship, you're qualified, just get, just keep on learning for the rest of your life. (Willis 1978)

This socialisation into work roles begins, therefore, long before you start work. Once work does begin further socialisation takes place. Sometimes the introduction to work is gradual, perhaps through a period of professional training, or an apprenticeship. Sometimes it is very sudden. The attitudes and beliefs which were built up before

163

work started will now be strengthened or modified in the real situation.

Learning to labour is not just learning a job, or even the attitudes that go with the job. It involves a great number of other things that need to be learned.

Consider what you would need to learn to become a doctor. Obviously you need to study medicine and know all about how the body works, what drugs do and how to cure people's illnesses. You also have to know how to communicate with other doctors: to know, for example, that 'cardiac arrest' means that someone's heart has stopped. But doctors need to learn more skills if they are to do the job of doctoring.

They must be able to deal with patients in a way which gives them confidence and reassurance. Doctors learn to develop a bedside manner which communicates confidence, expertise and peace-of-mind. They must also learn how to deal with matrons, nurses, relatives and troublesome patients and the other groups of people found in hospitals. All of these skills are learned informally, on-the-job but are vital if a medical student is to become a 'good doctor'.

In similar ways the toolmaker and the draughtsman must learn what it means to be a skilled workman and a member of the company staff.

The toolroom was a very different place from the unskilled 'shop' I had first been sent to on starting work. There were only four apprentices of whom I was the youngest. Right from my first day there, it was made clear to me that toolmakers were craftsmen, and as such superior to all the other workers. The ethos which has been described as 'the aristocracy of labour' was very present. At the centre of this ethos lay a strict adherence to very high standards of workmanship.

Four years later I left the toolroom for the 'jig and tool drawing office'. I have never experienced a more painful social dislocation. Gone was the ribald repartee that marked the beginning of another day in the toolroom. It was almost as if some ghost had whispered to each man on being promoted (from the toolroom) to the drawing office: 'Draughtsmen are gentlemen and members of the company staff and toolmakers are workmen and paid by the hour.' To the outside observer the status differences might have been difficult to detect, but to the factory worker they were as plain as the nose on his face. (Fraser 1969)

THE EXPERIENCE OF WORK

Work can be experienced in many different ways. Two men in the same office or at the same bench may experience their work quite differently. Work can mean different things to different people. To the boys studied by Paul Willis work meant money, boredom and

164

'having a laugh'. To the toolmaker it means skill and satisfaction. Goldthorpe and Lockwood have suggested three main types of attitude towards work.

Firstly, there is an *instrumental* attitude towards the job. The worker is in it for the money. His involvement in the job is usually low and it gives him little satisfaction. Work is kept separate from other areas of life except that it provides the money which makes the rest of life enjoyable. This kind of attitude is often linked to assembly line work as shown in a study of working on motor car assembly:

> If you work at Ford's on the line you let your mind go blank and look forward to pay day and the weekend. As one man put it: I just adapt to it. I suppose you could adapt to anything really. It depends on your circumstances. I'm married and I've taken out a mortgage. This affects your attitude to work. I just close my eyes and stick it out. I think about the kids and the next premium being paid. (Beynon 1975)

Secondly, there is the *bureaucratic* approach to work. Whereas the instrumental approach sees work as a job, the bureaucratic approach sees it as a career. The worker feels responsible to the employer and in return expects security and steady promotion. Money is not everything, though it is important. The work itself is valued and it often flows over into the worker's home life. Professional careers and 'white-collar' occupations are often linked to this attitude. The counting house (page 150) relied on this kind of attitude. It is likely that with the great expansion of white-collar work and its mechanisation, office workers today are moving towards an 'instrumental' attitude.

Thirdly, work can be seen as a social activity and can be important to people because of the social relationships involved. A steelworker describes one group he worked with.

> I knew some good fellows among the melters; in fact, I knew many, for mine was a friendly trade and it bred good men and it still does. It was a common thing for the furnace teams to enjoy each others' company and when that was so the time went by on wheels. I had a particular three working with me for a long time and I was secretly sorry when they were promoted elsewhere. (Fraser 1969)

This third attitude is built on the *solidarity* between workers in the factory or office.

Alienation

For many people, however, work provides little real satisfaction. Marx used the word 'alienation' to describe the separation of the worker from the product he or she makes. Car workers tell the story of a country lad who couldn't believe that he had to work on every car: 'Oh, no', he said, 'I've done my car. That one down there. A green one it was.' (Beynon 1975.) Such a story is funny because we accept that the assembly line worker seldom knows what happens to the thing he makes and certainly has no interest in what happens to it.

Blauner sees alienation as a sense of powerlessness in which the worker is unable to control the work process. Assembly-line workers often complain about the speed of the line and have been known to sabotage the 'track' in order to seize control and gain a moment's rest. Other aspects of alienation identified by Blauner are the meaninglessness of work, the isolation of the worker, and his self-estrangement – by which is meant the inability of the worker to express anything of himself in his work. Some jobs are obviously more alienating than others.

HOUSEWORK

Ann Oakley's study of housework (Chapter 4) looked at an activity which is seldom thought of as '*work*'. She found, however, that many of the features of factory work or office work also applied to housework.

The most valued feature of housework was the freedom it gave to the housewives to plan their own time. They valued their autonomy and felt that the best thing about being a housewife is that 'you're your own boss'. This freedom was, however, seen to be limited by the fact that housework had to be done and there were strong practical and moral pressures to get it done.

> Why do I clean the kitchen floor twice a day? Well, it's because she's all over it, isn't it? I mean it's not nice for a child to crawl on a dirty floor – she might catch something off it.
>
> Even though I've got the option of not doing it, I don't really feel I could not do it, because I feel I ought to do it. (Oakley 1974)

Housework was seen as monotonous and as never-ending.

> Housewives tend to be busy all of the time but they're not really doing anything constructive, are they? Well, I suppose it is constructive in a way, but you never really see anything for it and its all routine. (Oakley 1974)

Many of the housewives felt that housework was a very lonely occupation and looked forward to going out shopping in order to get away from the isolation of the house. It was also seen to be a job which, for many women, failed to give them any real interest in life. Many feared that they might become 'cabbages' and refused to even think

of themselves as housewives, preferring to write 'secretary' on official
forms.

Table 26. *What is best about being a housewife?*

Best thing	Number of answers mentioning
You're your own boss	19
Having the children	9
Having free time	5
Not having to work outside the home	4
Having a husband	4
Having home/family life	3
Housework	1
Other	2
Total	47

Table 27. *Worst things about being a housewife*

Worst things	Number of answers mentioning
Housework	14
Monotony/Repetitious/Boring	14
Constant domestic responsibility	6
Isolation/Loneliness	4
Must get housework done	3
Being tied down	3
Children	2
Other	2
Total	48

Source: Oakley 1974

Ann Oakley's study shows that housewives experienced housework
in many different ways but that for many their work was alienating in
the ways described by Blauner. They often experienced a sense of
powerlessness in the face of never-ending cleaning, washing and
ironing. Many of the daily tasks involved were meaningless and the
housewives often felt isolated and in danger of becoming 'cabbages'.

Leisure

Work is an activity which usually takes place in particular places, at
set times, and which is aimed at producing goods, services and wages.

167

We are stating these facts when we speak of 'place of work', 'going to work', 'hours of work' and so on. Leisure, on the other hand, involves more freedom in deciding when, or where, or why? People choose their own leisure activities. They are not imposed on them. Work involves a certain amount of control, or direction from above. At work people are never free to do just as they wish. A self-employed craftsman or shopkeeper knows that he must work or starve. Only a small minority are able to live without working. Even a tramp cadging fivepence for a meal is having to work at getting it.

Leisure is therefore the time left over when work is finished, or at least the main part of that time. For many people work overflows into leisure time. How would you classify travelling to work, or getting ready for work? Is time spent in these ways work time or leisure time? Work also carries over into leisure time when a worker has to bring work home with him. The executive who works on a report over the weekend, the commercial artist who has a piece of art work to finish. What about the young bank clerk or accountant who attends evening classes, in order to gain better qualifications for his job? Is this work or leisure? There are others who take on extra jobs in their leisure time, often for extra money but also for other reasons.

The dividing line between work and leisure is not a clear one. There are many activities which occur on the fringe between work and leisure. It might be easier if we reconsidered our original definitions. 'Work' and 'leisure' can each be viewed in two ways. 'Work' is something we do, an activity, but it is also a period of time. If we say 'we are working' we usually refer to the activity. When we refer to being 'at work' we usually refer to 'place and time'. We use the word 'leisure' in similar ways. Leisure time is that time outside working hours. A leisure activity is something we do for ourselves, not for someone who pays a wage. From this we can see that 'work activity' can take place in 'leisure time'. The executive with the report and the commercial artist are in this category. In a similar way 'leisure activity' can take place in 'work time'. The 'business lunch' which lasts from twelve to three, the odd game of cards when business is slack, are examples of this.

Work activities and leisure activities should be viewed together. What you do at work has some bearing on how you use your leisure. These patterns of work and leisure can now be considered.

PATTERNS OF WORK AND LEISURE

People who have jobs which allow them a large amount of personal freedom and responsibility, are often well educated and gain personal satisfaction from work find that their work *extends* into their leisure. There are no clear dividing lines and often work and leisure are seen as

168

one. Most doctors come into this group. They are seldom able to prevent work activities imposing on leisure time.

Another group adopt leisure activities which have very little to do with their work activity. We would say that their relationship between work and leisure is *neutral*; their leisure is seen as relaxation. Clerical workers and others with little freedom at work often fall into this group.

The third group of workers are those who get little personal satisfaction from work, who often find work dull and tedious. Leisure to them is an escape. They seek leisure activities which add colour to their lives, activities which are in *opposition* to the activity of work.

Within the last fifty years hours of work have been growing shorter. With increased automation they are likely to continue to do so in the future. More people have more leisure time; they are also better off. They have more money to spend on more leisure. This has led to many changes in leisure activities. Because the working-class groups have benefited most from this it has meant that leisure activities which were once for the rich alone are now enjoyed by all. Leisure has become more democratic. Mediterranean holidays are now within the reach of the vast majority of the population. An Adriatic beach in August will quite likely contain mill-workers from Burnley, clerks from Birmingham and bus-drivers from Bristol.

Leisure has become an industry with its own magazines, multi-million-pound budgets and television programmes. Bingo halls, yachting marinas, do-it-yourself shops, wildlife safari parks, evening classes and 'holidays in the sun' are all part of our 'leisure explosion'.

Trade unions and others

Over 12 million workers in the United Kingdom belong to trade unions. That is over 50 per cent of the total labour force. Trade unions play an important part in the industrial life of the nation. The foundations of the trade union movement were laid in the middle of the nineteenth century by men like Will Thorne of the gas workers, Ben Tillett of the dockers and William Allen of the engineers. It was on these foundations that twentieth-century unionists like Ernest Bevin and Walter Citrine built.

The main function of a trade union is to bargain with employers for better wages and conditions of work for the union's members. This is the central activity of all unions and is carried out on many different levels. The Trades Union Congress and the national executives of the unions are involved in political activities which protect the rights of the

169

worker. The area and branch officials of the union negotiate on a local level, while on the shop floor action is taken by shop stewards, conveners and the workers themselves. The greater part of this activity takes place at the level of the shop floor, involving only a few workers and the management. Many disputes are settled by discussion 'over the machine' by a worker and a rate-fixer, or in the works manager's office. Only a small minority get as far as strike action. When they do, demands for more money are often a camouflage which hides more basic disagreements. The 1970 Pilkington strike, which lasted for seven weeks and involved 8 500 workers, began over a mistake in wage calculations. Within days the workers were demanding a rise of £25 a week. Underneath it all lay a long-simmering feeling of powerlessness on the part of the workers; a desire, as one worker put it, to 'give Pilks a kick in the teeth'. The strike gave many of the workers a feeling of freedom and responsibility they had never known before.

In many industries unions maintain their positions by enforcing a 'closed shop' or an 'agency shop', in which all workers must belong to the union or at least pay an equivalent subscription to a charity of their choice. Membership of the union therefore becomes a basic requirement for getting a job and the union has control over entry into the industry. Such practices strengthen the union's hand in wage negotiations. Trade unions do perform other functions; providing insurance schemes, supporting research into industrial diseases,

Fig. 40. *Density of trade union membership*

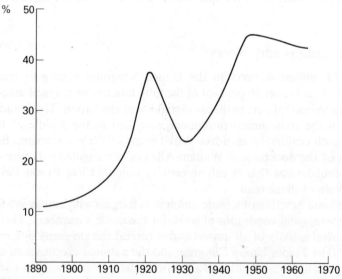

financing educational and other social activities, but these are less important than the central activity of wage bargaining.

TYPES OF TRADE UNION

British trade unions fall into four distinct groups, according to the types of workers included.

The largest unions, such as the Transport and General Workers' Union (T.G.W.U.) and the National Union of General and Municipal Workers (N.U.G.M.W.) contain workers from many different jobs. These are *general* unions. The T.G.W.U. has over two million members. The second largest union in the country is the Amalgamated Engineering Union (A.E.U.) with just over one million members. All members of the A.E.U. are engineers; they have the same trade, or craft, and the union is therefore a *craft* union. Most coal-miners belong to the National Union of Mineworkers (N.U.M.) which is an *industrial* union, having workers from only one industry. The final group are the *white-collar* (or blackcoated) workers who have their own unions.

These are not perfect divisions. The A.E.U. is a union for skilled engineers, therefore a craft union, but also the union for the engineering industry, therefore an industrial union. The Iron and Steel Trades Federation is the main union for the steel industry but has many white-collar members. Some white-collar unions are 'industrial' such as the National Union of Bank Employees (N.U.B.E.), whereas others are 'general' unions.

THE PATTERN OF UNION MEMBERSHIP

As the trade union movement adapts itself to new conditions, new unions appear and old ones amalgamate; the pattern of trade unions will change and the division into craft, industrial, general and white-collar unions may cease to be relevant.

In the last half century there have been many changes in the pattern of trade union membership. In 1939 there were 1 019 unions with a total membership of 6·3 million. The average union contained 6 000 members. By 1959 total union membership was up to 9·6 million but there were only 651 unions. The average membership had risen to 14·7 thousand. During this century the membership of trade unions has risen from only 2 million in 1901 to over 10 million today. Union membership has risen faster than the rise in the working population, so that the 'density of union membership' (the percentage of workers who belong to a union) has also risen. In 1901 12·8 per cent of the working population were union members; by 1964 this had risen to 42·6 per cent.

Unions are bigger. As there are also fewer unions to share this increased membership it has meant that some unions have grown very

171

large indeed. A long series of amalgamations and mergers have created a group of giant unions which together contain the majority of union members. Over half of the total trade union membership in 1963 belonged to one of eight unions which each contained over a quarter of a million members. One in four unionists in 1963 belonged to either the T.G.W.U. or the A.E.U.

This growth of trade union membership and its concentration in a few large unions has created powerful economic groups who are able to use their influence in the interests of their members.

White-collar unions

Growth in union membership has been greatest amongst white-collar workers. Some white-collar unions grew by over 100 per cent between 1948 and 1964, and the average rate of growth of industrial white-collar unions in that time was 76·6 per cent. This growth in white-collar unions may seem fantastic but, in fact, white-collar unions have only just about managed to keep up with the growth in the non-manual labour force. In central and local government in 1960 there was a total union density amongst non-manual workers of 83 to 84 per cent. In distribution and manufacturing industry as few as 12 to 15 per cent of white-collar workers were in unions.

Fig. 41. *The growth of white-collar unionism*

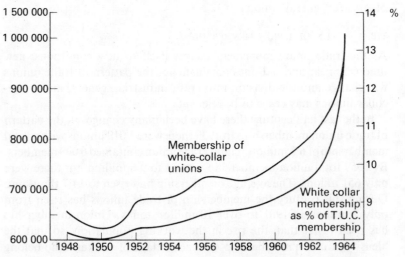

During the last ten to fifteen years there has also been a spread of trade unionism among women workers. Though there was a National Federation of Women Workers in the earliest years of this century

172

women have not, on the whole, played a very active part in union affairs. There are signs that this is changing and that women are becoming more union conscious, either joining existing male domin-ated unions or setting up their own female unions.

Fig. 42. *Women in unions (% of total membership)*

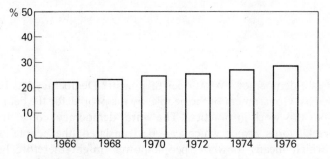

Professional associations

Many people who are not members of trade unions do belong to some form of professional association. Unlike unions these bodies do not negotiate with employers on behalf of their members. Their main function is to control the standards of entry into the profession and to discipline members who fail to maintain a professional standard. The Chartered Institute of Secretaries or the Institute of Personnel Management are examples of such bodies. Under 1971 Industrial Relations Act some of these professional associations have registered as trade unions to gain certain rights under the Act.

The employers

It is not only the workers who join together to protect their interests. Employers, too, have their associations. Within the Confederation of British Industry are a large number of groups of employers representing different industries. Each association provides a body of employers who are able to negotiate with trade unions at each different level. Through the Confederation of British Industry (C.B.I.) the employers are able to present their views to the government as the Trades Union Congress does for the unions.

173

9

People and Government

'Britain is a democracy.' What does this mean? Democracy has been described as 'Government of the people, by the people, for the people'. How does this work in practice? The word 'democracy' comes from two Greek words *demos* which can be translated 'the people' and *kratos* which means 'power': 'people-power' might therefore be a twentieth-century translation. But do people have 'power' in modern politics?

Democracy

The Greek city-state was the source of many of our ideas of democracy. In these city-states the citizens would meet together in the market-place and discuss the affairs of the town, electing certain of their number to undertake the work that was needed. The market-place would be fairly small and the size of the assembly would be limited to those people who could clearly hear the speakers on the platform. As only the adult men concerned themselves with politics this system worked fairly well.

REPRESENTATION

Britain is no tiny city-state, able to conduct its affairs in the market-place. The 'direct democracy' of Ancient Greece could never work in a modern nation-state with a population numbering tens of millions. Instead, we have a 'representative' or 'parliamentary' democracy. The people choose certain individuals to represent them in parliament. These 'representatives' choose a government which carries out the day-to-day business of running the country. We must now consider how far such an 'indirect democracy' is in fact 'government of the people, by the people, for the people'.

True democracy involves control by the people over the policies of the government. In this way democracy is different from dictatorship (rule by one man) or oligarchy (rule by a group). 'Democracy' has four basic features. First, the people have some form of control over the

174

policies of the government. During a British election each party outlines its policy. The people choose the party they prefer and if, after five years, they don't like those policies, they will not re-elect them. The ordinary person's influence over the government policy between elections is very slight though some influence is made possible by the activities of pressure groups. A second feature of true democracy is that all voters are equal. Each voter has one vote. There was a time when graduates of Oxford and Cambridge Universities each had two votes: a home vote and a university vote. This is not so today. Thirdly, people have the right to vote and engage in political activity. It is not a crime to oppose the government in Britain. People are allowed freedom of speech and freedom to hold meetings. And, finally, when people have exercised their equal rights the decision will be taken according to the wishes of the majority.

The British system of government

The centre of government in Great Britain is Westminster. Clustered around Parliament Square and Whitehall in London are most of the key institutions of government. The Palace of Westminster, or Houses of Parliament, contains the House of Lords and the House of Commons, made up respectively of Peers of the Realm and the elected representatives of the people. Every five years, if not before, the British people have the right to go to the polls to elect members of Parliament. The Leader of the Party which gains the most 'seats' in the House of Commons is asked by the Queen, in her position as Head of State, to form the Government. As Prime Minister he chooses his 'Cabinet' of leading M.P.s. From his supporters in Parliament the Prime Minister chooses men and women to lead the various departments of government, or ministries.

The House of Lords is not elected. In the past its members were the hereditary aristocracy and the right to sit in 'the Lords' was passed on from father to son. Today more and more of the active peers are appointed by the Government in recognition of their ability or service to the country. These are 'life peers' and only hold the title of 'Lord' or 'Lady' for their own lifetime. They cannot pass it on to their descendants. Life peers are chosen from all walks of life; but also in the House of Lords are twenty-four Bishops, the Archbishops of Canterbury and York and the Lords of Appeal, or Law Lords, who are High Court judges and act as the final Court of Appeal.

Debates in the House of Lords are presided over by the Lord Chancellor who sits on 'the Woolsack'—a reminder of the one-time importance of England's wool trade. The 'chairman' of the House of Commons is 'the Speaker'. He sits at one end of the House of Commons with the 700 or so M.P.s on either side of 'the Chamber', in front of him. On his right-hand side are the Government seats. The Prime Minister and Cabinet colleagues sit on the 'front bench'. Opposite them on the Speaker's left is the Opposition, with the Leader of the Opposition and his 'shadow ministers' on the 'Opposition front bench'. Behind the leaders of the two parties are their 'backbench' M.P.s. At the far end of the Chamber are the 'cross benches' where the members of the smaller parties and the independent members sit. Directly in front of the Speaker at the other end of the House of Commons is the 'Bar of the House'. It is from here that Black Rod, the Queen's representative, summons the House of Commons to hear the 'Queen's Speech' at the State Opening of Parliament.

The Queen cannot enter the House of Commons, instead the Commons go along, through the Central Lobby, to the Bar of the House of Lords from where they will hear the Speech from the Throne. In the Queen's speech the government lay down their policies and plans for action in the coming session of Parliament. It is, in fact, the Government's speech which the Queen reads.

The Queen is a symbolic Head of State, having little real power.

THE PROCESS OF LEGISLATION

Once the ceremony and ritual of the state opening is out of the way the two Houses get down to the business of running the country. Parliament's job is to legislate, to pass laws. The job of the Cabinet, assisted by the civil service, is to 'execute' the policies approved by Parliament. Parliament is therefore 'the Legislative' and the Cabinet and civil service – the Executive. The Law Courts, including the Lords of Appeal, make up the 'Judiciary'.

Acts of Parliament begin life as 'Bills'. It is usual for the Government to introduce a Bill, though 'private members' and individuals and organisations outside Parliament can do so. Once the Bill has been introduced (first reading) it is written out in its proposed form and then discussed in detail by the House of Commons (second reading), and by a Committee of M.P.s (committee stage), before it gets its third reading, and is 'sent upstairs' to the House of Lords. Here the process is repeated and eventually the Bill is ready, having been amended and approved by both Houses. It then receives the Royal Assent, the Queen's signature, which makes it an Act of Parliament. Voting in Parliament is called 'a division'. When a vote is to be taken the division bells are rung and M.P.s hurry past 'the tellers', who count the votes, into the lobbies, before returning to their seats to hear the result. Debates in Parliament are published daily in the publication known as *Hansard*, and the Government's proposals for new Bills are included in White Papers.

This very brief survey of the workings of Parliament gives some idea of how our democracy operates and the terms used in any discussion of political activities. Unlike other countries, Britain has no written constitution, or set of rules, governing the activities of parliament. The British Constitution is based on custom and tradition.

The voters

In Britain roughly 36 million people are eligible to vote. That is, they are British citizens over 18 years of age, not in prison, not certified insane, nor members of the Royal Family and are on the Electoral Register for the constituency in which they live. Their votes are fairly evenly divided between the Conservative and Labour Parties with a fair number going to the Liberals.

Table 27. *Voting in general elections (in thousands)*

Year	Conservative	Labour	Liberal	Other
1959	13 750	12 216	1 639	255
1964	12 002	12 206	3 093	349
1966	11 418	13 065	2 328	453
1970	13 106	12 141	2 109	900
1974	11 891	11 596	6 019	1 602
1979	13 978	11 509	4 313	1 699

Not everyone turns out to vote in an election. In the General Elections held in Britain since 1945 the average turnout has been around 80 per cent, going as high as 84 per cent in 1950 and as low as 73 per cent in 1945.

From these figures it would seem that 20 per cent, or two out of every ten voters, do not bother to vote. Is this in fact the case? It is likely that the proportion of electors who deliberately don't vote is less than this figure of 20 per cent. Electoral Registers are made up in October and come into force the following February. They are always a few months out of date. In that time people may have moved too far away to vote, some may have died, or left the country. People who are away on business, have moved, or are sick can vote by post, but many fail to do so in time for their vote to be counted. Possibly 8 per cent of the electorate are affected in this way, leaving only 12 per cent of deliberate non-voters.

These can be divided into two distinct groups. Those in one group do not vote because they do not agree with the policies put forward or with the actions of the parties, or candidates. They might be Liberal supporters in a constituency where there is only a choice of Labour and Conservative. Some may support a party but be so disillusioned with its policies and actions that they decide not to vote in protest. They would not go so far as voting for the other party. There may even be people whose views are changing and whilst they no longer support their old party, they may not have the courage to come right out and vote for the new one. In some cases people choose not to vote because it is a 'safe seat' and the candidate will get in easily whether they vote or not. We cannot tell how many of the 12 per cent non-voters fall into this group of deliberate non-voters. The other group of non-voters are those who are just not interested in politics. They see no point in doing anything out of their way. This group contains slightly more women than men, slightly more young and old than middle-aged, and slightly more poor people.

WHY DO PEOPLE VOTE AS THEY DO?

Political parties are very interested in finding answers to the question 'Why do people vote as they do?' Knowing who votes for them, and who does not, enables a party to aim its propaganda at the right people. Many explanations have been given for particular voting behaviour. It is often said that the working class votes Labour and the middle and upper classes vote Conservative. This cannot be true. If all working-class people voted Labour the Conservative Party would never win an election. Two-thirds of the electorate do manual jobs. Many of these must vote Conservative if the Conservative Party is ever to get into power.

Fig. 43. *Social class and political party*

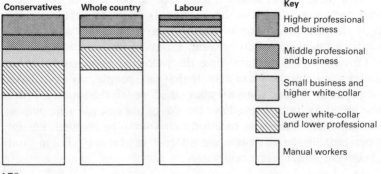

Conservatives   **Whole country**   **Labour**

Key

Higher professional and business

Middle professional and business

Small business and higher white-collar

Lower white-collar and lower professional

Manual workers

You can see from Fig. 43 that a large block of manual workers (working class) vote Conservative and some middle-class non-manual workers vote Labour. This problem of the working-class Conservative has puzzled social scientists for many years. Several possible explanations have been put forward. Working-class Conservatives may be 'deference voters'. Individuals who believe that the upper classes have the right to rule the country, and as the upper classes are thought to vote Conservative they, too, vote Conservative. They often feel that the Conservatives are the 'natural' rulers. George, in Chapter 1 on 'Banbury' would be a good example of a 'deference voter'. Another explanation looks at the way each voter places himself in a social class. This is known as 'self-assigned status'. A man may appear to belong to the working class. He may have a manual job and an elementary education, and live in a council house. But he may think of himself as 'middle class' and would choose to vote as he thinks the middle class votes. How each individual sees 'class' may also be important. In Chapter 3 we considered ideas of 'class ladder or class struggle'. Labour voters are more likely to see class in terms of conflict whilst Conservative voters see it in terms of a ladder. This, too, may account for the working-class Conservative voter.

The political life-style

It is not enough to consider voting behaviour only in terms of social class. Other factors have an influence. Voting behaviour has to be learned. This we call 'political socialisation'. Our 'political lives' pass through several stages. When we are very young politics mean nothing to us. As teenagers and young adults we begin to take notice. We begin to learn from the politics of our surroundings. The family is obviously important in this. A father's political views may well be passed on to the sons and daughters. Eighty-nine per cent of Conservative voters questioned in a survey by David Butler and Donald Stokes came from families where both parents were Conservative; 92 per cent of Labour supporters came from families in which both parents voted Labour. When the parents were divided in their political views 37 per cent of the children went for the Conservatives and 49 per cent to Labour. (Butler and Stokes, 1969.)

Parents have another influence over their children's politics. Personality is linked to political attitudes. A child who grows up with an attitude of suspicion towards anything new may not be impressed by a party which wishes to change things.

However, there may be influences which are stronger than the family.

A young person with Conservative parents who grows up in a neighbourhood which is strongly Labour, may adopt the attitudes of the majority of their friends instead of those of their parents.

Two more things need to be said about the influence of the family. First, children are more likely to be interested in politics if their parents are interested; secondly, the influence of the parents fades as the child grows into adulthood.

Finally, a lot may depend on the point of time at which each person's political views develop. Once a person has begun to commit himself to one party each new event is likely to strengthen his views. Therefore, the period of history when each individual began to be committed to a party is likely to influence the rest of his life.

It has been noticed that older people are more likely to vote Conservative – it was believed that this was due to some maturing influence in later life. But, it could be that these people began to develop their views at a time when support for the Conservatives was high. The 1920s and '30s was such a period and it was in these years that many of today's old people formed their views.

The roots of voting behaviour can be found in the early years of adult life. Once a choice has been made most voters find that life strengthens the attitudes which led to that choice. Each new election campaign creates the need to make that choice yet again.

The floating voter

Many election studies in the past have concentrated on 'the floating voter'. This character is supposed to act like a pendulum, swinging one way then the other, in response to the arguments presented by the politicians. It was thought that if one party increased its votes by 10 per cent over the other parties this was made up of 10 per cent of the voters changing their minds. Recent studies throw doubt on the very idea of a 'floating voter'. Changes in the results of different elections can be explained in four ways. First, there are those who have just reached voting age. They have not voted before and their opinions may fall on one side rather than the other. Then there are those who cannot find a candidate who exactly supports their view. Liberal voters may find themselves without a candidate and might choose to take what, for them, is second best and vote Labour or Conservative. Thirdly, there is the pool of non-voters we considered earlier in this chapter. As some people move out of this group others move in and this may be enough to tip the balance. Finally, there is a small group of people who do switch their vote from election to election.

The election campaign

General elections are held every five years, unless the Prime Minister asks the Queen to dissolve Parliament earlier. This might happen if a Government cannot maintain its majority in the House of Commons. A by-election is held in any constituency where the M.P. resigns or dies.

The proclamation of an election marks the beginning of a three-week campaign by each of the parties to capture as many of the votes as possible. But though we talk of 'an election campaign', it would be more accurate if we viewed it as four campaigns, each overlapping the others, each aimed at a different audience and having different aims.

THE LOCAL CAMPAIGN

First, there is the local campaign, carried out by party workers over a small area with only a few thousand voters. The local campaign consists largely of handing out literature, usually a printed election address from the candidate; canvassing as many as possible of those whose names are on the Register of Electors in order to find out who the party's supporters are; and going round on polling day reminding them to vote. In 1964 nearly one million people, or 3 per cent of the electorate, took part in local campaigns and 34 per cent claimed to have been canvassed. The importance of the local campaign lies in its encouragement of people to vote and the morale-boosting effect it has on the local party workers.

THE CONSTITUENCY CAMPAIGN

At the next level there is the constituency campaign. At its centre is the candidate. He may have been the constituency M.P. in the previous Parliament. He may be a local man or someone sent by the national office of the party. Whoever he is, and however hard he and his helpers work, he is unlikely to get his name across to everyone. In the summer of 1963 only 51 per cent of a sample of electors interviewed by Butler and Stokes could name their M.P. Even fewer could remember the names of other candidates. A survey in 1966 showed that hardly more than a quarter of a sample of electors knew their M.P.'s view on key issues and on some issues this fell to one-eighth. Voters voted for parties, not for the men and women who represented the parties.

THE NATIONAL CAMPAIGN

The third campaign is the national one. At this level the party leaders do battle through the mass media. It is a campaign of Press conferences and manifestoes, party political broadcasts and party images. As many

181

as 92 per cent of the electorate have claimed to follow the campaign on television and in the newspapers. The mass media are able to take elections right into people's homes. Despite this, most people's views remain as they were in the weeks before the campaign began. Advertising, television and the Press do not seem to have a great influence on voting behaviour during the campaign. More important is the 'image' of a party, or of a government, which people have built up during the previous years.

There have been suggestions that elections are won or lost by the actions of advertising agencies who try to 'sell' a party leader as they might sell soap powder. Richard Rose (1967) comes to the conclusion that whilst advertising politicians may be a useful way of passing on information, it does not really change attitudes. In any advertising campaign you cannot get away with selling a bad product for very long. In an election the 'product' is a party or its leader. If the voters have endured years of incompetent government and poor leadership they are not likely to be persuaded by an advertising campaign which offers them a 'new improved product' or 'dynamic leadership'. Advertising can never be better than the product it seeks to sell. A government's success in office is more important in winning an election than is three weeks of window dressing.

INFORMAL PRESSURES

The final type of campaign is very different. The local, constituency, and national campaigns are formal campaigns run by political parties and their helpers. This fourth campaign is an informal one. It has no organisation and is made up of ordinary people discussing the election as they go about their daily lives. In 1964 only 3 per cent of the Butler and Stokes sample had been actively involved in a formal campaign, but 12 per cent had tried to persuade someone to vote for a different party and 59 per cent had discussed the campaign. This informal campaign may be quite important in influencing the way people vote.

The parties

Political parties are an essential part of our political system. Without them it might well be impossible for democracy to operate. For many reasons our political system has operated through two major parties. It is a two-party system. America also has a two-party system, but on the continent of Europe most countries have multi-party systems. In multi-party systems governments are formed by a coalition of leading parties. Such coalitions are rare in Britain. Power usually goes to the one party with the most seats.

Fig. 44. *The structure of the Labour Party*

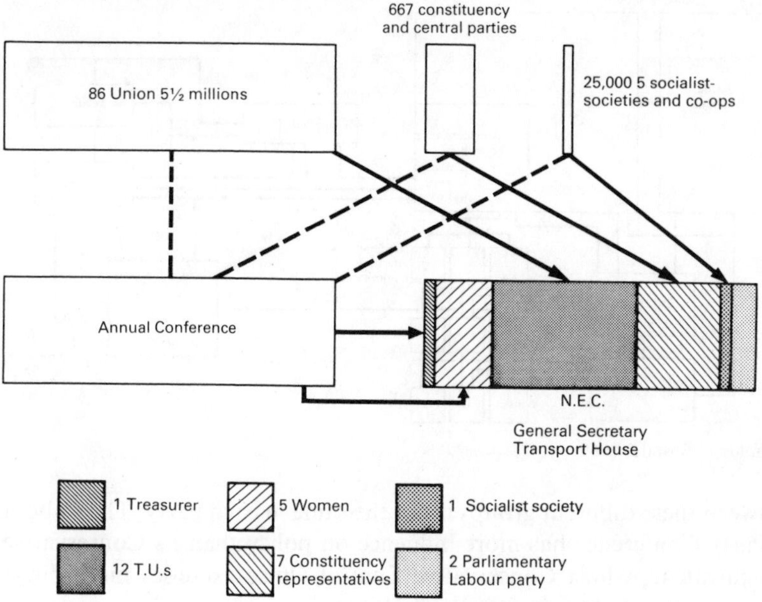

667 constituency
and central parties

86 Union 5½ millions

25,000 5 socialist-
societies and co-ops

Annual Conference

N.E.C.

General Secretary
Transport House

| | 1 Treasurer | | 5 Women | | 1 Socialist society |
| | 12 T.U.s | | 7 Constituency representatives | | 2 Parliamentary Labour party |

Source: Blondel 1969

Parties as we know them date from the middle of the nineteenth century. The modern Conservative Party grew out of a group of M.P.s who were known as 'Tories'. Their opponents, The 'Whigs', developed into the Liberal Party. These two parties grew strong in the second half of the nineteenth century. At the very end of the century the Labour Party appeared. Until the early 1920s Conservative and Liberal were the two major parties, but in the interwar years the Liberals lost much of their support and the Labour Party began to take their place. Since 1945 the Conservative and Labour Parties have both been Government and Opposition. The Liberals and other minority parties have had a very small share of the seats in parliament, though a larger share of the total votes in elections than you would expect from their number of seats. Both Labour and Conservative Parties have each developed their own patterns of organisation.

These vastly different party structures show four common elements. They each have a central bureaucracy which in effect manages the party. Each party has an Annual Conference at which delegates discuss matters of interest to the party. Party members express their views through the constituency party and other affiliated groups and M.P.s operate through the Parliamentary party. The balance of power be-

Fig. 45. *The structure of the Conservative Party*

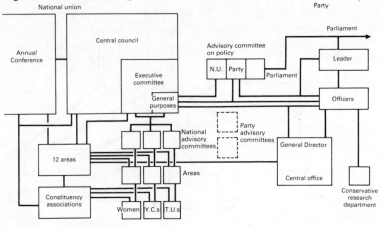

Source: Blondel 1969

tween these different groups is not the same in each party. The Labour Party Conference has more influence on policy than its Conservative equivalent; whilst Conservative Central Office exercises more direct power than Labour's Transport House.

The busiest time for any political party is during an election. Each party will have chosen its candidates long before and as soon as the election is announced, party workers will set to. Nomination papers are completed; election addresses are packed into envelopes; voters are canvassed; posters displayed and the faithful rallied. On election day supporters are reminded to vote, transport is laid on for the elderly, a check is kept on those who have voted and the laggards are given a further reminder. Later that night party workers will be at 'the count' to scrutinise the opening of the ballot boxes and the counting of votes. They will be present to cheer the successful candidate.

The election may be a peak of party activity but its success depends on the groundwork that has gone before. Apart from choosing candidates the Party, at all levels, decides on its policy on a variety of issues. Delegates from the local parties propose motions at conference and annual meetings which, in time, may filter through to become official party policy. Often this is supported by the work of research departments and by Labour's Fabian Society.

There is also a need to educate the party's supporters and to assist them in educating the electorate. Local meetings, lectures, weekend conferences, summer schools and party publications all help in this important function. And, because parties are voluntary organisations, some time must be spent on fund-raising. Subscriptions from members,

184

from trade unions or 'big business' are not enough to pay for the full-time staff, for 'between election advertising' and for election campaigns. Whist drives, bingo, socials and hunt balls are organised for the purpose of raising money. Such events also help to bring party supporters together socially and so strengthen their ties with the party.

THE PARTY'S IMAGE

An important feature of the average voter's view of the party is what is called 'the party image'. People associate particular policies or ways of life with particular parties. In a study which followed Labour's election defeat in 1959 Mark Abrams and Richard Rose showed that 89 per cent of Labour voters thought that the Labour Party stands mainly for the working class whilst 38 per cent thought that the Conservatives had a 'united team of top leaders'. Only 18 per cent of Labour voters felt the same way about Labour leaders. Mention of each party created a different picture in the mind of the voter. On the one hand Labour stood for the working man, out to help the underdog, supporting the social services; whereas the Conservatives 'would make the country more prosperous', had a united team of top leaders, would give more chances for a man to better himself, and so on.

In the years following their 1959 defeat the Labour Party worked to change their image. It became the party of economic progress; of 'white-hot technological revolution'. This change of image was claimed to be one reason for Labour's victory in the 1964 election. An important element in the party 'image' is the nation's view of the party leader, who may become Prime Minister.

Television and the Press tend to concentrate on the party leader and election campaigns are often built around him. A Labour poster used in 1966 just showed a picture of Harold Wilson and the slogan 'You know Labour Government works'. Some years before, the Conservatives had used an election poster which was simply a portrait of Tory Prime Minister Harold Macmillan. It didn't even need a caption.

When people go to vote they put their cross beside the name of a candidate. Behind that simple action are a mass of attitudes and beliefs which have been learned and practised and strengthened throughout adult life. The merits of the candidate, the policies of the party and the efficiency of the election campaign all come second to these political attitudes and beliefs.

Pressure groups

Modern governments do not carry out the task of running the country in isolation. Although governments are elected to run the country for five years the people do not just elect them and then let them get on with it. Each government department, member of Parliament or civil servant is under pressure from all sorts of groups within society. These 'pressure groups' differ from political parties in two ways. They do not fight elections and they are not interested in gaining power. Pressure groups usually have particular interests which they want the government to act upon. They are sometimes referred to as 'interest groups'. Often their interests go further than applying pressure to the government. The Automobile Association is a pressure group, which acts on behalf of the motorist. Thus the A.A. will push for government action on road safety, road building programmes, vehicle taxation, standards of garage maintenance, and other related subjects. It also provides breakdown services, holiday facilities and legal advice which are not political activities. Many pressure groups have this over-lapping of political and non-political activities.

TYPES OF PRESSURE GROUP

Pressure groups can be divided into two main types: those which seek to protect the interests of their members, and those which try to promote a particular cause. Such a division into 'protection' and 'promotion' groups can never be perfect. The A.A., for example, would try to protect its members from increased vehicle taxes and promote new laws on road safety. However, such a division of function is a useful one. An example of a 'protection' group in the local situation might be a ratepayers' association trying to protect residents from unsatisfactory or expensive council services. The Campaign for Nuclear Disarmament was a promotion group which tried to make the Government act on banning 'the Bomb'.

Pressure groups vary considerably in size, power and the methods they use. A large membership will not guarantee success. Some of the most influential groups have been very small. The campaign for an Independent Television Authority in 1954 was managed by a very small group of men. They were successful because the bulk of the general public supported their arguments and because they were able to persuade many influential people.

HOW PRESSURE GROUPS FUNCTION

Pressure groups operate in many different ways. Their main weapon is persuasion, and their best targets are those who actually take the decisions. Members of Parliament, senior civil servants and Cabinet Ministers are useful allies for a pressure group. M.P.s who are sympathetic to a group's views would agree to speak in Parliament whenever a relevant topic was under discussion and to ask questions at Question

Time in the House of Commons, seeking to gain support for the group's views. In return the pressure group would keep the M.P. up to date on the subject, often arranging tours or visits to keep him informed. In this way pressure groups help to make government more democratic.

Very often groups are unable to exert direct influence on the 'corridors of power'. In such cases they must seek to influence public opinion. They will try to get people to accept their views in the hope that the Government, or one of the political parties, will be persuaded by the sheer weight of opinion. In the 1972 coal-miners' strike the National Union of Mineworkers advertised in the daily papers. By presenting its case to the people it hoped to be able to force the Government to take action in ending the strike.

Fig. 46. *'It's Monday. But I'm not going down the pit today'*

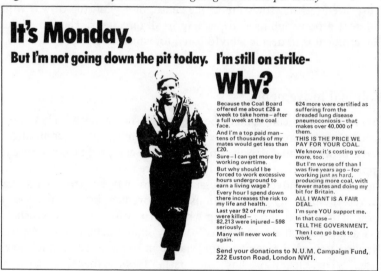

Source: The National Union of Mineworkers

Sometimes groups use less peaceful methods to impress their views on the public. Demonstrations, protest marches, and sit-ins often lead to publicity on television or in the Press. This draws the attention of the public to the group's demands. Housewives who block roads and hold up traffic have often found that the publicity helps in their fight for a pedestrian crossing or a footbridge. Very often it is the groups which are unable to put their views directly to the Government which need to demonstrate and protest.

Any attempt to persuade the Government depends on information.

187

A pressure group needs to prove that its case is right. To do this it needs to know the facts. Much time is spent in collecting information and passing it on to the appropriate government department. Evidence and information is also important to Royal Commissions and other government inquiries. A pressure group can make its views known by submitting evidence. Sometimes individuals who support the group's views are appointed to sit on commissions and inquiries. This gives them an even closer link with the government.

THE ROLE OF PRESSURE GROUPS

Pressure groups are important because they present the views of sections of the electorate to the Government between elections. They involve many people in the process of democratic government. They also provide a check on the Government's activities, making sure that the Government's actions are understood by the people. Governments must often feel that they are at the centre of a giant tug-of-war with different groups pulling and pushing in all directions. The job of the Government is to decide who to listen to, which way to go.

Political movements

Pressure groups can usually be recognised fairly easily. They have specific aims, a membership, a structure of officials and committees and a name to call themselves by. Often, however, political pressure is applied in other ways and by less structured groups. We would call them political movements. Pressure groups may be part of a wider movement and may give directions to a movement but the movement itself is broader than any group which exists within it. J. R. Gusfield has defined social movement as 'socially shared activities and beliefs directed toward the demand for change in some aspect of the social order'. This definition has four parts. Firstly, they are 'socially shared'. They do involve groups of individuals though often without the formal membership we would normally see in pressure groups. Secondly, they involve activities and beliefs. A movement is more than a sense of discontent or a feeling that things are not right in the world. Movements take action to change things and they share certain beliefs. Those beliefs lead, thirdly, to demands. In more formally organised movements these may lead to a manifesto laying down certain demands. Often they are just expressed publicly by those who share the aims of the movement. Finally, these demands are for change in the social order. Social movements are always concerned with change in some form or another. It may be change towards a particular view of the future, an ideal society or Utopia, or it may be change back to the way society was in the past.

At the centre of the movement there is usually an organised group around which there may be a committed membership. Further out, however, the movement is less structured and people's involvement is less.

Typical movements are movement for reform of the abortion laws, the environmentalist lobby, the women's movement, the 'clean-up Britain' campaign and the Campaign for Real Ale.

In the 1960s one of the best-known movements became known as 'Ban the Bomb'.

MASS MOVEMENT

For most of the 1960s there was considerable opposition to Nuclear Warfare and nuclear weapons testing. In Britain this opposition centred on the 'Ban-the-Bomb' movement at the centre of which was 'The Campaign for Nuclear Disarmament' (CND). The campaign worked through leaflets, public meetings and debates, demonstrations and an annual march from the Atomic Weapons Research Establishment at Aldermaston to London. It was through the 1965 Aldermaston March that sociologist Frank Parkin (1968) carried out a study of the movement. Sociologists who have attempted to explain the support for mass movements have often used the idea of alienation. It has been suggested that people who support movements such as CND share a particular view of their position in society, that they are in some way 'alienated'. They are 'in society' but not 'of society'.

One view sees individuals as isolated units with few links into society. These people turn to mass movements for social contact and a way of life. Thus the membership of CND might have been expected to have come from people who have few links with other groups in society. For most people these other groups provide a socialisation into democratic values, social relationships and personal contact, and a way of expressing particular views and interests. It has been suggested that democracy depends on such groups – political parties, trade unions, churches, voluntary associations etc – if it is to generate effectively. Mass movements, it has been thought, depend on 'alienated individuals' who are outside of this network of groups. Parkin's evidence does not support this view.

Eighty-four per cent of the older sample belong to at least one other organisation. Only 16 per cent could be defined as 'alienated' on this definition. The majority of CND members in Parkin's sample were middle class whereas in other studies of mass movements the 'alienated masses' come largely from the working class or from lower

189

middle class groups who saw their status threatened. These groups do not seem to have been important areas of recruitment for CND.

Table 28. *Membership of voluntary organisations*

	%
Membership in 1 or 2 organisations	49
Membership in 3 or 4 organisations	24
Membership in 5 or more organisations	11
Membership in no organisations	16
	100

Source: Parkin 1968

POWERLESSNESS AND REJECTIONS

Another view of alienation sees it as powerlessness. In modern society individuals can feel weak, unable to influence the course of events. It could be suggested that CND support came from people who felt that they had little power to change things. Parkin asked his respondents to say whether they agreed or disagreed with two statements:

1. Ordinary people cannot hope to change government policies.
2. There will always be war; it's part of human nature.

The replies did not suggest that CND members felt powerless. Ninety-seven per cent disagreed with the first statement and 87 per cent with the second.

A third view of alienation sees the supporters of mass movements as those who reject the dominant values of the society. In a wooden 'pluralist' society where people have freedom of speech and ideas there can be no single set of values which everyone holds. Parkin suggests that certain collections of values are more generally accepted and that other collections are likely to be seen as deviant. Support for the Royal Family, for example, is part of a collection of dominant values centred on the monarchy. Republicanism and opposition to the monarchy would then be seen as 'deviant values'.

When asked if they agreed or disagreed with the statement, 'The monarchy is an institution we should be justly proud of', Parkin's sample showed a clear rejection of the monarchy by all social classes. Their replies, supported by other evidence in the survey, suggested that CND members may well be alienated from dominant values in society. They are more likely to support 'deviant' values.

INSTRUMENTAL OR EXPRESSIVE

Political activity is usually regarded as activity aimed at achieving a particular result. We could say that people engaged in such activity

190

have an 'instrumental' approach. They seek to achieve certain ends. The means by which those ends are achieved are not particularly important. For some groups, however, the 'means' are important and may outweigh the 'ends'. The activity itself becomes the focus of politics and the aimed-for-results slip into second place. This is an 'expressive' approach to politics. People who 'stand up for their rights' or 'defend principles' are engaged in 'expressive' political activity. Fighting for a change in the Law which will benefit you directly (i.e. more money for school leavers) is instrumental. Most political activity combines instrumental and expressive aspects.

The CND sample were asked their views on the statement: 'Protests and demonstrations which fail to achieve their aims are a waste of effort'. If involvement in CND was largely instrumental you would expect most people to agree with the statement. Disagreement with the statement would indicate a more 'expressive view'. The survey showed that 86 per cent of the sample disagreed with the statement. For them participation in the movement's activities was enough in itself.

Parkin suggests that this more expressive emphasis points to the strong middle-class bias of the movement.

Civil servants

The role of Parliament is to legislate; to pass laws and decide on policy. Carrying out the laws and acting on the policy is the job of 'the Executive', which, as we have seen, is made up of ministers and civil servants. In all there are about three-quarters of a million civil servants, excluding those who work in government dockyards and industrial establishments. Most of these are engaged in routine clerical or administrative work, in employment exchanges, social security offices and for the Inland Revenue. One-fifth of civil servants work in London, mostly in 'Whitehall'. At one time all government departments were centred on a group of buildings in Parliament Square and along nearby Whitehall. The growth of government activities has forced many departments to move to new buildings further away from Parliament but it is still usual to refer to the central offices of the ministries as 'Whitehall'. As well as carrying out the routine work of government, administering the social services, collecting taxes, planning the environment and budgeting the nation's wealth, civil servants also advise ministers on their future policies. Senior civil servants investigate the likely result of a particular policy. They collect information, discuss the matter with interested groups and prepare a report for the Minister. Civil servants also undertake the drawing up of legislation to be put before Parliament.

The modern Civil Service still owes much to the pattern established by the mid-nineteenth-century Northcote-Trevelyan Report, but in recent years the reforms proposed by the Fulton Report (1968) and by successive governments have changed the pattern of the Civil Service.

The Northcote-Trevelyan idea of the Civil Service was founded on three basic principles: (1) a division of the Civil Service into grades or classes, (2) a policy of non-specialisation, and (3) recruitment and promotion within the Civil Service on the basis of talent and ability.

Traditionally civil servants belonged to one of three classes. The administrative class, mainly from universities, was in contact with ministers and advised on present or future policies. The executive class carried out the policies and the day-to-day business. The clerical class was responsible for the routine work of government. It was originally thought that a good administrative civil servant should not be an expert in a particular subject. There would be experts who would advise him, but he should be independent. He would be 'an able amateur', appointed because he was a capable administrator, not a specialist. A very large number of administrative civil servants therefore were graduates in history or classics, and few were scientists or engineers, who tended to be confined to their own specialist classes.

WHO ARE THE CIVIL SERVANTS?

It is very difficult to give a clear answer to this question. Not nearly enough is known about the top civil servants to give anything like a clear picture. Also, what evidence there is dates from before the Fulton Report and makes no allowances for changes that occurred as a result of the report.

Table 29. *Social background of higher civil servants in 1950*

	Percentage in the nation	Percentage in higher civil service grades
1. Higher professional	3	29·3
2. Lower professional	15	40·5
3. Skilled manual and lower non-manual	53	24·2
4. & 5. Semi-skilled and unskilled manual	29	3·0
Not given	—	3·0
	100	100

Source: Adapted from R. K. Kelsall 1955

The typical higher civil servant comes from a middle-class background. He has an equal chance of having been promoted from within the Civil Service, or of being appointed straight from university. If he went to university it was more likely to have been Oxford or Cambridge than either London or a newer university. And it is more than likely that his parents paid for his education, though the chances of his having been at Eton are only one in a hundred.

While this may be a picture of an average civil servant it is not without its exceptions. Twenty-five per cent of all administrative civil servants in 1950 attended state secondary schools. This has since increased. Probably 50 per cent of higher civil servants come from lower-middle-class backgrounds. However, as Kelsall's figures (see Table 29) show, the proportion of civil servants from each social class is very different from the proportion of that social class in the country as a whole.

Civil servants as a group are middle class. In the past their educational experience has been limited but this is changing. Recruitment of higher civil servants from the top ranks of industry and commerce will also serve to bring the administrators more into contact with the needs of the nation.

Who rules?

Politics is the study of the use of power. In theory in a democracy the people have power. In practice things are not so simple. It has been said that the British people have power once every five years, at elections. Between those times power passes to the chosen Government. But even this may not give a true picture.

Governments cannot do just as they like. They need the support of the people. They need the support of industry, commerce, trade unions, and so on, if they are to govern effectively. It is very difficult to pinpoint the real centre of power in the country.

Three theories attempt to identify those who exercise power in Great Britain.

ELITES?

Firstly, there is a theory of elites. An elite is a group made up of those people who hold the highest position in society. Elitist theories suggest that real power rests with the leaders of industry and commerce, with the top bankers, with the top civil servants. Government leaders would be involved in the activities of these elite groups and this would affect the way the country was run. For such a theory to be totally acceptable we would need to show that the elite was powerful enough to influence

193

the Government, and that it was united in the way its power was used. This might be true of a country ruled by a group of army colonels or by one political party. It does not seem to be true in Britain. There are many powerful groups which seek to exercise power in Great Britain but none have complete power and they are far from united. The Trade Union elite is clearly separate from the City Banking elite or from the Big Business elite. Certain elite groups may have a great deal in common. The Labour Party is closely tied to the trade unions; the Conservative Party to banking and business. But neither group could rule for long without at least some support from both unions and industry.

It may be that a theory of plural elites fits the facts better. The various elite groups each putting its own pressure on the Government. Groups having more or less power depending on their links with the Government of the day, with the voters having to decide which combination of elites rules best.

RULING CLASS?

A second theory is based on the idea of a ruling class, a group of people who have power because of birth or marriage into a class. The Conservative Party is sometimes regarded as the party of the ruling class. To support this theory it would be necessary to show that such a ruling class was united, that it was Conservative, unchallenged, and had power. If such a ruling class were in fact in power and unchallenged no other party would ever win an election.

Wilson and Lupton have shown how ties of family and kinship do link those in positions of influence.

However, they conclude 'that top decision makers as well as being linked by kinship, business interests and similar background, are also divided by competing, even conflicting interests'.

Fig. 47. *A ruling class?*

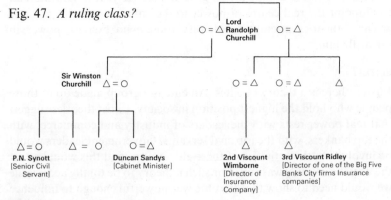

It is not enough to be born into the right family. Leaders in industry and politics must be able to satisfy the shareholders, or the voters, that they can do the job. An industrial concern may have a peer of the realm on the board as a figurehead, but figureheads have no power. As educational opportunities develop and more people are pressing for top jobs the benefits of family and class are likely to diminish still further.

THE ESTABLISHMENT?

The final theory of the centre of political influence is based on the idea of 'the Establishment'. Whereas the ruling elite is based on economic and political power and the ruling class on family, 'the Establishment' is based on the acceptance of tradition. The roots of the Establishment are thought to be in the public schools, its strength in the Civil Service and Conservative Party, and its soul in the Church of England. These different parts are thought to be held together by a desire to see things continue as they are, without change. Support for the idea of 'Establishment' rule might be found in the view that both Labour and Conservative Governments follow similar lines of action. The party in power seems to be limited in its ability to change the course of events.

In the end we must conclude that none of these theories is completely true. Power is spread among a large number of different groups. The voters have absolute power every five years. Parliament has power between elections. The Prime Minister and Cabinet exercise day-to-day power. But Parliament and Prime Minister must keep one eye on the electorate if they wish to be returned at the next election. They must also be mindful of the Press and television which often stand between rulers and ruled. Civil servants have powers but they can only act at the behest of a Minister, and there is always some interested pressure group watching to see that things are done fairly. And finally there is the Law, which can always be used to test the rights of the citizen against the power of government. Power is spread widely and is always subject to checks and restraints. No one individual or group has absolute power.

10

Rich and Poor

He is of noble wealth and birth. So is she. Between them they own or have a stake in a sizeable chunk of Scotland and London. Now they have announced their engagement – and one day their fortunes will come together in a multi-million golden cascade. The 21-year-old Duke of Roxburgh and Lady Jane Grosvenor, 22, were pictured together at the Duke's home, 100-room Floors Castle in Roxburghshire, Scotland. As befits the occasion, the photographer too was an aristocrat, the Earl of Lichfield, who is Lady Jane's brother-in-law. *Daily Express*, 24th August 1976, quoted in A. Giddens' 'The Rich', *New Society* 14.10.76.

How unusual are the Duke of Roxburgh and Lady Jane Grosvenor? Are they all that is left of a dying aristocracy whose wealth has been reduced by taxes and inflation or are the rich, like the poor, always with us.

Income and wealth

Before we can answer these questions we must consider what 'being rich' means. We can judge how rich someone is on the basis of firstly what they earn, that is their income, and secondly, on the basis of what they have, which we would call their wealth.

In Fig. 48 we can see the official view of the distribution of income. The graph shows quite clearly that those people who are in the top 10 per cent of income-earners receive over 26 per cent of the total income before tax. The remaining 90 per cent of earners have to make do with the remaining 74 per cent of total incomes before tax. The bottom 10 per cent of earners only have 2·5 per cent of incomes to share among themselves before tax, though their proportion, while still low, does improve after taxation is taken into account. The inequalities are even clearer when we consider that the top 1 per cent shared 5·7 per cent of total incomes before tax (3·9 per cent after tax) and the top 5 per cent shared 16·7 per cent (13·6 per cent after tax).

The graph also shows that taxation does seem to have had some effect on the actual income people receive after tax is paid. Those with the smallest incomes pay little or no tax whereas those with the highest pay considerably more. However, this graph may not give us the whole picture. It is based on taxation returns and on people's *money* income. Taxation figures for the very rich are always likely to under represent the true figure. 'Tax avoidance', or taxation planning, as it is more politely known, may often reduce an individual's apparent income. It is likely that the real incomes of the rich are more likely to be understated than those of the poor. In addition there is the problem of 'fringe benefits' or perks. Many employees receive additional benefits which do not count as income. They may have a car or a house which goes with the job, their children's school fees may be paid, they may even have interest-free loans for season tickets or house purchase. The benefits tend to be worth more the higher you are in the firm. Company directors generally receive more perks than managers and managers more than manual or clerical workers. These benefits are difficult to measure. It is however clear that they are more

Fig. 48. *The distribution of personal income before and after tax*

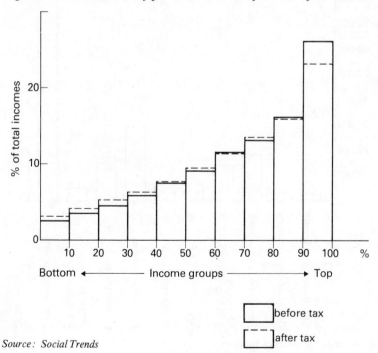

Source: *Social Trends*

valuable to the higher income groups than to the lower groups. If anything they help to make the rich richer. Peter Townsend has calculated that when taxation and fringe benefits are taken into account the position of the richest 10 per cent has changed little in the last twenty years.

The second factor in 'being rich' is wealth. This can be made up from many different things. Your wealth includes any money you have under the mattress or safe in the bank, the value of your house if you own one, your household possessions, shares in building societies or with the Stock Exchange, Premium Bonds, Savings Certificates, mink coats, diamond bracelets and priceless Picassos. All of these things add up to your total wealth.

The ownership of wealth is even more concentrated than income. The top 1 per cent of wealth-holders own over a quarter of all personal wealth and the top 5 per cent own over one-half. This position has not

Fig. 49. *The main types of private wealth*

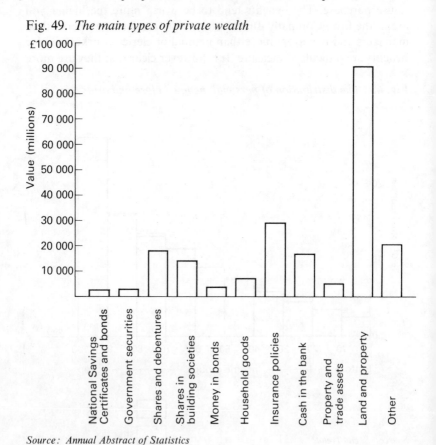

Source: *Annual Abstract of Statistics*

changed greatly since the beginning of the century. In 1911 the top 10 per cent wealth-holders owned 92 per cent of all wealth, in 1960 they owned 83 per cent. Estate Duty returns do suggest that the small group of the most wealthy, the top 1 per cent, has shrunk in size since 1911. Whereas they then held 69 per cent of all wealth, by 1960 their share had fallen to 42 per cent. However, while the share of wealth held by the top 1 per cent declined, the share of the next 4 per cent down the ladder increased. This could mean that there are less very, very, wealthy people and more not so very, very, wealthy people; or that the wealth has been shared around the families of those very, very wealthy people in order to escape from taxes on inheritance. Early in this century estate duties brought in over 16 per cent of the government income. At the present time they bring in less than 4 per cent. Estate duty is another form of taxation which the rich have learned to avoid.

The rich

The world of the very rich is made up of three distinct groups of people. These groups are often closely interlocked with each other. The first group is small and on its own relatively unimportant. It is made up of those who could be counted as 'instant rich'. They are the pools winners and the pop-stars whose wealth is derived from activities which bring in very large incomes, often in a very short period of time. Though they may appear frequently in the press and on television they are not a particularly important section of 'the rich'. Most of the rich have either inherited their wealth (and along with it status and prestige), through established aristocratic families or through industry and commerce. Traditionally the British upper class was made up of the landed aristocracy whose members could often trace their ancestors back to William the Conqueror. Their wealth was in great country estates and their income came from farming. There are still many such families though not all of them are rich. Those that have kept their position have usually done so by merging with that other group of the rich – the commercial and business elite.

Whilst the base for the aristocracy was in the countryside, the base for the business elite is in the city, and more precisely in the City of London. It is here that the big banking and financial concerns operate. The Stock Exchange, the Commodity Markets, the Merchant Banks and the Bank of England are all based in the City of London where fortunes can be made and lost very quickly. The 1960s were a period of property speculation and asset-stripping when some individuals

199

made themselves into millionaires overnight. These people were the exceptions. The greater amount of city wealth is either in the hands of long-established banking and finance families such as the Rothschilds, or is owned by industrial or commercial magnates such as Jules Thorn or Isaac Wolfson. Often these families began with a self-made entrepreneur who built up the firm from almost nothing into a vast financial empire. The business, industrial and commercial rich may have had the money but often lacked status. The aristocracy had the status but for the last century, at least, have lacked the money. Today's rich are a combination of these two groups combining income, wealth and status, and often considerable power.

Poverty

You could say that the poor are all of those who are not rich. But what does it mean not to be rich? Compared to a property speculator with a fortune of £27 million most people seem poor. Yet if you ask them if they are poor they will deny it. The problem with poverty is one of defining it. Is poverty a fixed line below which people become poor? Is it a way of life, or a feeling that people have? This is a problem which has concerned sociologists and others for many years.

The earliest attempts to define poverty were based on the view that a family required certain basic commodities if they were to survive. If they were unable to provide these things then they were in *primary* poverty.

Seebohm Rowntree carried out a series of studies of poverty in York in the first half of this century. With the help of the British Medical Association he drew up a shopping list of necessary foods which should form part of a balanced, if meagre, diet for a man and his wife and three children under 14. To the cost of this basic diet Rowntree added an amount for clothing, fuel and light and sundries. Other items bring the weekly bill to just over £5. This was Rowntree's poverty line. Families which existed below this line were said to be living in *secondary* poverty. At a still lower level were those families which were completely destitute and were in primary poverty.

The idea of a fixed poverty-line based on the necessities of life creates difficulties. There is no guarantee that people will spend their money in the way laid down by the British Medical Association or any other official body. In normal life people do not agree about what their basic necessities are. Whilst a healthy diet may be important, some luxuries may be just as necessary – a night out at the pictures or a couple of bottles of brown ale for example. If you start asking people

Fig. 50. *Rowntree's shopping list*

Table 1. **Dietary for man, wife, and three children (based on B.M.A. Report on nutritional needs, published 1950)**

Breast of mutton – 2½ lb. at 8d. per lb. (imported)	1.	8.
Minced beef – 2 lb. at 1s. 4d. per lb.	2.	8.
Shin of beef – 1½ lb. at 1s. 6d. per lb.	2.	3.
Liver – 1 lb. at 1s. 6d. per lb.	1.	6.
Beef sausages – 1 lb. at 1s. 3d. per lb.	1.	3.
Bacon 1¼ lb. at 1s. 11d. per lb. (cheapest cut)	2.	4¾.
Cheese – 10 oz. at 1s. 2d. per lb.		8¾.
Fresh full cream milk – 14 pints at 5d. per pint	5.	10.
Herrings – 1½ lb. at 8d. per lb.	1.	0.
Kippers – 1 lb. at 1s. per lb.	1.	0.
Sugar – 3 lb. 2 oz. at 5d. per lb.	1.	3½.
Potatoes – 14 lb. at 9 lb. for 1s.	1.	6½.
23½ lb. Bread – 13½ loaves at 5½d. each	6.	2¼.
Oatmeal – 2 lb. at 6d. per lb.	1.	0.
Margarine – 2½ lb. at 10d. per lb.	2.	1.
Cooking fat – 10 oz. at 1s. per lb.		7½.
Flour – 1¼ lb. at 9½d. per 3 lb. bag		4.
Jam – 1 lb. at 1s. 2d. per lb.	1.	2.
Treacle – 1 lb. at 10d. (in tins)		10.
Cocoa – ¼ lb. at 8½d. per ¼ lb.		8½.
Rice – 10 oz. at 9d. per lb.		5½.
Sago – ¼ lb. at 9d. per lb.		2¼.
Barley – 2 oz. at 9d. per lb.		1.
Peas – ½ lb. at 10½d. per lb.		5¼.
Lentils – ¾ lb. at 10½d. per lb.		8.
Stoned dates – ½ lb. at 10½d. per lb.		5¼.
Swedes – 6 lb. at 2½d. per lb.	1.	3.
Onions – 4½ lb. at 5d. per lb.	1.	10½.
Apples – 4 lb. at 5d. per lb.	1.	8.
Egg – 1 at 3½d.		3½.
Extra vegetables and fruit	1.	6.
Tea – ½ lb. at 3s. 4d. per lb.	1.	8.
Extras, including salt, seasoning, etc.		9.
	47.	4.

(1 shilling = 5p, 47s 4d = £2·37)

about poverty they will immediately draw comparisons. People see themselves as better off than some and worse off than others. Each individual relates his or her own position to the positions of other people. Poverty is relative. It is not a fixed line. Ideas of what poverty is change from time to time and in different places. A diet including half-a-pound of stoned dates and six pounds of swedes may have been 'poverty' in York in 1950. It would be regarded as more than enough in some part of the world where different standards of poverty are applied. A reasonable definition must relate poverty to the accepted standards within the wider society. If it is usual for families to own a refrigerator, a washing machine or a colour television then to be without one can be taken as a sign of poverty. We need to consider poverty in relation to the general standards within society.

It is therefore important to distinguish between poverty which is absolute – Rowntree's primary poverty – and relative poverty. A society may have few people living in absolute poverty but will still have a problem of relative poverty where large numbers of people are surviving at a level which most of their fellow countrymen would find unacceptable.

The idea of relative poverty is an important one but it does leave the sociologist with a problem. If the shopping list approach of Rowntree is abandoned, and we base our views of poverty on a person's position relative to the rest of society, how do you answer the question 'who is poor'? In this situation the sociologist must begin his answer 'well, it all depends . . .'. This is obviously not good enough if we want to get a clear idea of the number of people who might be in poverty or if poverty is disappearing or increasing. To get over this problem most social scientists use as a basis the level at which the government, through the Supplementary Benefits Commission, pays out Supplementary Benefit to people in need. It is not in any way a true measure of poverty. The S.B.C. scales may in fact be below the level at which we would say people are in poverty but it is a measure of poverty which is often used.

RELATIVE DEPRIVATION

Poverty is relative in another sense too. The poor are those people who are deprived of the things other people take for granted. But do people in fact see themselves as deprived? Do the poor, whoever they may be, see themselves as poor? Very few people look at advertisements for expensive watches and fast cars and say 'I can't afford that, therefore I'm poor'. Such things are outside of their frame of reference (Chapter 3). In normal life people relate their position to those around them.

One of the areas in Banbury studied by Margaret Stacey was known as The Village. Wychtree Road runs through The Village with the council estates at one end in Upper Wychtree Road and the private houses in Mayfair Drive at the other.
Between the two is Wychtree Terrace where Mrs Kingpin lives.

> She has strong links with many households in Wychtree Road as well as Wychtree Terrace and is the centre of an extensive gossip network. She distinguishes sharply between the Upper Wychtree Road people who 'live like pigs', 'drag up' their children and are a 'thieving lot' for whom she has no time, and the Mayfair Drive residents who are 'a cut above themselves' and a 'bit snobby'. (Stacey 1975)

Mrs Kingpin views her position in The Village relative to her neighbours. In that she is less well-off with not such a nice house as those who live in Mayfair Drive she is 'relatively deprived'. Compared to the residents of Upper Wychtree Road however she feels quite prosperous.

Poverty therefore is relative in so far as individuals lack things that others take for granted. Deprivation is relative because people see themselves within a fairly narrow frame of reference and not in the context of the wider society.

The idea of relative deprivation has been developed by Runciman who argues that people may fail to see themselves as deprived not only because they make comparisons within a fairly narrow frame of reference but also because they have come to see their situation as an inevitable part of the way society is organised. Poverty is seen to be natural and is justified as a normal part of life. This view suggests that inequality is inevitable and can never be changed. Poverty is even seen as a virtue, as in the old song 'she was poor but she was honest'. Such a view can be used as a justification for the continuance of poverty and as an explanation for the failure of any attempts to remove it. It is an ideological viewpoint (Chapter 7) which serves the interests of the wealthier classes.

Who are the poor?

In his early study of poverty in York, Seebohm Rowntree saw that 'the poor' were not a fixed group of people. During their lives people would go in and out of poverty as their circumstances changed.

'The life of the labourer', wrote Rowntree, 'is marked by five alternating periods of want and comparative plenty. During early childhood, unless his father is a skilled worker, he will probably be in poverty; this will last until he, or some of his brothers and sisters, begin to earn money and thus augment their father's wage sufficiently to raise the family above the poverty line. Then follows a period in which he is earning money and living under the parents' roof; for some portion of this period he will be earning more money than is required for lodging, food and clothes. This is his chance to save money . . . this period of prosperity may continue after marriage until he has two or three children, when poverty will again overtake him. This period of poverty will last perhaps for ten years, i.e., until the first child is fourteen and begins to earn wages; but if there are more than three children it may last longer. While the children are earning, and before they leave the home to marry, the man enjoys another period of prosperity – possibly however only to

203

sink back into poverty when his children have married and left him, and he himself is too old to work. (Rowntree 1961, quoted in Coates and Silburn 1970)

Rowntree describes a 'cycle of poverty' through which people pass during their lives. The disadvantages experienced by each generation passing through this cycle of poverty are passed on to the next generation. Mothers from the poorest social groups have smaller babies and risk more infant deaths.

Table 30. *Birth and social class 1973*

Social class of mother	Stillbirths per 1 000 of all births	Average birthweight (grams)
I	7·4	3 359
II	8·5	3 346
III	11·2	3 273
IV	13·5	3 244
V	16·2	3 163
All classes	11·6	3 262

Source: Social Trends

Fig. 51. *Health and social class*

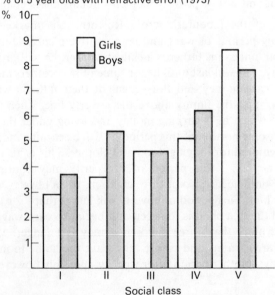

Eyesight

% of 5 year olds with refractive error (1973)

Fig. 52. *Health and social class*

Tooth decay

% of 5 year olds with tooth decay (1973)

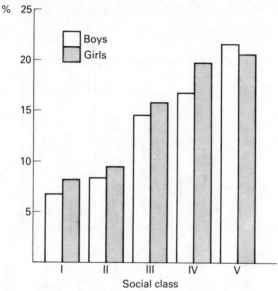

Fig. 53. *Health and social class*

Height of school children at the age of 14 (1973)

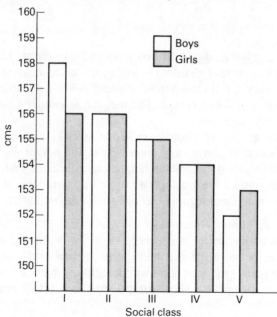

Fig. 54. *Health and social class*

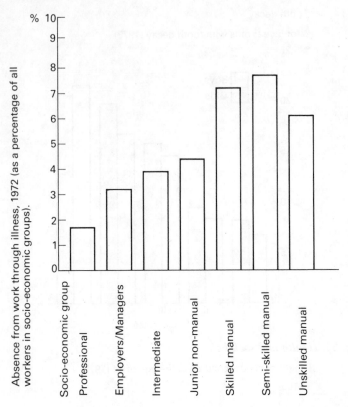

Twice as many babies die in the first week of life in social class V as in social class I. Even though infant mortality has fallen steadily throughout this century social class V mothers have never been able to catch up their sisters in social class I. The inequalities which exist at birth continue throughout life.

Particular groups of people are more at risk than others. The families of the unemployed and the low paid, the sick or disabled, the elderly, single parents and their families and families with three or more children stand the greatest risk of getting into debt, of suffering the worst housing, inadequate diets and the poorest health.

Frank Field has written that
the cycle of inequality is complete. Even in death the significant differences between the rich and the poor stubbornly remain. We have seen that wives of professional groups have a far greater chance of giving birth successfully than the wives of semi-skilled

and unskilled workers. The children of professional workers have a far greater chance of surviving the first year of life, and then of living longer.

These children are unequal when they start school and continue to draw away from their peers from poorer homes. The cycle of inequality is reflected in the income earned, the status at the workplace and in the housing rich and poor families occupy. These class differences appear again in the difference in health, and finally in death.

Despite growth in the national wealth the age-old inequalities remain. The position of the poor has improved. But so, too, has that of the rich. It is as if the poor have been placed on an escalator which gradually lifts their position. But the rich, too, are on board their own escalator which is moving just as fast, if not faster. (Field 1974)

Fig. 55. *Overcrowding, 1972 (percentage of households in each socio-economic group with no spare rooms)*

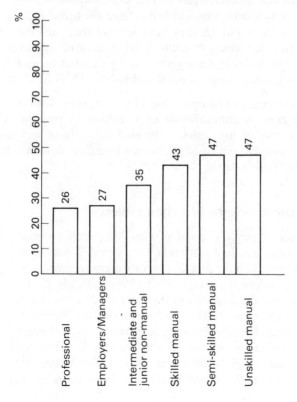

A culture of poverty

Poverty, as we have already seen, can be understood (a) as not having enough money for the basic essentials of life or (b) as being relatively deprived in comparison to other groups. Sociologists who have worked among people who live in, or near to, poverty have noticed that poverty has other important features. Poverty appears to produce its own attitudes and beliefs, its own behaviour and its own way of life. Coates and Silburn, in a study of a poor district of Nottingham, commented:

> In nearly every interview we detected a basic sense of hopelessness or powerlessness. Although the degree of resignation or despair may vary from one man or woman to another there are still few people who express unqualified self-confidence or optimism. This is not to say that people in St Ann's are perpetually gloomy, far from it. One is constantly aware of a warmth, generosity, and humour – so often more characteristic of the poor than of those with more to lose. The difference we would emphasise is that cheerfulness and optimism find an exclusively private expression.
>
> The overwhelming majority fail to have any broad social expectations, almost as though they have learned that such expectations are beyond their reach or control. When cheerful optimism is felt, it is not because things are getting any better, but because they are not getting much worse. (Coates and Silburn 1970)

An American anthropologist, Oscar Lewis, has described this characteristic of poor neighbourhoods as a 'culture of poverty'. Poverty becomes a way of life which is handed down from generation to generation with its own customs, its own language, its own values and view of the outside world.

Solving the problems of urban poverty

The 'culture of poverty' point of view led people to believe that to reduce poverty you had to change the culture. It was largely on this basis that both Labour and Conservative governments attempted to tackle the problem of poverty in the 1960s and early 1970s.

A string of official reports in the early 1960s drew attention to the problem of the inner cities. The Milner-Holland Report focused on housing in London, the Plowden Report looked at Primary Schools, Seebohm considered the social services and Ingleby, children and young persons. The problem came to be called 'urban deprivation'. It was believed that the problems of the inner cities were caused by the disorganisation of the people who lived there. If you could help the people to get themselves organised then they would break out of the 'culture of poverty' and the problems would be solved. First you had to find how to get people organised. A large number of separate projects were set up to do this. Urban aid was to 'provide for the care of our citizens who live in the poorest or most overcrowded parts of our cities and towns. It is intended to arrest, in so far as it is possible by financial means, and reverse the downward spiral which afflicts so many of these areas.' (Home Secretary, James Callaghan, addressing Parliament 2.12.68)

The E.P.A. or Education Priority Area projects sought to establish 'the kind of partnership between parents and teachers in relation to children that there should be in an ideal community'. The Neighbourhood Schemes put large sums of money into particular problem neighbourhoods. Inner Area Studies looked in detail at the problem of local authorities in six local areas. In 1969 the Home Office established 12 Community Development Projects which were based on three assumptions. 1. It was the deprived who were the cause of urban deprivation. 2. The problem could be solved by overcoming apathy and encouraging self help. 3. Local research into the problem would bring about changes in local and central government policy.

In the 1970s came yet more projects but the approach began to change. It became recognised that 'the problem of urban deprivation cannot be tackled effectively by means of special compensatory programmes of the self-help or community development type'. The attack on 'the culture of poverty' had not worked.

The fault lay in the very idea of a 'culture of poverty'. The first criticism that was made was that if such a thing as a 'culture of poverty' did exist it was a result of deprivation and not a cause of it. To remove the poverty you had to remove the fundamental causes which very often lay outside of the deprived community. The Inner City Study Projects and the Community Development Projects both pointed out very clearly that 'social disorganisation' was not the root of the problem. The real problem lay in a shortage of jobs caused by closing factories and by insufficient investment in new ones. C.D.P. argued that instead of putting the blame on the poor the government should look more critically at the way industry was organised in a capitalist society. The second criticism of the 'culture of poverty' rejects the whole existence of a separate culture. This criticism is based on studies of poor communities which suggest that the attitudes and values of the poor are no different from those of 'rich' society.

Liebow, in a study of 'Tally's Corner' found that the unemployed men who hang around the corner placed little value on work. However the jobs the men were always offered were low-paid and had low status. 'The rest of the society', remarked Liebow, 'holds the job of dishwasher and janitor in low esteem if not outright contempt. So does the street-corner man.'

Coates and Silburn's study of St Ann's in Nottingham came to a similar conclusion. Rather than belonging to a separate culture they suggested that the people of St Ann's shared the same hopes and values as the rest of the people of Britain. Their poverty forces them to be realistic about what is possible and about what they can achieve.

The welfare state

Government action against poverty, ill health, unemployment and deprivation is not confined to the urban poverty programmes. The origin of the Welfare State goes back to the early years of this century when health and unemployment insurance were first introduced. Modern governments accept that they have a responsibility for the wealth and wellbeing of the nation. This has not always been so. The Acts of Parliament which form the basis of Britain's system of health, welfare and social security date from the end of the Second World War. Before that time governments were only prepared to accept responsibility for certain groups, or for the very poor. Most people had to make their own arrangements for insurance and medical care.

THE BEVERIDGE REPORT

The turning point came with the publication in 1942 of the Report of a committee of civil servants headed by Sir William Beveridge, on Social Insurance and Allied Services. In his Report, Beveridge described five freedoms which were the right of every man, woman and child in the country. These were freedom from want, disease, ignorance, squalor and idleness. The Report proposed a comprehensive system of social welfare for all. The idea of the state, or the community, providing for the needs of the least fortunate was not new. The Poor Law of 1601, the 1834 Poor Law and the 1911 People's Budget are earlier examples of state action. Men and women like Charles Booth, Edwin Chadwick, Octavia Hill, Eleanor Rathbone, Sidney and Beatrice Webb each made their own contribution. The Beveridge Report was unique in bringing so many ideas together to provide for people's needs, 'from the cradle to the grave'. The proposals of the Report were contained in a long series of Acts of Parliament passed between 1944 and 1948. The 1944 Education Act

is discussed in Chapter 6. It was followed by the Family Allowances
Act 1945, the National Insurance Act 1946, the National Insurance
(Industrial Injuries) Act 1946, the National Health Service Act 1946,
the Children's Act 1948, the National Assistance Act 1948, and others.
Many of these Acts of Parliament have since been amended or replaced
by new legislation but the pattern of the Beveridge Report remains.

FROM WOMB TO TOMB

The idea of a Welfare State is built around four basic concepts. First,
there is the principle of social security. Richard Crossman has described this as a 'cushion of security against hardship due to unavoid-
able misfortune' which could lead to considerable hardship for the
worker and his family. Workers could insure themselves privately
against such catastrophes but many failed to do so. The Welfare
State does it for them; providing compulsory National Insurance
against accidents. Another misfortune might be ill health. In this
case the state provides a National Health Service out of taxation. The
second principle was that of 'equality of entitlement'. One of the
lessons of the Second World War was that basically all men have the
same needs. A rich man's house was as likely to be hit by a bomb as
was that of a poor man. All men should be entitled to the same basic
social welfare. A duke may collect the same pension, be treated in the
same hospital, send his son to the same school, as a dustman. Above
this basic minimum individuals could make their own arrangements,
but the basic minimum was there as a right. The families of all lower
paid workers have a right to the Family Income Supplement. All
unemployed men have a right to industrial training and to the services
of an employment exchange.

Central to all ideas of social welfare is the principle of concern for
the individual. Because people have different needs and different circumstances they must be treated differently. A probation officer or
child-care officer must treat each case on its individual merits, even
though this may seem unjust. The final principle of the Welfare State
is that of participation and community involvement. Ordinary, local,
people serve on the Board of Managers of local primary schools as
well as on the Regional Hospital Boards, and other bodies.

SOCIAL SECURITY

An important part of the Beveridge scheme was for a national system
of social security. There had been limited schemes of health and
unemployment insurance before but Beveridge progressed a scheme
which would cover everyone. It was to be based on a government-run
insurance scheme to which everyone contributed the same amount.

211

The benefits of this scheme were to be available to all. At the outset therefore the scheme has three important features.

Firstly, it was a contributory scheme, secondly payment was on a flat-rate and thirdly benefits were universal.

In time, however, these features were changed. Whilst it remained contributory it was clear that Beveridge's hopes for a self-financing scheme were not justified. The government increasingly subsidised the scheme from taxation. The flat-rate paid by everyone was replaced by a two-tier system by which an additional 'earnings-related' payment gave many workers a higher level of benefit. Their contributions, and therefore, what they received at retirement, or if made redundant, was related to what they earned.

Many people had, and still have, a great dislike, or even fear, of the means-test – the declaration of income and resources before a social benefit can be received. For many it brings back memories of the 1930s when men had to prove that they were destitute before they could receive help. Social Security after the Second World War was not charity. It was an insurance paid for by all and therefore available to all as a right. Professor Richard Titmuss wrote 'There should be no sense of inferiority, pauperism, shame or stigma in the use of a publically provided service'. This principle of universalism without means-test was not supported by everyone and strong arguments developed in favour of selective rather than universal benefits. Firstly, it was considered to be a wasteful use of limited resources to provide for everyone equally irrespective of their needs. Benefits it was argued should go to those in greatest need. The means-test enabled the providers of social services to know what people's needs were. Secondly, some politicians felt that it was morally wrong to give people something for nothing. People should stand on their own feet and should only be helped when in real need. Thirdly it was feared that universalism would mean that more and more of the nation's resources would be spent on social services and less would be available for investment and the needs of industry. The Conservative Party in particular had favoured a move towards selective benefits and away from universalisation. The Family Income Supplement is one example of a selective benefit. It is available only to those families whose income is below a certain level and provides a cash payment as well as free prescriptions, free school meals and other benefits. Means-tests are also used for rent rebates, payments towards home-helps, university grants and day nurseries.

The opponents of selectivity argue that it is in fact less effective in helping those in need. The stigma of claiming such benefits and the complexity of many forms prevents many from seeking help. It has been estimated that in 1975 non-take-up of benefits for those under retirement age was £175 000 000. Probably a quarter of those who should receive Family Income Supplement fail to claim. Often people do not know that they can claim these benefits, or they claim too late. It is likely that many of those who fail to claim are those in greatest need.

Another result of means-tested selective benefits is the creation of a 'poverty-trap'.

You would normally expect a person who gets a pay-rise or works more overtime to be better-off. The 'poverty trap' can mean that someone who receives means-tested benefits is in fact worse off if they work longer hours or get a pay-rise. This is because means-tested benefits fade away at the point where income tax begins. Whereas one week a wage-earner received a wage plus benefits a pay rise the next week could mean that he not only loses the benefits but also starts to pay tax and is worse off. There have been attempts to reduce the effect of the poverty trap by introducing lower tax rates for low-paid workers and by taking some groups out of the tax system altogether but they have not removed the problem completely.

It can be seen that social security has moved a long way from its original principles. It is a very complicated system involving large numbers of civil servants to check claims, pay out benefits and in-vestigate 'scroungers'. Despite this vast administration and sums of money spent the social security system does not seem to have succeeded in removing poverty.

The voluntary organisations

Long before the phrase 'Welfare State' was first used, voluntary organisations were involved in social welfare. The earliest schools, hospitals and poor relief came from private charities and though the state has taken over responsibility for these things the voluntary bodies still exist and perform useful functions.

While the Welfare State usually provides a basic minimum, volun-tary groups are able to provide much-needed extras. The National Health Service provides all that is needed to make a hospital patient well. There are doctors and nurses, operating theatres and X-ray equipment. Because funds are limited, hospitals are seldom able to provide a library or a hospital shop, or a bedside radio service. These facilities are often provided by voluntary groups, by groups of 'hospital friends' or by a Rotary Club. These important extras involve fund raising and voluntary workers to run them. Raising money and

213

organising voluntary workers are two important functions of voluntary organisations. They enable the welfare services' scarce resources of money and manpower to be used more effectively.

In some parts of the Welfare State the voluntary organisations have a far more important role to play. In the Children and Young Persons Act 1969 the officers of the National Society for the Prevention of Cruelty to Children are 'authorised persons' able to bring a young person before a juvenile court. Similarly Dr Barnardo's is a recognised agency for the care of children, working with local councils. This partnership between voluntary body and state or local authority should not be underestimated. Very often it is the voluntary organisation which introduces a new idea or a new solution to a problem. Later, when its value has been proved, the state may step in and give it finance or even adopt its ideas for its own purposes. Family Planning, Citizens Advice Bureaux, community care of the mentally ill are all schemes which began in a small way and were later supported by the state. Voluntary bodies are often able to provide a testing ground for new ideas.

Sometimes this 'testing ground' function of the voluntary organisation goes as far as sponsoring or even conducting research into a problem. Cancer research is an example of this. The money available for research through the government-backed Medical Research Council is limited. By raising funds from voluntary bodies, scientists are able to increase the amount of research being carried out. Voluntary bodies also have a certain independence from the government. This can be important if the organisation wishes to act as a pressure group, applying pressure on the government. Groups like the Child Poverty Action Group and Disablement Income Group are primarily concerned with this pressure-group function. They provide an independent check on the activities of the Welfare State. They also try to keep the public informed and to educate people. 'Shelter', the National Campaign for the Homeless, is an example of a voluntary body which devotes considerable effort to education.

Voluntary organisations have a very important part to play in the Welfare State. They perform useful functions in providing additional resources, initiating new ideas, involving voluntary workers and educating the public. The welfare society is a partnership between state, local authority and voluntary organisation.

11
Crime and Deviance

Crime is generally thought of as a problem in society. Frequently we are told that crime is getting worse, that the crime-rate is rising and that law and order are becoming more difficult to maintain. But what exactly is crime? How do we know that it is rising? and what has it to do with law, and with order? Can sociology help us to answer these questions?

Crime is universal

To begin with we must understand that there is nothing unusual about crime in society. There is no society in the world which exists without crime. There may be differences in the things people in different societies *count* as crime but no society is without crime in some form. This is not really very surprising. For there to be no crime, everyone would either have to think alike, which is obviously impossible, or they would have to be so tolerant that any actions would be permitted, even murder. In the end every society has a point where it says these actions are wrong and wrongdoers must be punished. Having said, however, that crime is found in all societies, what people count as crime, and what they do about it differs from society to society. They also differ at different times and even in different parts of one society.

Having begun with the idea that crime is usual in society, we must recognise certain basic features of what we call crime. For any action to be a crime it needs to be defined as 'crime' by people or individuals who have the power to do so. Parliament can make laws, so too can judges, but as we shall see later in this chapter there are other 'definers' – the police and the newspapers, for example. This means that what counts as 'crime' can change from time to time, and from place to place, laws change and actions which were once permitted become criminal.

Secondly, for an action to become a crime it needs to be decided by a legal process which will involve not just the police as 'law enforcers' but also magistrates, judges, juries, counsel and so on.

Before continuing to look at crime in more detail it is important to get a basic idea of how the law works and who is involved.

THE LAW

Law in England is made up of two strands. Parliament has the power to make laws. These laws are known as statutes. Sometimes Parliament gives power to make laws and regulations to other bodies. Government departments and local councils for example can make regulations which have the force of law as long as these regulations are not themselves against the law or in any way against the will of Parliament or the courts. As well as statute law there is the older tradition of common law. Statutes can never be designed to cover every possible event. Times change, new problems arise and statutes need to be interpreted. This is done by the courts of law. The decisions of the courts become 'precedents' which guide judges on how they are to proceed in the future. This is the basis for common law. It lays down the principles upon which judgements will be made. This does not mean that judges can do what they like. Parliament always has the power to decide what the correct interpretation is and can always pass a statute to close a 'loophole' should one appear. Just as Parliament has the power to change the law against 'precedents' laid down by the courts, so too can the courts give judgement against the Government when it breaks the rules.

As well as two kinds of law, statute law and common law, there are also two kinds of court. On the one hand there are courts which deal with offences against the law. These are criminal courts. Many court cases deal with disputes between individuals where no law has been broken and these are dealt with by civil courts. Robbery is a matter which would be dealt with by a criminal court whereas a civil court would deal with disputes over contracts, including business contracts, property and marriage.

Most criminal cases are 'non-indictable' which means that they are less serious than 'indictable' cases and will therefore be dealt with by the lower courts. The magistrates court, which has a magistrate (or justice of the peace), instead of a judge and jury deals with over 90 per cent of all criminal cases including some of the less serious 'indictable' offences. More serious cases are dealt with by the crown courts. The Old Bailey in London is an example of a more famous 'crown court'. Civil cases are dealt with by county courts or by the various divisions of the high court.

When someone is allowed to 'appeal' against the verdict of a court,

216

the case is taken to a higher court and possibly to the House of Lords which is the final court of appeal.

Offences by young people are dealt with separately. The law defines people under 14 as 'children' and those between 14 and 17 as 'young persons'. Many cases involving children and young persons will not get into court. They are likely to be dealt with by the Police Juvenile Bureaux or by social workers. Children under 14 are not held to be criminally responsible. Should a 'child' get into serious trouble with the law, the juvenile court would sit as a 'care proceedings' and seek to ensure that the child received whatever help or care was needed. Much of the work with children and young persons is carried out by social workers.

The enforcement of the law involves other groups of people as well as the courts. Most obvious amongst law enforcement agencies are the police. There are over 125 000 policemen and women in the United Kingdom assisted by a further 79 500 civilian employees, traffic wardens and part-time special constables. In addition there are the separate police forces for the railways, airports and military bases. On a number of matters, Parliament has also given powers of law enforcement to certain specialised groups of people. Factory inspectors, weights and measures officers and public health officers all have powers of law enforcement.

Other groups are concerned with the treatment of offenders. Probation officers prepare reports on people who are being taken before the courts and supervise those who are put 'on probation' as an alter-

Fig. 56. *The courts of law*

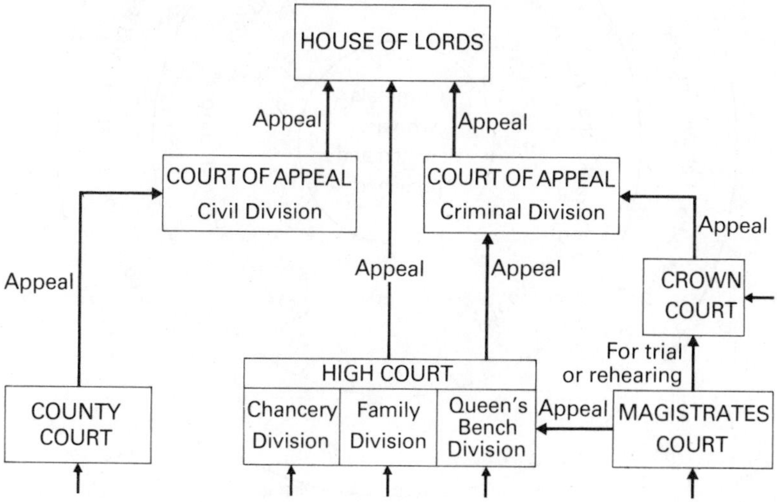

217

native to prison. Social workers have a similar role for those under 14. There are then the prisons and remand centres to which the courts may send convicted persons or those awaiting trial.

SOCIOLOGY AND CRIME

In their attempts to understand crime and other forms of deviant behaviour, sociologists have used different ways of looking at the problem. Some have thought of crime as a kind of illness which has particular causes and which can be prevented and cured. Others have viewed crime not as a disease but merely as a particular type of action which becomes 'criminal' because people with the power and authority to do so 'label' it as criminal. For this group of sociologists the way actions are labelled is more important often than the actions themselves. A third approach looks at crime in the context of a society in which most property is owned by a fairly small group of people who use their power to keep those with little property under control. In these debates about crime and deviance there is a basic problem of whose view of crime is correct. On the one hand there are

Fig. 57. *Views of criminals and deviance*

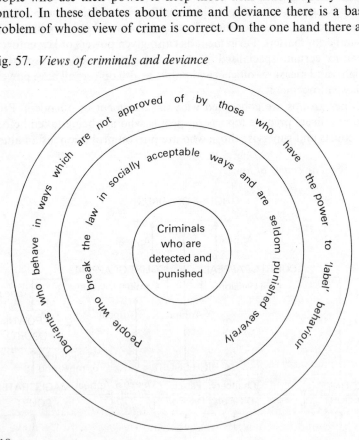

those sociologists who accept the everyday definition of crime. They are often termed criminologists. They see crime as certain activities which the law says are criminal and which are therefore wrong. A wider view sees crime as activities which would be generally thought to be wrong but which may not come to the attention of the courts. Edwin Sutherland pointed to this kind of wrongdoing in his study of 'white-collar crime'. These are crimes, usually committed by 'persons of respectability and high social status' in the course of their normal work. Business fraud, tax evasion and even free use of the firm's telephone all come into this category. A yet wider view sees crime as merely one form of deviant behaviour in a society which contains many forms of deviance. To understand crime you need therefore to understand deviance and how it arises. As well as problems of perspective and definition sociologists must also consider why they should study crime. Can the sociologists remain neutral? Is it possible to study something as important as crime or deviance for its own sake without having some interest in the uses to which that knowledge is put? Some sociologists accept that their role is to provide answers to questions posed by the law enforcers. They seek to provide the information which will guide the actions of judges and policemen, prison governors and probation officers. Other sociologists wish to remain independent, free from the influence and interference of those in authority. Indeed, they would argue it may be more important to study those in authority than to study the criminals themselves. These problems are basic to the study of crime and deviance and will appear again as we examine various approaches in more detail. You should consider your own viewpoint and discuss it with others.

Explaining crime

In looking for reasons for criminal behaviour, sociologists have worked from two types of explanation. Firstly there is a way of explaining crime which looks for causes in each individual. Crime is seen as a personal action caused by physical characteristics. This type of model could be called genetic as it is usually based on the study of genes and the chemistry of the body. An Italian scientist, Lombroso, developed a theory on these lines in the nineteenth century. Criminals he claimed would easily be recognised by their physical characteristics, and he produced drawings that showed basic criminal types.

Lombroso's theories are not generally accepted today though some scientists still think of crime as having a basically biological cause.

The second type of explanation is concerned not with the make up

219

Fig. 58. *The criminal man from Lombroso's* L'uomo Deliquente, *1876*

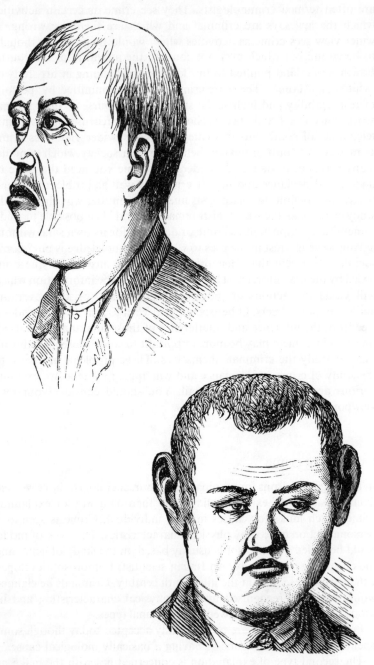

of the individual but with the social environment within which the individual lives. Most sociological theories are based on some variation of this type of explanation which could be called 'environmental'. You will not have to think very hard to realise that crime is unlikely to have one single cause, whether you are concerned with one particular crime or with crime in society it is clear that there are many causes. Most theories of criminal behaviour are in fact 'multi-causal'.

In the 1920s Cyril Burt carried out a psychological and sociological study *The Young Delinquent*. He argued that there was no single explanation for criminal behaviour. Over 170 different causes were studied. Many of these were basically 'genetic' and in Burt's view were likely to be the major cause in roughly 35 per cent of the cases studied. The remaining 65 per cent were caused by mainly environmental factors. Burt's genetic, or physical causes, included low intelligence, temperament and physical infirmity.

Few sociologists today would be quite as confident as Burt in attempting to give percentages to particular genetic and environmental 'causes' of crime. Burt himself admitted that 'between what is instinctive (genetic) and what is acquired (environmental) there is no sharp clean-cut division', and also that no test could ever satisfactorily separate the two aspects. Most modern sociologists would say that Burt over-emphasised genetic influences and included as genetic many factors which were largely environmental.

ENVIRONMENTAL INFLUENCES

If genetic factors are not as important as Burt suggested more attention must be given to environmental influences.

One line of argument is based on the view that to become a law-abiding adult the child needs to be socialised into the important values of society. If that socialisation is not adequate or effective then the child will be likely to become a delinquent. This argument concentrates on the idea of family socialisation and on the effect of the family in a child's early life. Young children learn the difference between right and wrong at an early age. Naughty children are punished – with a smack or by being sent to bed. Punishment may also take the form of being denied affection. 'Mummy doesn't love naughty children' may be the kind of punishment used. Good behaviour on the other hand is usually rewarded, by a kiss and a hug or by actual rewards like a sweet or a biscuit. In so-called *normal* families rewards and punishments are given fairly and consistently. Naughtiness, if discovered, leads to punishment; being good gets a reward. What counts as 'being good' or 'being naughty' is usually clearly defined and reliably enforced. When this does not happen the socialisation is said to be faulty

221

Fig. 59. *The criminal area*

Rates of male juvenile delinquents, Chicago 1927–33

Rates per 100 male population in 10–16 age group

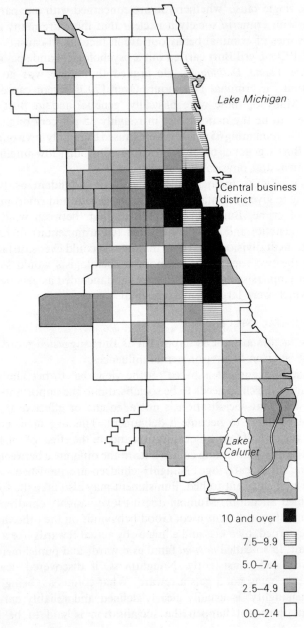

Lake Michigan

Central business district

Lake Calumet

10 and over

7.5–9.9

5.0–7.4

2.5–4.9

0.0–2.4

222

because criminals are therefore thought to be those that are not given the right kind of upbringing. The problem with this approach is that it tries to build its argument on the idea of a *normal* upbringing.

You have only got to look around you to see that family life differs very much from family to family. We must therefore treat any ideas of a 'normal' upbringing with some caution. What writers often refer to as 'normal' upbringing, or *correct socialisation*, is often the socialisation they are used to. Socialisation is also important when you consider the effects your friends have on you. 'Getting into bad company' or 'mixing with the wrong sort' are often given as explanations of criminal behaviour.

The American sociologist Edwin Sutherland recognised this in his theory of *'differential association'*. For Sutherland the way people learn to be criminals is much the same as the way other people learn not to be criminal. It just depends on the group from which you learn. The more closely you are involved with a group the more you learn from them. Other studies have taken a broader view and have tried to relate criminal behaviour to the environment in which people live.

Shaw and McKay studied the official statistics for crime in Chicago in the 1930s. They saw the city as a pattern of circles, like an archery target. At the centre was the business and entertaniment area of downtown Chicago. Surrounding it was a ring of older housing (called the 'zone of transition') which though once prosperous had now fallen upon hard times and was the home of a shifting population of unskilled workers and immigrants. Beyond that lay the settled working-class communities surrounded in turn by the better-off residential areas and on the outer ring by the upper-class estates. On Shaw and McKay's evidence crime was centred on the 'zone of transition'. Even though the population of this zone was continuously changing, the delinquency rate remained the same. This zone of the city, it was suggested, lacked the established community sense to be found elsewhere. It was socially disorganised and this contributed to the crime rate. Shaw and McKay's 'ecological' theory has been criticised. In describing social disorganisation they neglected many aspects of the community which were not criminal. In addition their concentric zones do not fit the maps of other cities. They did, however, point to the fact that rates of delinquency are often higher in particular environments.

Who becomes delinquent?

Researchers who try to study the causes of criminal behaviour often have difficulty in studying a normal (non-criminal) group of people.

Very often in the past criminologists have concentrated on studies of people who have already been convicted of criminal acts. Statements about the causes of crime are often made only on the basis of the evidence of those who have committed crime and seldom with comparable evidence on non-criminals in similar situations. This often means that researchers are looking back into the criminal's past in an attempt to explain his present behaviour. Frequently the evidence they require is lost or forgotten or wasn't recorded as no one thought it important enough.

The Cambridge study on delinquent development attempted to overcome these problems and to find the basic causes of crime among young people. Four hundred and eleven eight-year-old boys were selected from 6 primary schools in an area of North London. The boys all came from a fairly settled working-class area of North London. Information on the boys was collected in three ways:

1. The boys themselves were either interviewed or tested five times – at the ages of 8–9, 10–11, 14–15, 16–17 and 18–19.
2. Their parents were interviewed in the first year of the study and then once a year until the boys left school.
3. Criminal records of the courts and the police were used to keep a check on any offences committed by the boys.

The whole study lasted ten years and at the end was still in touch with over 94 per cent of the original sample of boys.

At the end of the study the researchers had evidence on over 150 different factors which might have had an influence on a boy's behaviour. These included the family background, housing, progress and behaviour at school, intelligence, height, health, friendship groups and criminal records for each of the 411 boys studied. On the basis of police and social services records the boys were grouped under four headings:

(a) Boys with more than one conviction.
(b) Boys with one conviction only.
(c) Boys with no convictions but who were known to the police through the juvenile bureaux or an unsuccessful prosecution.
(d) Boys with no convictions who were not known to the police.

In addition to the official records of delinquency the study also asked the boys themselves about their criminal acts. This evidence showed that the vast majority of boys had committed some kind of minor offence. Ninety-three per cent had let off fireworks in the street, over 90 per cent had seen an (X) certificate film when they were under age. A few boys had committed more serious offences such as housebreaking (7 per cent), shop-breaking (12.7 per cent), theft from cars (14 per cent). These self-reported crimes did not always match up to

224

the official records. The official figures would seem to understate the true extent of criminal behaviour.

When the evidence on official and self-reported criminal acts is compared to the possible causes of crime, five factors stood out as important:

(a) low family income
(b) large family size
(c) at least one parent with a criminal record
(d) low intelligence
(e) parental conflict or lack of discipline.

The boys who suffered from at least three of these factors were statistically more likely to be in the group of persistent offenders.

The Cambridge study is useful in that it points to certain basic problems which would seem to affect criminal behaviour. Some questions did remain unanswered. The differences in self-reported crime and the official records may indicate some form of police bias. The boys in the delinquent groups may have fitted particular stereotypes of criminals more so than equally delinquent boys who were classified as non-offenders. It is not clear how far such a study of a fairly small group of boys in one area of London helps us to understand who becomes delinquent at other times and in other places.

Most importantly, however, the study emphasised the need to consider the effects of a number of inter-related causes of crime.

> The Cambridge study on delinquent development suggests that delinquency arises from a complex interaction between the individual home atmosphere, the personal qualities of the boy and the circumstances in which the family live . . . a multi-causal theoretical approach seems necessary. (West and Farrington 1973)

Different amounts of crime and delinquency in different areas of cities or among different groups of people can therefore be explained in a number of ways. Poor housing conditions, large families, low wages may all be linked to crime but they need not be definite causes. Many people who live in poor housing, have large families or low wages do not always turn to crime. We may still be left with many of our questions about the causes of crime unanswered.

MERTON'S VIEW

Robert K. Merton has put forward a theory which may take us a little further forward in our search for explanations. Merton was concerned not only with crime but with other forms of deviant behaviour also. He recognised that instead of being a result of a breakdown in law and social control, deviance may in fact be a result of the very way society is organised. In their lives people want many things. They may want wealth, success, power, or just a comfortable home and a little peace and quiet. Merton calls these 'goals'. Some of the goals are encouraged by society. Others are not. Within society there are different ways of achieving these goals. Some of these ways of achieving the goals are approved of, and some are not. The ways the goals are achieved he called 'means'.

Most people have *goals* of which society generally approves. They want to earn a decent wage and to live in reasonable comfort. They use accepted *means* to achieve their goals. They work hard, spend their money carefully and try to make ends meet. Merton calls this approach 'conformity'. Other people have similar goals but may choose to use different means. They may use means which are not generally approved.

They will use other means to achieve their goals. They may turn to crime or ways of making a living which do not meet with general approval. Merton calls these 'innovators'.

A third group accept the means but ignore the goals. These are termed 'ritualists' and while they work within the system they have no idea of where they are going or what they want from life. Merton includes two more groups – retreatists and rebels – who reject both the goals and the means. The 'retreatists' reject goals and means by dropping out of society. The rebels seek to change the society. You could probably recognise each of these types in your school or college. Schools and colleges have their own goals – being educated, passing exams, etc. They have means by which these goals are achieved: working hard, writing essays, turning up for classes, etc.

The *conformists* intend to pass their exams and do all that is expected of them. In extreme cases they are called 'swots'. The innovators want to succeed but they will use other methods. They may get higher marks by 'borrowing' other people's work. They may cheat in exams. Ritualists don't really know why they are at school. They don't have much ambition but they do all of the work just the same. Retreatists gave up long ago. They don't care about the exams and they don't bother with studying. Rebels think the whole system is rubbish and try to change it. They may want to abolish exams or make lessons voluntary. In particular they want to change what schools stand for.

Merton suggests that these different approaches are the result of the way society is organised. Certain goals – success, wealth, prestige etc – are encouraged within society. Many people however are not able to obtain these goals in ways of which society approves. They therefore adopt means which are seen as deviant.

Crime, therefore, arises when people are unable to achieve the *goals* which everyone regards as normal by the *means* which society accepts.

SUBCULTURE

A further approach to the problem of crime also recognises that criminal activity is concentrated in certain localities. Instead of blaming the physical environment – bad housing, unemployment and a lack of amenities – attention is directed towards the attitudes and values the people share. It focuses on the cultural factors.

The American sociologist Albert Cohen used the idea of subculture to describe the ideas and values of particular areas which were against the values of the whole society. In Cohen's view there was a kind of 'anti-culture' produced by problems of 'getting-ahead' in a world dominated by middle-class values. He suggested that young people in working-class areas become frustrated because they cannot gain the success which middle-class values suggest they should. This leads to a sense of rejection and turning to gangs and teenage groups where they can be accepted on equal terms. In Cohen's view delinquency and crime are the result of this status frustration imposed upon working-class youth, by middle-class social values.

A slightly different view which also focused on the idea of sub-culture was developed by Walter Miller, another American Sociologist. Miller's view of sub-culture is broader than Cohen's. For Miller certain working-class communities are centred on a way of life which itself encourages certain kinds of behaviour. The desire for working-class youths to show that they are tough, quick-witted and daring combined with a belief in 'luck' are likely to bring them into conflict with the law. 'Getting into trouble' is seen as a normal aspect of slum life, as normal as being unable to pay the rent.

ADOLESCENT BOYS IN EAST LONDON

Peter Willmott considered these theories in his study *Adolescent Boys of East London* (1966). Many of the boys who were interviewed recognised the conflict between the values within their own community and the values demanded for success outside.

'There's a proper way of speaking everyone should have', said a 17-year-old clerk, 'and I'm trying to get it, I'm trying to change my accent to sound my aitches and say "good evening" instead of "watcher" and "goodbye" instead of "ta-ta".'

'You have to talk a bit different to what you do at home,' said a 15-year-old would-be bank messenger, 'that's if you want to get on

227

well. Because you're in the City and talking to all posh people. You want to be able to mix with the right sort of people.'

Most of the boys interviewed rejected such changes.

'I don't want promotion. I just want to stay ordinary,' said an electrician's mate aged 19, 'a friend of mine went into a bank. He had to change his voice and now he says "Hallo"; you'd think he was a poof.'

'I couldn't change the way I spoke,' said a butcher's boy aged 18. 'I've been brought up like that. I know my way around here, anywhere else I feel out of place.'

Theories of 'status frustration' may have fitted some teenagers but it did not explain all of the delinquent behaviour. Delinquency in Bethnal Green was usually fairly trivial. Forty per cent of offences in the area involved stealing, often fairly minor theft though with some more serious 'breaking and entering'. Theft was more common among the younger teenagers. Older boys were more likely to be caught 'taking and driving away' cars or motorbikes, or riding a motorcycle without a licence. One in eight crimes involved some form of hooliganism or violence. Downes' research in a nearby part of East London showed that from the age of 20 the chance of being involved in crime falls rapidly.

Many of the boys interviewed by Willmott regarded stealing as 'normal behaviour'. An 18-year-old commented.

'We used to thieve now and again, same as anyone else, but I don't think we was bad, it was just the normal thing to do.'

And a 16-year-old was probably exaggerating only slightly when he said: 'There's not a boy I know who hasn't knocked something off at some time or another'. A friend who was present commented: 'They're not thieves or anything like that, they're just normal'.

On the surface there appeared to be a 'cult of toughness' among the boys of Bethnal Green. It was generally thought to be 'manly' to stand your ground when threatened or to fight someone if they abuse you. In Peter Willmott's view this toughness was more 'a matter of folklore than everyday behaviour'. Much of it was talk without action.

Any hostility the boys did feel was usually directed at adults, often those in authority – the police or council caretakers. It took the form often of shouted insults or vandalism, rarely of deliberate physical violence. Willmott concludes that rejection and frustration do cause some boys to turn to crime but that there are many other boys in similar positions who manage to 'go straight'. For most of the boys delinquency is fairly trivial, part of the basic tension between adolescents and the adult community and encouraged by the peer group, which begins to lose importance as the boys get older and as their attention turns to courtship and the prospect of marriage.

An alternative view

So far in this chapter we have concentrated on the approach we described as 'criminology', which attempts to find the causes of crime so that 'the problem' of crime can be solved. We have already seen how some sociologists have criticised this approach. They argue that sociologists ought to be looking at problems like crime from an independent viewpoint. Instead of accepting the popular view of crime and working from there the critics say that sociologists should be prepared to reject the popular view and seek to understand crime truly sociologically. To do this the sociologist must make his own questions and not take those questions which society – in the shape of judges and policemen and newspaper journalists – prepares for him.

Traditional criminology they argue has taken a one-sided view, only studying the criminal. More important perhaps is the study of those who decide what crime is and how certain actions become labelled as 'crimes'. This alternative approach is often called 'transactional' theory because it sees crime as the result of a 'transaction' between those who have the power to say what crime is and those who are called 'criminal'. A further criticism is that traditional criminology only looks at certain kinds of actions which have been called 'crimes'. It fails to consider behaviour which, though not criminal, is still thought by many people to be wrong, or at least not normal. For this reason many sociologists prefer to focus not on crime but on deviance. This is often known as *deviance theory* or as *labelling theory* because of its concern for how certain acts become 'labelled' deviant. We shall be using the term 'deviance theory' to cover all of these alternative views including 'transactional' approaches and 'labelling'.

DEVIANCE

One of the best summaries of the deviance approach comes from the book *Outsiders* by American sociologist Howard Becker.

> . . . deviance is created by society. I do not mean this in the way that it is ordinarily understood, in which the causes of deviance are located in the social situation of the deviant or in the 'social factors' which prompt his action. I mean, rather, that social groups create

229

deviance by making the rules which when broken constitute deviance and by applying these rules to particular persons and labelling them as outsiders. (Becker 1966)

From this point of view deviance is not a quality of the act a person commits but rather a consequence of the application of rules and sanctions to an 'offender'. The deviant is one to whom the label has successfully been applied; deviant behaviour is behaviour that people so label. In the first part of the passage, Becker is taking a different approach to that of Albert Cohen or Miller who see 'causes' of crime in society. Instead of focusing on the environment which might cause people to break rules Becker looks at the way rules are made and applied. To Becker deviance is not about the way people behave but about the way others label that behaviour. Deviance is seen then as 'a transaction' between someone who behaves in certain ways and those who have the power to label that behaviour and to apply rules to it.

This view of deviance therefore centres on three important questions:

(a) Why is certain behaviour labelled 'deviant' in the first place?
(b) In what ways do people come to be labelled deviant and have certain rules applied to them?
(c) What are the effects of this labelling both for society and for the individual?

When sociologists try to answer these questions they are building their answers on certain assumptions. Firstly, deviance is relative. That means that actions which may be acceptable in one place or at one point of time may not be accepted elsewhere or at a different time. For example, killing people is legally acceptable in times of war if the person killed is an enemy. Killing people is not acceptable in the normal way of life whoever it is who is killed. However, Parliament could decide to re-introduce the death penalty for certain crimes in which case it is within the law for certain people – i.e. public executioners – to kill certain people – i.e. properly convicted criminals.

A second assumption is that people's ideas of what is acceptable or unacceptable can be influenced and that this affects how they react to particular situations. Deviancy theorists are, for example, interested in the way newspaper and television affect people's ideas of what is normal and what is deviant.

Thirdly, there is an assumption that certain people have the power to act on their beliefs about deviant behaviour. The police can arrest people whom they believe to be breaking the law. Often they have to use their discretion and this can mean that certain kinds of 'deviance' become singled out for action. Magistrates and judges also have the power to make statements which people generally listen to.

Fourthly, by labelling someone's actions as deviant, this can have an effect on the person who is labelled. If people say that you are 'idle' or 'nutty' or 'thick' or 'kinky' enough times you may well begin to believe them and even to act in the way 'idle', 'nutty', 'thick', or 'kinky' people are supposed to behave. A final feature of this approach is the idea of deviancy as a process, as something which happens with one event leading into another making it difficult to say which is a cause and which an effect.

We can see these ideas at work in Stanley Cohen's study of Mods and Rockers.

Mods and Rockers

Mods and Rockers were separate groups of teenagers. You could recognise a Mod by his rather snappy suits, or by the fur-lined parka he wore when riding on his scooter. Rockers on the other hand preferred motor-bikes and wore jeans and leather jackets. A study by Alan Little showed that both groups were basically made up of working-class young people with only slight differences in success at school, or earnings at work. In the early 1960s, however, Mods and Rockers were a 'problem'–especially at seaside towns on Bank Holiday week-ends. After the Easter Monday 1964 the newspaper headlines were:

'Day of Terror by Scooter Groups' *(Daily Telegraph)*
'Youngsters beat up town–97 Leather Jacket arrests'
(Daily Express)
'Wild Ones invade seaside–97 arrests' *(Daily Mirror)*

Magistrates spoke of 'sawdust Caesars' and great public concern was shown about what many people felt was a serious social menace. The Mods and the Rockers were society's most feared 'deviants'. How did it all come about? Who gave them this distinguished position?

Stanley Cohen, a British sociologist, studied the history of the Mods and Rockers and the way in which they became notorious. In addition to interviews with the young people themselves and with magistrates, local councillors and others involved, Cohen also studies the way in which the newspapers dealt with the problem.

It all started with 'an event'.

Clacton is an East Coast resort not particularly well known for the range of amusements it provides for its younger visitors. Easter 1963 was worse than usual–it was cold and wet. The shopkeepers

231

and the stallholders were irritated by the lack of business and the young people milling around had their own irritation fanned by rumours of cafe owners and barmen refusing to serve some of them. A few groups started roughing it around and for the first time Mods and Rockers factions, a division at that time only vaguely in the air, started separating out. Those on bikes and scooters roared up and down, windows were broken, some beach huts were wrecked, one boy fired a starting pistol in the air. The vast number of young people crowding the streets, the noise, everyone's general irritation and the often panicky reactions of an unprepared and under-manned police force made the two days rather frightening. (Cohen 1967)

Cohen goes on to show that there were also some 'troublemakers' present who represented a hard-core of youths and most had criminal records.

From 'the event' there grows 'a myth'. Cohen argues that the deviant event makes people search for reasons and that the event itself becomes magnified. 'Violence and damage' were regular head-lines, yet the damage was not really very great. At Whitsun 1964 it added up to £400 at Brighton, £250 at Margate and £100 at Bourne-mouth. Only one in ten of those arrested were charged with offences involving violence. Another aspect of the myth was that 'the riots' were bad for business, keeping people away from the seaside – deck-chair hirings at Brighton were 8 000 down over the Whitsun week-end 1964 – but it was one of the coldest Whit Mondays for many years.

Myths about the affluence of the teenagers were also unfounded. The young people brought before the Clacton Magistrates after Easter Monday 1963 had an average of 15 shillings (75p) each for the whole week-end. The take-home for these young people was no more than the average for their age group. These beliefs about the Mods and Rockers were important. They were the basis on which 'society' justified its action against the deviants. Sociologists would describe them as 'stereotypes', that is when certain characteristics of a group are applied to all individuals in that group. Thus any young person wearing a fur-collared anorak was likely to be labelled 'a Mod' and if he arrived by train at a seaside resort on a Bank Holiday was likely to be put back on the train by the police. The myths justified the measures taken to control what was seen by many as a social problem. For example bail was often refused for very trivial offences and a number of magistrates' verdicts were later reversed on appeal.

Informal agents of social control also took up extreme positions. On the initiative of a group of Senior Aldermen and councillors the Brighton Council overwhelmingly passed a resolution calling for the setting up of compulsory labour camps for Mods and Rockers. A group of Yarmouth businessmen and hotelkeepers set up a Safeguard Committee which seriously debated setting up road-blocks outside the town to prevent any invasion. (Cohen 1967)

These were all part of the process of amplification which turns a series of delinquent acts into a major social problem.

Stanley Cohen argues that, at its simplest, this process involves six stages. In real life things are not always as simple but the stages provide a way of understanding 'Mods and Rockers'.

At the root of the phenomenon was the *initial problem*. The roots of this could be found in the position of young people in the early 1960s. They were better off than they had been ten years before. They were earning more and had more to spend. Against this they were still not accepted as adults. From this they developed distinctive ways of behaviour and styles of dress which gave the young people an appear-ance of separateness. The Who, one of the leading groups of the Mod era, sang:

> People try to put us down,
> Just because we get around,
> Things they do look awful cold,
> Hope I die before I get old.
> This is my generation baby.

This development of deviant action and style is the *initial solution*. This leads to a *reaction*. A myth develops which involves misunder-standings and stereotypes. The myth makes others sensitive to the problem. Forms of control are called for and the problem begins to grow. Cohen calls this *the generation of the control culture*. The enforcement of law and order against the deviants *separates* them off still further from the main body of society and increases the deviance. In the end the forces of law and order can say 'there, we told you so, there was a problem but we have contained it and brought the trouble-makers to justice'. The myth is *confirmed* (see Fig. 60).

POWER AND CONSENSUS

In the end, any study of crime and deviance of law and order must come down to the question of power. When the police or the courts enforce the law they are using their power to maintain order in society. Sociologists would say that they are agents of social control. But where does their power come from, and how is it used? One answer is that the law enforcers – the police, judges, prison governors, traffic wardens, park-keepers, teachers and others – gain their power,

Fig. 60. *Creating a myth*

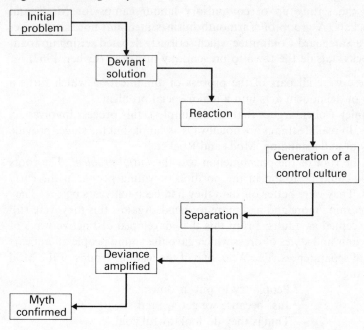

through a chain of responsibility, from the elected Parliament which in turn gains its power from the people who elect it. This means that the power and authority of the law enforcers depends upon the agreement of the ordinary people of the country. This is described as a consensus view and is based on the idea that each person gives up a little of their freedom to the state so that the state can use that freedom to keep everyone in order. This consensus also means that most people believe that it is in their interest for law and order to be maintained. The consensus view sees society as normally law-abiding and peaceful with the law there to prevent any occasional breakdown of order.

The alternative view is based not on consensus but on conflict. Society is not naturally law-abiding but is instead a mass of conflicting interests. The law seeks to keep the conflict under control. Those who take this view of society will point to the unequal distribution of property, wealth and power as the main causes of conflict. The law is seen as the way in which those who have power and influence control those who don't. This control is not only of course through the official 'law enforcers' like the police and the courts. Those who hold a 'conflict view' would say that control is also maintained by influencing what people think and their beliefs of right and wrong.

The mass media, education and the family play an important role in this aspect of social control. 'Order' is maintained in all sorts of social groups in many informal ways. If you want to test this kind of social control for yourself try pushing into a long queue at the front instead of going to the end. No one has the legal power to force you out but considerable 'informal' pressure will be used.

Crime and deviance is very much about the exercise of power; the power to define what is criminal or deviant, the power to control and punish those who misbehave, even the power to inflict pain or death. On the other hand crime and deviance may themselves be attempts to gain power. The thief attempts to gain power over property that is not his in a society where property is valued. The vandal may, using the only way he can, exercise power in a world which makes people increasingly powerless. The worker who puts a spanner in the assembly line may be using the only method possible to gain some control over his own work. Actions which are often said to be senseless may make great sense to those who do them even though such actions could not be condoned. Whether we call them criminal or deviant or not depends very much on our view of society and on the nature of law and order.

CRIMINAL STATISTICS

Sociologists have two main sources of evidence about criminal activity. Firstly, there are official sources which record the numbers of crimes reported, court appearances, sentences and other similar information. This information is provided by the police, the courts, prisons etc. and is collected together in *The Criminal Statistics for England and Wales* published by the Home Office each year. Secondly, there is the evidence collected by sociologists for their own purposes. This tends to be limited to particular areas or groups of people and usually focuses on the attitudes and behaviour of individuals and groups. Information on crime, especially official statistics, need to be used with care. Whilst the statistics are accurate in terms of crimes reported and cleared up, or sentences given, there are a number of reasons why they may not fully indicate the extent of real crime. If a crime is not reported to the police it is unlikely to become part of the statistics. There are cases where it is not realised that an offence has been committed. Often the victim of the offence does not wish to report the crime, either because they are a willing victim, as with illegal abortion or some sex offences, or because they have a close relationship with the offender and would not want them to be in trouble with the police. It is not unusual for the victim of sex offences to be too embarrassed to report the crime unless it is of a serious

235

nature. Parents might not report acts of indecent exposure through a desire to protect their children from unpleasant questioning.

In other cases crime is unreported because the victim has little faith that anything can be done to improve matters or because they themselves are antagonistic to the police. Much poaching goes unreported because many people believe that country people have a right to the occasional pheasant or hare. Finally, there are those offences which are never detected and are known only to the criminal. Exceeding speed limits in built up areas is a common motoring crime which is only rarely detected.

More problems arise when we try to compare crime rates in different years. Changes in the law and in administration can produce apparent changes in the number of particular crimes. Cases of shopbreaking dealt with by higher courts fell from 8 848 in 1962 to 2 803 in 1963. This was almost entirely due to the Criminal Justice Administration Act which allowed such cases to be dealt with by magistrates' courts.

Finally, there may be occasions when juries are reluctant to convict for certain crimes or when offenders plead guilty to a lesser crime in return for evidence regarding other crimes with which they have been involved.

The problem of comparing crime rates is made more difficult by differences in police activity. Changes in police man-power or lack of resources can have a considerable effect on the detection rate and the number of crimes cleared-up. The police do not prosecute every crime they know about. They have considerable discretion. They may give 'a caution' or even ignore certain offences through lack of time to prosecute. The pattern of motoring offences in particular varies from place to place.

In some areas the police are tough on vehicle checks and unsafe tyres whereas elsewhere they concentrate on speeding offences. All of this has an effect on the level of reported crime.

CRIME TRENDS

Despite all of the problems of the criminal statistics it is still possible to get a general idea of the pattern of crime in Britain as a whole. It is quite clear that recent years have seen an increase in the amount of known crime. The two main areas of reported crime are theft and offences involving motor vehicles. This is a sign of the greater opportunities that exist for crime in our society. Modern supermarkets with their goods on open shelves make shoplifting much easier. More cars mean more motoring offences. There has also been an increase in large-scale organised crime.

Offences of violence against the person and criminal damage have

Fig. 61. *Reported crime (U.K.)*

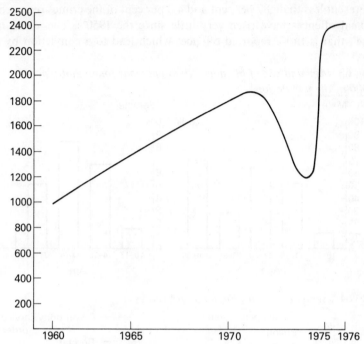

Fig. 62. *Types of offence 1976 (England and Wales)*

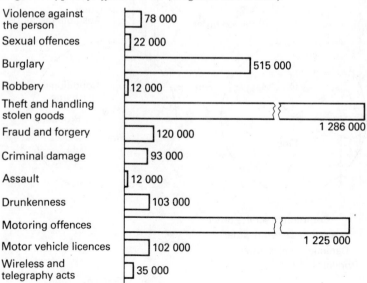

237

shown the largest increases in the past twenty years though they still represent less than 3·7 per cent and 4·3 per cent of the crimes reported. Sexual offences have risen very little since the 1950's. The 'clear-up rate', that is those reported offences which lead to a conviction by a

Fig. 63. *Age and sex of offenders 1976 (persons found guilty per 1 000 of the population)*

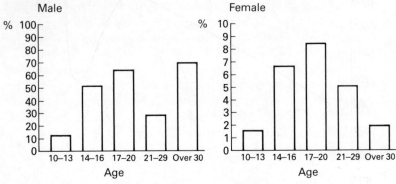

Fig. 64. *Sentences 1976 (England and Wales)*

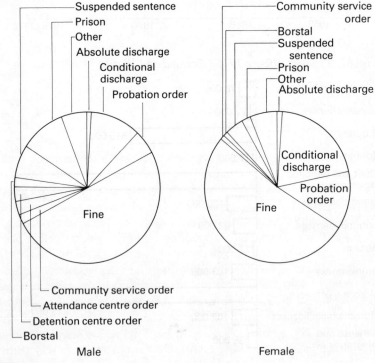

court, varies from year to year but is usually between 40–45 per cent of the known crimes.

The typical offender in our society is a boy, of school age, committing an offence with or without violence against property, or an older teenager involved in theft or vandalism. Men are generally more likely to commit than women though the crime rate among women is growing. The most likely punishment for any type of offence is a fine. Alternative punishment such as attendance centres – at which offenders attend on Saturday afternoons – and community service orders – involving offenders in work for the community – are used for a small number of offenders.

Police manpower has risen as the crime rate rises though nearly all police forces have less men than they could employ. In recent years there has been a rapid increase in the number of women police officers and in the number of civilians who assist the police in their duties, including traffic wardens.

Table 31. *Police forces (England and Wales) (thousands)*

	1961	1966	1971	1976
Policemen	72.7	82.5	91.8	101.0
Policewomen	2.3	3.2	3.8	7.0
Special constables	47.6	41.9	30.0	21.4
Cadets	3.3	4.1	4.5	3.7
Traffic wardens	0.3	2.7	5.8	5.9
Civilians	11.8	18.2	28.1	34.6

Crime in the news

For most people their closest regular contact with real crime is in the pages of their daily newspaper or on the television news. Crime is something you read about or see on the television. Our ideas about crime depend very much upon the way in which it is presented in the media. Not all media crime however, comes under the heading of 'news'. Crime is also entertainment. On television, crime is portrayed in plays and films and the same heroes often appear in paperbacks and at the cinema. Usually we keep 'news-crime' and 'entertainment-crime' separate as though one is the real-life world while the other is make-believe. Such a division is not wholly accurate. The methods by which a news story and a piece of fiction are created are in some ways very similar. Firstly, crime fiction has a basis in reality. Some fictional stories are based on real-life events. This is not the only way reality

239

provides a basis for fiction. Crime stories may not have happened in real life – but they could have done. They seldom stray far from what might have happened. The characters are modelled on roles and relationships which we recognise from real life. 'The police', the criminal, 'the innocent bystander', the victim, are all characters we can recognise. Crime fiction does not have to invent totally new characters.

Secondly, the way a crime novel is written depends very much upon the values held by the people who make up the audience. At the end of the story the 'good guys' usually win and law and order triumphs. Entertainment-crime does, however, go a certain way beyond real life. The fiction writer or the television dramatist produces a story which entertains. It must be 'exciting' and 'gripping', holding people's attention and making them buy the next novel or watch the next programme. There is often a basic formula of suspense, violence, intrigue, romance, danger and suspicion. Put together in the right order they produce a readable book or an exciting film. Entertainment-crime is basically concerned with a product which needs to be sold to an audience and that audience must come back for more.

Newspapers are also a product. They need to be sold in very large numbers and people must be persuaded to carry on buying them day after day after day. This means that the basic rules for producing crime-news may not be very different from the rules which affect entertainment-crime.

News begins with events but not all events are news. Producing a newspaper means making a selection, or in fact a series of selections, from the available events. These selections are based on the idea of news value. A good journalist is trained to recognise 'news value' in a story. A good story has something about it which is unusual, unexpected or dramatic or which contains tension, romance or human interest. These are characteristics which do not differ greatly from those found in a good novel or a television play.

> 'There is this thing called a news story', commented a crime reporter on a national newspaper, 'I don't know how to recognise it, it's experience, I suppose. It's an odd quality. You can put six reporters in a court and they sit through six hours of cases and they'll all come out with the same story'. (Chibnall 1975)

In the course of an average day, a journalist comes across many events, reports, or leads which might produce a story. He or she selects on the basis of their potential news value. Often a story will need to be written-up in a way which adds to its news value. Words will be chosen which emphasise particular aspects of the event and interpretations will be given. Another crime reporter commented that

240

news stories were 'cliches set to music – you select the right cliche and write it up to suit the particular circumstances. Something like "tug-of-love" identifies a particular story and its theme.' (Chibnall 1975)

Reporters are not alone in selecting and shaping the news. Their stories are passed on to the sub-editors and those above them. Their role is to make further selections and to shape the news until it is ready to go into the paper. They have been described as 'gatekeepers' because of their role in restricting the amount of news that can pass through. A copy-editor studied by an American sociologist used 1 297 column inches out of the 11 910 inches which were supplied to him. Their selections are, once again, based on the idea of news value though they also select on the basis of the newspaper's own policies.

The selecting and shaping of the news which takes place at these various levels has considerable influence on how crime is reported. A study by Roshier showed that the level of crime reporting in five British daily newspapers did not change much over a thirty-year period. There was no evidence to suggest that an increase in crime rates led to an increase in crime reporting. On one national daily the space given over to crime actually fell at a time when crime rates were rising fastest. Roshier also found that there was no connection between levels of particular crimes and their coverage in the press. Manslaughter, murder and drug offences involving the well-known were given far greater coverage than theft or motoring offences which affected a far greater number of people. In the words of a crime reporter, 'company fraud is a difficult thing to write about . . . there's no violence, no drama.' (Chibnall 1975)

THE CRIME REPORTER

In the newspapers studied by Roshier there was also a tendency to place greater emphasis on the results of successful police action than the actual 'crimes solved' rates would have justified. The picture which emerged was one of more effective police activity than was in fact the case. This may have been a result of the particular way in which crime reporters work.

Crime reporters are an elite group in Fleet Street. Chibnall estimates that there can be no more than 70 journalists who regularly report on crime and the police and that less than a third of these are full-time crime reporters. As a group they are the main channel of most of the news about crime. The news they handle is not strictly 'crime' news. It is police news, for the crime reporter's major source of information is the police.

Much of his time is spent establishing relationships with police officers who can give him the news he wants. Crime reporters need to

241

be trusted by their informants and to be able to provide favours in return for the information given. The relationship between the crime reporter and his police contacts is often very close. As one reporter put it: 'over the years you get to know a copper . . . they're not just business contacts, they're friends'. (Chibnall 1975)

This relationship can affect the news which is reported. The crime reporter is unlikely to publish a story which might offend the police as this could put a stop to further information. Similarly he might include a story which is clearly favourable to the police or which helps the police in their investigations.

> Often the police will issue information which makes a good story and say, 'well, if you print this it may help us catch this guy', usually it's a case of leaking information that the police are getting closer. Well when he hears this the guy gets jumpy. (Chibnall 1975)

Particular problems arise when a crime reporter gets hold of a story of police corruption. He could suppress, or write it up anonymously, or hand it over to a colleague. Seldom would the story be given to another crime reporter. Journalism is a competitive activity. The search for a scoop or an 'exclusive' story goes on all of the time. The only way a crime reporter can be sure of his share of exclusives is to keep as close as he can to his one main source of stories – the police. This closeness inevitably affects the way the crime reporter does his job and the view of crime which is presented in the news.

Steve Chibnall points out that 'Most crime reporters see their professional responsibilities toward the public as entailing the support of the police in the battle against crime. This means they are obliged to defend and promote the interests of the police.'

CONCLUSION

We can see therefore that in trying to understand crime in our society we need to take into account a number of factors. We must consider the social influences which are likely to lead to criminal or deviant behaviour; we need to look at the way deviance is defined and the way in which it is presented. Crime and deviance have been of particular interest to sociologists because they reflect society's view of what is normal and acceptable behaviour. By understanding crime and deviance we can also get a better understanding of what counts as normal.

12
Religion in Society

Sociologists have been interested in religion since the very earliest days of the subject. Some of the founders of sociology even thought that sociology would replace religion. Marx, Weber and Durkheim each considered the way religion affected the societies they knew. Their influence is still important.

Marx thought religion was like a drug. He called it 'the opium of the people'. He saw religion as one of the ways in which the ruling class prevented the oppressed workers from rising in revolt. Religion, with its promise of 'treasure in heaven' was often the only source of hope for those who had no chance of 'treasure on earth'. Durkheim also saw religion as central to the way society worked. For society to operate effectively it needed a set of beliefs and values which held everything together. For him, religion was the moral glue of society. Religion was at the basis of social life and part of the way men understood the world.

Weber's contribution is more far-reaching than that of either Marx or Durkheim. He looked at the way religious ideas related to other areas of life, particularly to the way the economy was organised and he considered how religious groups themselves operated. Many of the basic ideas we will use in considering religion in society come from the writings of Max Weber.

In this chapter we will consider three main aspects of the sociology of religion. Firstly, what is religion and how can it be studied by sociologists? Secondly, how do religion and religious ideas affect other areas of social, economic and political life? Thirdly, how do religious groups operate and how can they be better understood?

Before looking at these three questions, we must consider one question which should not concern sociologists. That is the question 'is religion true?' All sociologists have their own ideas about such a question, and as ordinary people would no doubt have an answer. As sociologists it is not a question they can even attempt to answer. Questions of religious truth are a matter for theologians not for sociologists.

In October 1978 over 900 people living in a religious community in Guyana, called the People's Temple, apparently committed suicide by drinking fruit juice mixed with cyanide. They believed that others were about to take away all that they had worked for, that their only form of survival was death. One of the leaders of the movement wrote to a journalist shortly before he died, 'A man who hasn't found something to die for isn't fit to live, well we've found something to die for and it's called . . . social justice'.

Most people would say that the members of the Guyana People's Temple were wrong in their beliefs. Few people believe that suicide is the only way to prove your faith. But, people did believe such things, the suicide did take place and hundreds died. The People's Temple and its beliefs were a 'social fact'. To understand it fully the sociologist must put his own beliefs on one side and try to see such 'social facts' through the eyes of those who do believe. It is not the sociologist's job to prove or disprove the truth of such beliefs, merely to understand them.

What is religion?

Some would argue that the People's Temple was not really a religion. In many ways it seems more like a political or social movement. There is little mention of God in the Temple writings and even the faith healing depended upon belief in the powers of the Temple leader, Father Jim Jones.

Fig. 65. *How religious do people think they are? 1968–69*

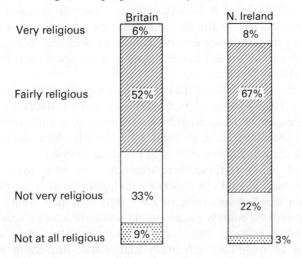

Source: Religion in Britain and Northern Ireland (I.T.A. 1970)

This problem of actually saying what religion is, is an important one in sociology. We can see the problem more clearly if we consider someone who goes to church and ask ourselves the question – 'is that person religious?' We could answer that people who go to church are religious because they go to church, that evidence of churchgoing is reliable evidence of religion. You can probably already see the problems of this point of view. Firstly, it is a circular argument in which churchgoing is evidence of religion and religion is a cause of churchgoing. This is obviously not a sound argument. Secondly, and more important, it assumes that the *action* of going to church automatically indicates what the person *believes*. Belief in God may not be the only reason for going to church. There may be social reasons. Perhaps going to church on Sunday is an accepted thing to do, or a sign of social status. There may be very practical reasons for going to church. It may be that young people go so that they qualify for membership of a church youth club or because it is a good place to meet people. Others may go because they enjoy the music or like singing hymns. There could be many reasons for going to church which have nothing at all to do with religion. It is also quite likely that many people who regard themselves as religious, who hold religious beliefs, may never go to church.

Social scientists must therefore be careful in separating the way people behave (their actions) from what they believe. Church-going means different things to different people. Understanding the meaning that religion has for people is an important part of the sociology of religion.

This still leaves us with the problem of defining religion. We have to decide which meanings or beliefs can be counted as religious. You could say that 'religion is a belief in spiritual beings'. Under this definition any belief in the supernatural or things beyond our earthly experience is religious.

Therefore, believing in luck, or horoscopes, or ghosts is religious. This sort of definition tends to include more than it excludes. Another 'inclusive' definition is that religion is that which is of 'ultimate concern'. If, therefore, your ultimate concern is that Leeds United win the F.A. Cup then you could say that 'football mania' is a kind of religion.

Inclusive definitions such as these are not very helpful to the sociologist. They include too many things to be useful for comparison or analysis. Sociologists often find it easier to work with narrower, exclusive definitions based on particular evidence or events.

This does not solve the problem. You still need to decide what evidence you are going to use as a basis for your definitions. You could use evidence of what religion does. Durkheim wrote that 'religion is a system of beliefs which unite those that believe in them into a single moral community'. He defined religion in terms of what it does, or its function. We would say that it is a functional definition. Alternatively you could use a definition in terms of what religion is. This sort of definition normally selects a few important characteristics of any religion and uses them as a basis for defining it. Religion could be defined in terms of the belief in things which are beyond human activity and in terms of symbols which relate to those beliefs.

Defining religion is a problem, and one which cannot easily be solved. Sociologists use many different definitions, some are broad and inclusive, others are narrow and exclusive, some look at what religion does and others at what it is. It is important that when you read about religion you ask yourself why certain actions and beliefs are being labelled 'religious'. Ask yourself what kind of definition is being used.

CAN YOU HAVE A SOCIOLOGY OF RELIGION?

If religion is about beliefs, spiritual beings and the supernatural, how can it be studied by sociologists? It has been argued that because religion is individual to each person it can never be understood by science, even by social science. Sociologists would not in general agree with this view. Religious beliefs do not exist in a vacuum. Believers live in a social world. Their beliefs are acquired through social contact and are expressed in social behaviour.

The hermit in his cave lives by beliefs he learned from other people. Holy scriptures and religious writings communicate particular ideas and beliefs to human beings who live in social groups. The child goes to school or classes to learn about the Bible, Talmud or Koran, the adults belong to a church, synagogue or mosque, they are led and guided by a priest, rabbi or imam. Religion is a *social* phenomenon. It is, as we have already seen, a social phenomenon which is built on particular beliefs and meanings. These beliefs make up the cultural aspect of religion and make it possible for us to distinguish, for example, between religious groups and other groups such as political parties or social clubs. In studying religion we need to consider both its social and cultural aspects. To consider the social areas of religion, such as church attendance or religious obedience, without the cultural areas, such as what people believe, would give an inaccurate and one-sided view.

Religion and society

An important interest for the early sociologists of religion was the relationship between the beliefs people held and the social, economic and political organisation of society. For Durkheim the beliefs could not be separated from the way society was held together. The most elementary forms of religion began, he argued, when bands of primitive hunters came together. The feelings of friendship and togetherness which developed grew into rituals which, in the course of time, came to be regarded as sacred. In such a way religious beliefs grew from the very existence of society. They served to hold the society together and provided a basis for moral rules and social order. Durkheim went on to stress the evolutionary character of religion. Elementary forms of religion evolved into more advanced forms as primitive society itself evolved more advanced patterns of social organisation. At each stage religion provided the basis for social solidarity, and held the society together. Durkheim's approach has been the basis for a sociology which analyses religion in terms of the functions which religion performs. By using an open or 'inclusive' definition of religion Durkheim implies that any system of beliefs which functions to hold society together is religious. In this way nationalism and communism may be defined as religious. They are sometimes called 'functional alternatives' for religion because they carry out similar functions of social solidarity.

Durkheim's views have been criticised by other sociologists. His arguments were based upon what he took to be elementary forms of religion found among the Arunta Aborigines of the Australian desert. More recent studies have shown that even more elementary religions exist and their religious systems do not support Durkheim's view. Durkheim's functional definition has also been criticised because it is so broad that it includes many belief systems which should not really be termed religious. The idea of social evolution has also been rejected by many who question the idea that societies develop upon a straight path from 'primitive' to 'advanced' and Durkheim's approach has failed to show *how* religion changes. Whilst such criticisms are important they should not lead us to reject Durkheim's work which points to an important connection between patterns of belief and the organisation of society.

Another approach to the relationship between religion and society is found in the work of Max Weber. Whereas Durkheim was concerned with religious beliefs and social patterns, Weber's interest centred upon beliefs and the economic system. In the sixteenth and seventeenth centuries there grew up in parts of Europe a new class of capitalists whose wealth was based on the development of industry. Dominant among them were wealthy Protestants who followed the beliefs laid down by John Calvin. Weber noted that there was a great similarity between the religious beliefs of these new capitalists and the

247

beliefs of Calvinism. Both sets of beliefs placed great stress upon the individual being responsible for his own success and salvation. Both emphasised the need for diligence and hard work which was for the glory of God. In his study of *The Protestant Ethic and the Spirit of Capitalism* Weber showed how these two sets of beliefs were linked, the one supporting the other. The theory has been questioned. It has been shown that there were capitalists who were not Calvinists and that much capitalist development came before Calvinism became important. However, Weber's thesis shows that religious ideas can form the basis for economic values. Weber emphasised that whereas the Catholic monk had a 'calling' to prayer and devotion the Calvinist saw his life as a 'calling' to work hard and to live simply. Industrious-ness and sober living were a duty to God. To the Calvinists salvation could not be earned. It was predestined by God. Your work and success in this life was a sign that you stood among the chosen few who would inherit the kingdom of heaven.

Whilst Durkheim pointed to social solidarity and Weber emphasised the economic implications of belief other writers have looked to the political implications of religion. Marx viewed religion as part of man's alienation. Religion was something that man had produced but only served to maintain his oppression. 'Religion', he wrote, 'is the sigh of the oppressed creature, the heart of the heartless world, just as it is the spirit of the spiritless situation. It is the opium of the people.' (Karl Marx and Frederick Engels, *On Religion* 1844)

This kind of approach can be used to explain the impact of Methodism upon England in the eighteenth and nineteenth centuries.

During the 70 years before 1850 almost every country in Europe experienced a political revolution except for Britain. Why was Britain not affected? The rise of Methodism may provide part of the answer.

The origins of Methodism lay in the Church of England. When George Whitfield and John Wesley went out to preach to the people they did so because the Church of England had failed to keep the allegiance of the working people. The people who flocked to hear the Methodist preachers and who later formed the backbone of the new churches and chapels were mostly drawn from the ranks of the skilled artisans, the better-off members of the working class. Methodism gave them hope for the future and a way of using their talents. For many it provided an education and a bridge into the middle class. The values and beliefs of Methodism were, however, the values of the political and religious establishment. Methodism served to dampen down revolutionary feeling rather than encourage it. Methodism carried religion to the working people and with it there went a message which provided a justification for inequality. Each man's lot was appointed by God who will reward the sacrifice in the life to come. Methodism may have been one of the most effective means of social control to influence the English working classes.

The work of Durkheim, Weber and Marx provide us with valuable insights into the way religion is tied to the social, economic and political structure. They look at religion as it affects whole societies whereas other sociologists have focused upon smaller-scale issues and the operation of particular religious groups.

Church and sect

One of the first things that you notice when looking at religious groups is their diversity. Walk through any large town and you are likely to pass the places of worship of a great variety of religious groups. Some are local branches of large religious organisations, others are part of a looser federation of religious bodies and some may even be completely independent with no links to any other group. Churches like the Church

Fig. 66. *Changes in membership of religious groups (1970–75)*

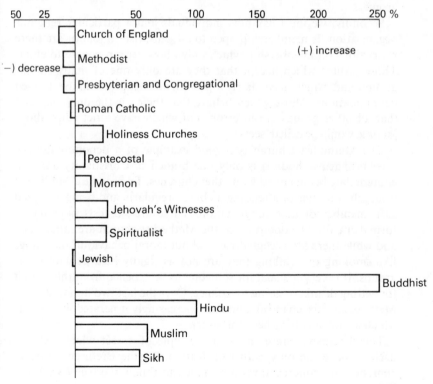

of England or the Roman Catholic Church are very large indeed. In Britain alone these churches have nearly five million members between them without counting all of those people who may call themselves 'C of E' or 'Catholic' without ever going to church. The Salvation Army, The Society of Friends, Christian Science and other groups are also widely scattered across the country and have links with many other countries. The Church of England has over 17 000 church buildings in Britain. The Church of Christ, Scientist has less than 300.

Size is an important feature to consider, but it is not the only way in which religious bodies can be compared. An alternative would be to separate those groups known as 'churches' from those we might term 'sects'. In general churches are larger than sects but size is not the most important difference. It is more important to compare their attitudes to the wider society and their particular belief and practices.

This becomes clearer if we consider two main questions. Firstly, how does the religious group see itself and its beliefs? Does it believe, as many groups do, that there is only one path to heaven and that they alone hold the key, or does the group accept that there are many different views of religion and that it is only one of a large number of groups?

Secondly, we must ask how individuals join a particular religious organisation. Is membership open to all who wish to join or are there restrictions on membership which only allow certain people to enter. Those groups which accept that they are only one of many similar groups and which have fairly open membership would be termed denominations. Those which believe that their's is the only way and that all other groups are in error, and which have strict rules about joining, would be called 'sects'.

The Methodist Church is a good example of a denomination. It accepts that Methodism is only one branch of Christianity and can contemplate being united with other churches. To become a Methodist is largely a matter of attending a church regularly and being accepted as a member of that congregation. There are no tests of entry or formal rituals. The doctrines of the Methodist church are fairly open and while there are accepted views about moral behaviour and things like smoking or drinking they are not as rigidly held as with other groups. It is very unusual for someone to be expelled from the church for getting drunk, or going to a dance. Over the last two hundred years Methodism has changed and has increasingly tolerated behaviour which would once have been forbidden.

The 'Exclusive Brethren' is an example of a sect which believes itself to have the only path to salvation. To the Brethren all other churches and congregations have failed to follow the true (Brethren)

250

way and are therefore 'in sin'. The Brethren keep themselves as much apart from society as is possible. They have not, as have some sects, taken themselves completely out of society, by setting up isolated communities in distant places. They do, however, maintain a high level of separation while still living and working within non-Brethren society. The focus of Brethren life is the family. Every meal is seen as a re-enactment of Christ's Last Supper and non-members may be excluded from it. This means that members of a family who remain outside the sect may have to eat alone. Failure to keep to the strict rules which forbid dancing, the cinema and other 'worldly' entertainment could lead to expulsion from the sect.

Between the extremes of the closed sect and the open denomination are a variety of other groups with different beliefs about themselves and the world. Some groups do change their ideas and beliefs and may become more sectarian or more like denominations. They may accept more worldly values or they may reject them.

TYPES OF SECT

The basic division into 'church-type' movements, or denominations and sects can be taken a little further by considering the various types of sectarian groups that exist.

Not all sects cut themselves off from the world as do the Exclusive Brethren. Many groups are very involved in the world's affairs, for many different reasons. Bryan Wilson has listed seven main types of sect in terms of the ways in which they see the world and their own beliefs.

The *conversionist* or evangelical sects are involved in the world because they want to change it. Their mission is to bring people to salvation. Many Gospel Churches and Evangelical Assemblies come within this group. Their time is spent crusading for religious revival. Whereas such groups seek to evangelise in order to change the world other groups look forward to a time when the world will itself change. In particular, *revolutionary* sects look forward towards the Millenium, or the Second Coming of Christ. The Jehovah's Witnesses are a group which have always had a very clear idea of what will happen at Armageddon when'only the saved will inherit the Kingdom. These two approaches – the conversionist and revolutionary are often closely linked and are very different from the approach of the third type, the *introversionist* sects, which, like the Exclusive Brethren, seek to withdraw from the world.

A fourth type of sect, the *manipulationist* sect, differs from those already described because its members accept the world instead of

251

rejecting it. Sects of this type believe that they have special ways of gaining those things which all desire. Good health and a successful career are things which most people think are important. Manipulationist sects believe that men and women are only denied these things because they have not learned how to live the right sort of lives. Scientology, for example, teaches that people can be more successful if they clear their minds of unhealthy 'engrams' which prevent them from reaching their full potential.

Health and healing are important to many religious groups. They are central to the beliefs of '*thaumaturgical*' sects. Thaumaturge comes from a Greek word meaning wonder-worker. Such sects do often claim to 'work-wonders'. In particular they often believe that contact can be made with the dead whose help can be gained for the problems of the living. Spiritualist churches come into this group.

Wilson concludes his list of sect-types with the *reformist* sects, which seek to remain in the world while seeking to change it through social and political pressures (such sects are often very close to becoming denominations), and finally with *Utopian* sects which withdraw themselves completely from the world in order to live perfect lives in a new society.

These seven types give us an indication of the varieties of sect which exist in the world and some of their beliefs and practices. They are not seven completely watertight categories. Many real-life sects combine aspects from a number of different types. The Church of Jesus Christ of Latter Day Saints (Mormonism) is an example of a large sect which combines features of many of these different types. In the middle of the last century the Mormons cut themselves off from the rest of America by migrating West into the uncharted territory of Utah. The values they held were, however, the same values of success and achievement which were part of the 'Great American Dream'. The early Mormons believed that with the establishment of their church Christ's promises had been fulfilled and that America was the home of the new Millenium. Today the Mormons are very much an evangelical, conversionist group. A period of missionary service is an obligation for all young Mormons. Such a sect has every appearance of being a denomination, only keeping its sect-like character through its emphasis on its special knowledge and beliefs.

THE BEGINNINGS OF A SECT

Studies of religious groups have shown quite clearly that the organisation of sects, denominations and churches varies and that it is quite usual for groups to change. A sect may become established, its doctrines and pattern of membership may become more open, and it will become a denomination. A denomination may also change in the reverse direction. Where did it all start? How do religious groups come into being, and why?

One of the best known examples of the beginnings of a religious group is found in the New Testament. We can use it here as an example of the development of religious groups in general. In the four Gospels and in the Acts of the Apostles we find a detailed account of how the Christian Church began. Jesus was obviously a very impressive individual. He was a leader with considerable abilities who had the power to make others follow him. This is clear from any reading of the Gospels. He preached in a land which was occupied by a foreign army, ruled by a weak 'puppet' king where the established religious authorities were either powerless or collaborated with the enemy. There were revolutionary 'liberation' groups but they had little success. Because of his teaching and its effect on the people Jesus was executed. His followers escaped but later began to reorganise. They formed a tight little group which had considerable initial success preaching the words of Jesus. Their success was so great that some of their numbers had to give up preaching and attend to the day-to-day administration of what had by now become a Jewish sect. An official leadership developed and there grew up a need to communicate Jesus' sayings to those who had never heard him. Written records were essential. The teaching became particularly important when Christianity ceased to be an offshoot of the Jewish faith and began to take in Greeks, Romans and others. For its first few hundred years Christianity was a religion for slaves and the oppressed. It was not until the Roman Emperor Constantine made it an official religion that it became an established religion.

If we analyse the rise of Christianity, we can see a number of features which are common to the origins of many religious movements.

Firstly, there was a leader with considerable influence and authority. His authority was not a traditional authority such as that exercised by the main religious leaders, the Pharisees, nor was it the legal authority exercised by the Romans. This authority was a part of the personality of the leader. Weber uses the word 'charisma' to describe this kind of authority and Jesus is a good example of a leader with charismatic authority.

There were, secondly, a group of followers with a very strong belief in their charismatic leader. Later some of these followers would become leaders. Their authority was derived from the authority of Jesus. Many of these men and women had particular skills of organisation and teaching.

Thirdly, there was a body of people who were in some way deprived.

253

Many were very poor, others lacked power or sense of belonging as a result of Roman rule, many were physically handicapped.

Fourthly, the movement began as an offshoot of one religion and ended up as a religion of its own.

Finally, as the movement grew a greater proportion of its time was devoted to administration and less to the work of preaching, healing and so on and there developed a need to socialise the second generation into the group's beliefs.

If we bring the story up to date we can also see that what began as a sectarian religion ended up as an established church and that new sects began to arise out of it. The process started once more with new charismatic leaders, new followers, in answer to new needs out of which came new organisations.

The same pattern can be taken and applied to many other groups. Of particular importance are the role of the charismatic leader who leads the breakaway from the established groups, and the form of deprivation experienced by the followers. There is some evidence that particular kinds of deprivations lead to the establishment of particular kinds of church or sect.

Glock and Stark have identified five kinds of deprivation which may influence the evolution of a sect. *Economic* deprivation is another way of saying that people are poor. *Social* deprivation occurs when they lack power or status. *Organismic* deprivation occurs when individuals have a serious physical handicap. *Ethical* deprivation is caused by dissatisfaction with the values or ideals of the wider society and *psychic* deprivation is a state of despair and hopelessness. Liston Pope, in his study of churches in the mill towns of North Carolina, found that those churches which catered for the poorest and the most powerless members of society were those which practised 'ecstatic' religion. Other churches referred to them as 'Holy Rollers' because of their peoples' practice of dancing and rolling on the floor, often in a trance. This link between economic/social deprivation and 'ecstatic' religion has been noticed in studies of other groups. Similarly links can be made between other forms of deprivation and particular groups.

The origin of any religious movement can be related to particular social circumstances. To the sociologist religions don't just happen, they arise from social situations and involve leaders and followers, needs and aspirations.

Religion in Britain

Table 32 gives us a general picture of the pattern of religion in Britain. What does it mean and how reliable is it?

Table 32. *Church membership 1975*

	Members (Thousands)	Ministers (Numbers)	Church Buildings (Numbers)
Episcopal Churches			
Church of England	1 862(a)	14 379	17 212
Church of Wales	133(b)	896	1 720
Episcopal Church in Scotland	78(a)	235	335
Church of Ireland	176	375	495
Other	6	66	68
Other Churches			
Baptist Churches	256	2 394	3 560
Methodist Churches	596	3 098	9 138
Church of Scotland	1 042	2 261	1 964
United Reformed Church	175	1 795	2 068
Other Presbyterian and Congregational Churches	539	1 508	3 492
Roman Catholic Churches	2 413	8 032	4 100
Other Trinitarian Churches	574	9 239(d)	7 379
Mormon Churches	100	5 260	160
Jehovah's Witnesses	79	7 000(a)	600
Spiritualist Churches	57	233	594
Other Churches	70	164	1 001
Other religions			
Jews	111(c)	400(a)	315
Buddhists	21(a)	172(a)	30(a)
Hindus	100(a)	100	120(a)
Muslims	400(a)	1 000(a)	800(a)
Sikhs	115(a)	—	75

Notes
(a) – Estimate
(b) – Easter attendance
(c) – Heads of households (men and women)
(d) – Includes part-time ministers

The table divides religious groups into three sections: Episcopal Churches; other Churches; and other religions. The Episcopal churches grouping is dominated by the Church of England which is the 'established' church. Otherwise known as the Anglican Church, the Church of England has never held a real monopoly of religion.

Until the early nineteenth century it did have a very powerful position as the law prevented anyone who was not an Anglican from holding political office. At the present time it is only the ruling monarch who must still be a member of the established church. The 'Other Churches' section of the table lumps together a wide variety of groups from the Methodists, who separated from the Church of England in the eighteenth century, to the Roman Catholics from whom the Church of England itself separated two hundred years before.

Of the three columns: Members, Ministers and Church buildings, the last is probably the most reliable. At least most people are agreed about what a church building is even allowing for the fact that 'other religions' call them by different names. The problems of counting 'religious' buildings are, however, small when compared to the problems of counting members and ministers. It is a table in which it pays to read the small print first.

Church membership is an impossible thing to measure. What is a 'church member'? To be a member of the Church of England or the Roman Catholic Church you need to be baptised. For many people baptism, or christening as it is often wrongly called, is a ritual which takes place when they are still babes-in-arms. For full membership of these churches and the right to receive the Holy Communion you also need to be confirmed. You will notice that membership of the Church of Wales is based on 'Easter Attendance'. All active church members of Catholic and Episcopal churches are expected to attend the Easter Communion service. So Easter attendance may be a reasonable measure of membership. In other churches different 'membership rules' apply. Baptists regard adult baptism as a sign of church membership. Methodists are usually 'card carrying' members. When we get down to the 'other religions' section the problem of membership becomes immense. 'Jew' and 'Sikh' are not only religious terms they also apply to a particular community of people. The fact that the Jewish figure includes 'heads of households' suggests that it is based on the Jewish community as an ethnic group rather than the active members of synagogues. It is not very surprising that not many of the figures for 'other religions' are given as estimates.

In the same way that definition of memberships vary so do definitions of minister. Some churches have elaborate hierarchies of deacons, priests and bishops. In some the 'ministry' could include 'priests' who have little 'ministerial' functions. They may be worker-priests in the week and clergymen on Sundays. Some may be full-time members of monasteries. Some religions do not even have professional priests. The Jewish rabbi is a teacher with a role very different from that of the Church of England vicar.

256

This table indicates some of the very real problems which arise when you attempt to put numbers to any area of religion. All religious statistics need to be approached with caution. Figures such as these can only give a very rough guide to the real pattern of religion in Britain.

The pattern of religion

When we look more closely at the evidence of religious activity and belief some sort of pattern emerges.

Fig. 67. *Who is most religious? 1968*

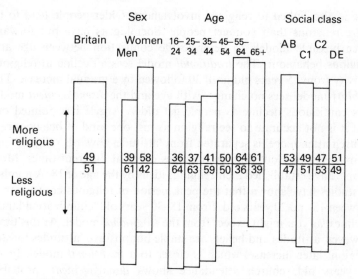

Source: *Religion in Britain and Northern Ireland* (I.T.A. 1970)

SEX DIFFERENCES

Women are more likely to be involved in religion than men. They are more likely to go to church, to pray regularly and to believe in God. Such differences are not, however, the same for all religious groups. American studies have shown that in Eastern Orthodox churches men are in the majority and we can see a similar pattern among Jewish congregations in Britain. The proportions of men and women in Roman Catholic churches are fairly similar whereas in Christian Science men are outnumbered by four to one. Argyle has suggested that such differences are caused by a combination of social and psychological factors. Women, he claims, are more likely than men to

257

experience feelings of guilt and are therefore attracted to churches which promise salvation. Protestant denominations which have the higher proportion of women members emphasise God as a father figure whereas men are more attracted to churches, such as Roman Catholic, which place emphasis on the Virgin Mary as the Holy Mother. It may also be possible to explain the greater religious involvement of women in terms of 'relative deprivation'. Luckman points to difference in religious activity between working and non-working women and suggests that religious involvement may be linked to other economic and social roles. Women who go to work and have careers are less likely than other women to participate in religion.

AGE

Age is also linked to religious involvement. Older people tend to be more religious than younger people. Sociologists have put forward three possible models to describe the connection between age and religious behaviour. The *traditional* model sees a decline in religious activity from 15 years old until 30 followed by a gradual increase. The *stability* model sees no changes with age and the *disengagement* model sees continuous decline as people get older. Argyle has pointed out that it is not accurate to see religion as just one kind of behaviour. If 'church attendance' is separated from 'attitudes towards religion' and from 'belief in God' different changes occur at different times. Most people have established their religious ideas by the age of 18. A number of studies have shown that the peak period of religious conversion is between 15 and 20 years old. From 18–30 years old 'church attendance' declines, as you might expect from the *traditional* model. At this time, however, attitudes and beliefs are stable but positive 'attitudes toward religion' later increase, which is closer to a *traditional* model. From 60 years old, church attendance shows *disengagement*, probably because people are less active and prefer to watch religious programmes at home on the television to actually going to church. Attitudes and beliefs both show an increase at this time which supports the *traditional* pattern. The evidence shows clearly that religious ideas and behaviour do not stay the same throughout life. As we grow older our views and behaviour change.

SOCIAL CLASS

Religious behaviour and attitudes are linked to the social class of the individual. Writing in 1851 at the time of the Census of Religion Horace Mann commented, 'it is observable how absolutely insignificant a portion of the congregations is composed of artizans'.

The middle class are often thought to be more religious than the working class. This need not be true. Middle-class religion is often more obvious than working-class religion. It involves a religion of 'doing' rather than a religion of feeling. American research studies by Demerath showed that the lower classes were less likely to be church members but more likely to hold certain beliefs. Middle-class religion centred on a 'social gospel' and calls to help one's fellow men whereas more working-class groups emphasised salvation and hope for the life to come. This difference in emphasis also affects the denominations supported by different social classes. The larger denominations such as Church of England, Methodist and Presbyterian/Congregationalist, have a largely middle-class membership, whereas sects and 'independent' churches draw more upon the working class. There are, however, certain variations to this pattern. The Roman Catholic church has a large working-class following and some sects such as Christian Science have strong middle-class membership. Links between religion and social class also influence voting behaviour and may explain why Roman Catholics are more likely to vote Labour and why Anglicans tend to vote Conservative. The traditional link between the Methodist Chapels and the Labour Party may also explain the strength of the Methodist Labour vote.

THE GEOGRAPHICAL SPREAD OF RELIGION

As well as differences in age, sex and social class religious behaviour is also affected by geographical differences. Often different factors overlap. Social class affects where people live. Social class differences in church-going will, therefore, affect the location of particular churches. There are also historical factors which have influenced the location of religious groups. The most important of these has been migration.

When people move they take their religion with them. On arrival at their new home they seek out others of the same faith and seek to establish a religious community. When large numbers of people migrate their common beliefs and religious culture often form the basis of the community. We can see this clearly in the religious groups which surround the ports at which immigrants arrive.

At the end of the nineteenth century many thousands of Jewish refugees arrived at the London Docks. They came to escape persecution in Eastern Europe and were often destitute. On arrival they sought the help of their fellow Jews and eventually settled within a short distance of the docks. Synagogues were founded and Jewish industries were set up. As the people became established they began to move away into more desirable areas and new Jewish communities developed. Each stage of migration led to the establishment of new synagogues, food shops specialising in kosher foods, Jewish schools and social activities. Some members of the Jewish community drifted away and were absorbed into the wider community, often through intermarriage. For many their 'Jewishness' provided a basis for their identity in a strange land. Religion helped to hold the community together.

The same pattern is still being worked out in the districts surrounding London's docks today and around many other ports of entry. The new immigrants are from India, Pakistan and Bangladesh or from the West Indies. In East London the Jewish community has been replaced by a Muslim community. The synagogues have given way to mosques, kosher butchers to halal food shops and in the narrow streets Ahmed and Rasul now work in the rag trade once dominated by Cohens and Benjamins.

Whilst migration between countries can help us to understand the location of particular religious groups we must also consider migration within one country. For example, Methodism is much stronger in the Isle of Wight than in the surrounding areas of Hampshire and Dorset. The reasons for this are to be found in two historical events. Firstly, the success of the early Methodist preachers like George Whitefield and John Wesley in spreading their faith in Cornwall in the eighteenth century. Secondly, the migration of one group of Cornish Methodists from Cornwall to the Isle of Wight in the nineteenth century. On this basis Methodism became established on the Isle of Wight.

A similar pattern can be seen in Corby in Northamptonshire. Whereas most of the East Midlands has a fairly mixed pattern of Church of England, Methodist, Baptist and other churches, Corby is strongly Presbyterian. Once again the reason is migration. Earlier this century the Scottish steel firm of Stewarts and Lloyds opened a new factory on the iron-ore deposits which surrounded Corby. They brought with them a skilled force of Scottish workers who brought with them their church.

Migration does not always involve large groups who moved together. Migration can be the result of other factors. The Jewish community is well established at a number of seaside resorts. This is partly due to the desire of many Jewish families to stay at kosher hotels within reach of a synagogue when they go on holiday and to the wish of many older people to retire to the seaside while still keeping to their beliefs and practices.

RELIGION IN THE CITY

Patterns of migration, social class and age come together when we look at religion in the city. Most cities have more churches than they need. This is partly due to movements of population and a general decline in churchgoing but also is a result of the over-enthusiasm of our Victorian great-grandparents who built more churches than even they needed. It would be wrong, however, to base our ideas of city religion solely on the numbers of empty churches.

Most city churches were built and are still owned by the larger denominations. We have already noted that the membership of these denominations is largely middle-class, a group who tend not to live in the central parts of cities. The middle classes either build their own churches in the suburbs or on the housing estates or they travel to worship at certain prestige churches in the heart of the city. Religion in the poorer areas of the city is also likely to involve a number of smaller groups meeting in far less obvious buildings.

In the suburbs the church is often a social as well as a religious centre. The Sunday services share the church notice-board with details of dramatic societies, tennis clubs, scouts, cubs, guides and brownies. Going to church is merely part of a pattern of wider social contacts.

In attempting to make sense of the pattern of religion in Britain we need to consider the way these different factors work together.

Fig. 68. *Religion as leisure*

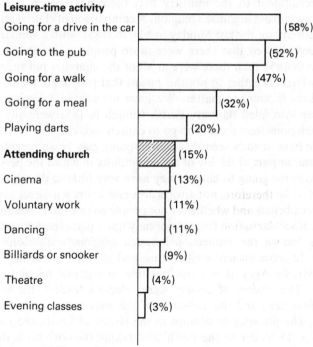

Leisure-time activity

Going for a drive in the car	(58%)
Going to the pub	(52%)
Going for a walk	(47%)
Going for a meal	(32%)
Playing darts	(20%)
Attending church	(15%)
Cinema	(13%)
Voluntary work	(11%)
Dancing	(11%)
Billiards or snooker	(9%)
Theatre	(4%)
Evening classes	(3%)

Source: Young and Willmott 1973

261

Population movements, age, sex, social class, all work together to produce a very complex pattern of religious activity.

Secularisation

The term 'secularisation' is often used to describe a process which is thought to be affecting religion in modern societies. 'Secular' is the opposite of 'religious' and *secularisation* means 'becoming less religious'. It is almost taken for granted that society today is in some way less religious than society in the past. For the sociologist of religion the idea of secularisation creates many problems. We have already considered the problems of defining and measuring religion. If it is difficult to define and to measure it is going to be very difficult to decide if it is diminishing. Different meanings people give to the word *secularisation* add to the problem.

The most obvious meaning of secularisation is that people are less religious. This means usually that less people go to church and Thomas Luckman has in fact called this 'a decline in church-oriented religion'. It is quite clear from the evidence on church-going, from the rate at which church buildings are being closed down and from the decline in recruitment to the ministry that there has been a considerable drift away from organised religion. A comparison of church attendance in Banbury on the last Sunday in March, 1851, with a similar Sunday in 1968 showed that there were more people in the Parish Church alone in 1851 than there were in all of the churches put together 117 years later. Whether or not this means that people are themselves less religious is another matter. We have no way of knowing that the people who filled Banbury Parish Church in 1851 were any more or less religious than those who go to church today.

We have already seen that church-going may be an accepted social custom, or part of the life of the community in which the person lives. Motives for going to church may have very little to do with religious belief. It is, therefore, not always accurate to draw a direct connection between beliefs and whether or not people go to church. An alternative view of secularisation focuses not only upon participation and church-going but on the connection between religious institutions and the state. In some ancient civilisations, and to some extent in Europe in the Middle Ages, it was not possible to separate religion from the state. The leaders of society were religious leaders, the laws were religious laws and the authority of the state rested upon the will of God. The presence of bishops in the House of Lords, the monarch's role as 'Defender of the Faith' and taking the oath on a Bible in a court of law are evidence of the connection between church and state in Britain. Whether these are examples of meaningful links between religion and the state or just hollow rituals is open to much debate.

A further problem arises when we try to discover when any religious decline began. Very often people speak about a 'golden age' when churches were strong and religion dominated the world. It is very difficult to decide when that 'golden age' might have been. It certainly was not during the Victorian period. The 1851 Census of Religion showed quite clearly that going to church was a middle-class activity. Nearly twenty years earlier Thomas Arnold, a leading churchman and headmaster of Rugby School, had commented 'it does not do to talk to the operatives (factory workers) about our pure and apostolic church. They have no respect for it. The church as it now stands no human power can save.' The most likely period for the title of 'golden age' is perhaps the twelfth century when the power of the church appeared strong and religion widespread. It can be argued, however, that the church in this period of history was so powerful and so closely aligned with the interests of the state that it was scarcely a religious organisation at all. Other candidates for the 'golden age' title might be Europe in the fourth century A.D., or Ancient Greece, or even the very dawn of civilisation. It is very difficult to agree on the most appropriate period.

Ultimately we must come to the view that secularisation has never been a consistent 'decline of religion'. Patterns of religious belief change and different ages have quite different features. The search for a golden age may be a wild-goose chase. David Martin has pointed out that 'when change becomes automatically secularisation then Europe has been secularised so often that it is difficult to see how any religion can be left.' (Martin 1969)

Although we may not get very far in a search for a 'golden age' it is clear that in recent history there has been some separation of social, political and religious institutions. The increased popularity of civil marriages gives us one example of this change.

Table 33. *Civil and religious marriages*

United Kingdom, 1971–76				
	Religious marriages		*Civil marriages*	
	1971	*1976*	*1971*	*1976*
Total Marriages (thousands):	278	212	181	194
Percentage of all marriages:	61%	52%	39%	48%
Percentage change	−23%		+22%	

Source: Social Trends

Religious activities are playing a smaller part in people's lives and have less influence over political events. Whereas at one time church leaders were also political leaders, any modern bishop who comments upon politics is likely to be told to 'get back to his prayers'. This is all part of a general separation of church and state.

So far secularisation has been discussed only in terms of the relationship between religion and other areas of social life. We can also use the concept to consider changes which have taken place within religious groups. One of the main features of most religions is an interest in the 'other world'. Religious language includes words like 'heaven' and 'hell' and 'the life-hereafter' all of which indicate a concern for the 'life-beyond'. We often refer to individuals as being 'other-worldly' when we mean that they do not have a great interest in the problems of this life but are thinking about spiritual matters. However, religion is not only concerned about the life-hereafter. When people pray, or seek religious help, it is often to enable them to get on better in this life. When people were asked about the situations in which they were most likely to think about God, most gave examples of illness or bereavement or serious personal trouble. 'Death' was the one word most likely to make people think of God. While this does suggest an 'other worldly' attitude it is also clear that people do turn to religion to sort out the problems of this world. This is a form of secularisation. It shows a move away from religion which is concerned with spiritual matters towards a religion which is firmly based on worldly success. Studies of religious writings, for example, have shown that health, and wealth and success in this life have often been the aim of people who prayed or wrote testimonies thanking God.

This move from 'other-worldly' interests to 'this-worldly' interests can also be seen in the way many religious groups are organised. Peter Berger has suggested that many modern churches run on the same basis as big business in a market economy. They use the same techniques of management, they measure success in terms of the numbers of souls saved or donations pledged in any year and may even move into co-operation with other religious groups where it is thought likely to increase their share of the 'market'. Berger sees the religious scene as a market place of competing groups, 'the religious tradition, which previously could be imposed, now has to be marketed. It must be "sold" to a clientele that is no longer forced to buy. The pluralistic situation is above all a market situation.' The development of religious advertising with hard-sell and soft-sell techniques, campaigns, door-step witness and street-corner evangelism may be evidence for Berger's point of view.

Secularisation also involves the way people think about the world quite separately from any system of organised religion. All religions contain beliefs and mythologies which help them to explain why things are like they are. These beliefs explain not only spiritual matters but also human relationships, differences in opportunity and in success and the workings of the natural world. If you are poor, or persecuted, or handicapped, religion can provide a reason and a hope.

The Bible says, 'How blest are those who know they are poor; the kingdom of Heaven is theirs . . . How blest are those who have suffered persecution for the cause of right; the kingdom of Heaven is theirs.' (Matthew, Chap. 6.) It is important to remember, however, that in the past religion has also attempted to explain the natural world, as well as the social and spiritual worlds. The movements of the sun and the planets, creation, the shape of the earth's surface and many other physical phenomena have been explained by religion. Often this has brought religion into conflict with science. As scientific discovery has developed it has shown that the natural world obeys physical laws which can be determined by experiment and by reason. This has led to a change in the way people think and in the ways they explain things. At one time it was believed that God created the earth in 4004 B.C. at 9.30a.m. on October 23rd. Adam and Eve were created on October 30th. Today we know far more about the nature of evolution and would not attempt to explain the origins of mankind in purely mythical or religious terms. Our ways of thinking about cause and effect now depend far more on science than they do on religion. This 'rational' approach to understanding the world does not, however, confine itself to explaining the physical universe. Sciences like psychology and sociology also help us to explain the social world rationally. Secularisation of the way we think implies that men and women now look for reasons for all aspects of human life in science and reason and not in religion.

While there can be no doubt that the growth of science has led to a change in the way people understand the world we should not fall into the trap of pretending that we all are rational creatures all of the time. Superstition is still a feature of many people's lives. Abercrombie and others have described this as 'the God of the Gaps'. They found that superstition was far more commonplace than many people had previously thought and that it was important in people's lives.

Over three-quarters of the sample touched wood in certain situations and almost half of them threw salt over their shoulders if some was spilled. There is then a big jump to belief in lucky numbers (22%) and charms (18%), the evasion of ladders, and the belief that black cats bring good luck (both 15%). Only one in ten people thought the number 13 was unlucky. (Abercrombie and others 1970)

265

Though people claimed to perform these actions, it is not certain that the actions have meaning for them. They could just be habits which could easily be broken.

We tried to discover more about the beliefs behind the practices by asking people whether or not they became uneasy if, for some reason, they did not perform the right action in the appropriate circumstances. Here it seems that the less common superstitious practices are more actively supported by those performing the actions. Nearly all of those who thought the number 13 unlucky said they would feel uneasy living in a house numbered 13. Just under half of those who tried to avoid ladders (for non-secular reasons) said they felt uneasy if they failed to do so, whereas only 8% of the wood touchers expressed a similar attitude. (Abercrombie and others 1970)

It is clear that though science and reason do form the basis for the way in which we understand and explain the world, for a significant number of people superstition and religion are still important.

Secularisation is, therefore, a topic which is difficult to pin down. In attempting to determine whether secularisation has taken place, and how it affects people's lives, we need to take into account a number of important factors. It is not enough to support the argument that secularisation has taken place solely on the basis of attendance at church on Sundays. We need to consider why people go to church, how the church sees its role in society, how people understand the world and the relationship between religious and other institutions.

References

ABERCROMBIE, N., BAKER, J., BRETT, S., and FOSTER, J., (1970) 'Superstition and Religion: the God of the Gaps,' *Sociological Yearbook of Religion* Vol. 3, SCM Press.

ASCH, S.E., (1951) in *Groups, Leadership and Men* (ed. Guetznow) Carnegie Press.

BECKER, H., (1958) 'Problems of Inference and Proof in Participant Observation', *American Sociological Review*, Vol. 23, No. 6.

BECKER, H., (1966) *Outsiders*, Free Press.

BEYNON, H., (1975) *Working for Ford*, E. P. Publishing.

BLONDEL, P., (1969) *Voters, Parties and Leaders*, Penguin.

BUTLER, and STOKES, (1969) *Political Change in Britain*, Macmillan.

CHIBNALL, S., (1975) 'The Crime Reporter: A Study in the Production of Commercial Knowledge', *Sociology*, Vol. 9, 48-63.

COATES, and SILBURN, (1970) *Poverty: the Forgotten Englishmen*, Penguin.

COHEN, S., (1967) 'Mods, Rockers and the Rest: Community Reaction to Juvenile Delinquency' *Harvard Journal*, 12, No. 2, 121-30.

COMMUNITY DEVELOPMENT PROJECT, (1977) *Costs of Industrial Change*.

DOUGLAS, J. W. B., (1964) *The Home and School*, MacGibbon and Kee.

FIELD, F., (1974) *Unequal Britain*, Arrow Books.

FLORENCE, P. S., (1961) *Ownership, Control and Success of Large Companies*, Sweet and Maxwell.

FRASER, R., (1969) *Work 2*, Penguin.

GAVRON, H., (1970) *The Captive Wife*, Penguin.

GOLDTHORPE, J. and LOCKWOOD, D., (1969) *The Affluent Worker in the Class Structure*, Cambridge University Press.

GOLDTHORPE, J. and LOCKWOOD, D., (1968) *Industrial Attitudes and Behaviour*, Cambridge University Press.

HARGREAVES, D., (1967) *Social Relations in a Secondary School*, Routledge and Kegan Paul.

HOGGART, R., (1957) *The Uses of Literacy*, Chatto and Windus.

JACKSON, B., and MARSDEN, D., (1962) *Education and the Working Class*, Routledge and Kegan Paul.

KELSALL, R. K., (1955) *Higher Civil Servants in Britain*, Routledge and Kegan Paul.

KELSALL, R. K., (1957) *Report on an Inquiry into Applications for Admission to Universities*, Association of Commonwealth Universities.

KENDALL and SMITH, (1939) *Table of Random Sampling Numbers*, Cambridge University Press.

LOCKWOOD, D., (1958) *The Blackcoated Worker*, G. Allen and Unwin.

MARTIN, D., (1969) *The Sacred and the Secular*, Routledge and Kegan Paul.

MAYER, K., (1955) *Class and Society*, Random House.

MYRDAL, A., and KLEIN, V., (1968) *Women's Two Roles*, Routledge and Kegan Paul.

NEWSON, J., and NEWSON, E., (1971) *Patterns of Infant Care in an Urban Community*, Penguin.

OAKLEY, A., (1974) *The Sociology of Housework*, Martin Robertson.

PARKIN, F., (1968) *Middle Class Radicalism*, Manchester University Press.

REES, A. D., (1950) *Life in a Welsh Countryside*, University of Wales Press.

ROSE, R., (1967) *Influencing Voters*, Faber and Faber.

ROWNTREE, S., (1961) *Poverty: A Study of Town Life*, Macmillan.

SCHOOLS COUNCIL, (1970) Working Paper 27, *Cross'd with Adversity*, Evans/Methuen.

SHARPE, S., (1976) *Just Like a Girl*, Penguin.

STACEY, M., (1960) *Tradition and Change*, Oxford University Press.

STACEY, BATSTONE, BELL and MURCOTT, (1975) *Power Persistence and Change: a Second Study of Banbury*, Routledge and Kegan Paul.

WEST, D. J., and FARRINGTON, D. P., (1973) *Who Becomes Delinquent?* Heinemann Educational.

WILLIS, P., (1978) *Learning to Labour*, Saxon House.

WILLMOTT, P., and YOUNG, M., (1960) *Family and Class in a London Suburb*, Routledge and Kegan Paul.

268

WILLMOTT, P., (1966) *Adolescent Boys of East London*, Routledge and Kegan Paul.

WISER, W., and WISER, C., (1969) *Behind Mud Walls*, University of California Press.

WOODWARD, J., (1968) *Management and Technology*, H.M.S.O.

YOUNG, M., and WILLMOTT, P., (1957) *Family and Kinship in East London*, Routledge and Kegan Paul.

YOUNG, M., and WILLMOTT, P., (1973) *The Symmetrical Family*, Routledge and Kegan Paul.

Further Reading

A successful grasp of sociology depends heavily on the student's ability to relate sociological ideas and methods to a wide range of events and situations. Reading around the subject is therefore very important. Students should make full use of the excellent range of books which are now available, many of which have been written specifically for the G.C.E. 'O' Level student. Reference has already been made to the Longman's Social Studies Series edited by Richard Cootes. The four foundation texts in Series One: *Enquiring About Society* by David Jenkins; *The Family* by Richard Cootes; *British Government* by Philip Gabriel; and *Production and Trade* by Brian Davies and Derek Hender are all relevant to the sociology student. The shorter Series Two titles include: *The Social Services* by David Whittaker; *Education and Society* by Alan O' Donnell; *Crime and Punishment* by Robert Roshier; *Leisure* by Susan Dickinson; *Population* by Michael Richards; *Race Relations* by Mercia Last; *Marketing and Advertising* by Michael Snell; *Industrial Relations* by Ian Wortley; *Religion in Britain* by Peter North; and *Women and Society* by Susan Dickinson.

More detailed coverage of similar topics is provided by the Aspects of Modern Sociology Series edited by John Barron Mays and Maurice Craft, published by Longman. *A Sociological Portrait*, edited by Paul Barker, Penguin 1972 contains a series of essays on aspects of sociology and would be useful reading for the more advanced student. In addition to basic textbook reading students should attempt at least one original sociological study. Many of these are available in inexpensive paperback editions. They are also available from public libraries. *The Captive Wife* by Hannah Gavron, Penguin 1968; *Family and Kinship in East London* by Michael Young and Peter Willmott, Penguin 1962; *Just Like a Girl* by Sue Sharpe, Penguin 1976; *Poverty the Forgotten Englishmen* by Ken Coates and Richard Silburn, Penguin 1973; *Power, Persistence and Change* – a second study of Banbury by Margaret Stacey and others are all readable studies which give an idea of how sociologists go about their work. Extracts from some of these books and from a range of other studies are included in many of the readers currently available. *The Sociology of Modern Britain* edited by Eric Butterworth and David Weir, Fontana 1975 provides a good selection of short extracts.

A sociologist's reading list should not be limited to books by sociologists or about sociology. Fiction and biography are very valuable sources of back-

270

ground information and ideas. *Kes* by Barry Hines, Penguin 1969; *Walkabout* by James Vance Marshall, Penguin 1963; Nina Bawden's *Carrie's War*, Penguin 1974; *Lord of the Flies* by William Golding, Penguin 1960; *The Seige of Babylon* by Farrukh Dhondy, Macmillan 1978; and Laurie Lee's *Cider with Rosie*, Penguin 1959 all explore the relationship between individuals and particular social circumstances. A full list of useful fiction and biography would be very long indeed. Many stories have also been made into films. The six thematic anthologies in the Longman Imprint Series provide useful short stories on *The Minority Experience, The Experience of Prison, The Experience of Sport, The Experience of Colour, The Experience of Work,* and *Breaking Away*.

Finally students should keep their reading up-to-date by making use of journals and newspaper articles. New Society and its regular insert for students, Society Today, is particularly valuable.

Information on new publications for social science students and regular book reviews are contained in The Social Science Teacher, the journal of the Association for the Teaching of the Social Sciences. Information on A.T.S.S. may be obtained from them at 85 Dorchester Rd, Solihull, West Midlands.

Appendix

Examination questions

A selection of examination questions, some of which are from past papers of the Associated Examinations Board are included to give students and teachers an indication of the range of question styles which are used by examining bodies. The questions included illustrate the types of questions which have been set in the past on the main areas of the subject. The types of questions used are reflected in the examination papers of most Boards.

Copies of past papers can be obtained from the relevant examination boards.

1 Urban living and rural living are different mainly because of contrasts in the social environment rather than the physical environment. What are the major differences between these social environments? (AEB 1978)

2 (a) How can towns and cities be described as 'anonymous' when they are frequently so crowded?
  (b) To what extent does the anonymity of urban life help to explain the higher crime rate in towns as compared with rural areas? (AEB 1978)

3 'Marxists believe that modern industrial societies are divided into two major classes according to the ownership or non-ownership of capital or property...
  'In Britain official statistics published by the Registrar General describe social class and socio-economic group in terms of occupation' (S. R. Parker *et al. Sociology of Industry* 1967)
  How useful are the above ways of looking at stratification in modern Britain? (AEB 1979)

4 Social class is an idea used by sociologists to help them understand different kinds of social behaviour.
  Explain what may be meant by social class and show how sociologists use the term. (AEB 1978)

5 'Beer has developed as a man's drink. It takes some getting through and long practise. Women who plunge in and order a pint give a reckless, if un-conscious challenge to the man's right' (Anne Garvey, 'Women in Pubs', *New Society*)

What does this extract suggest about the traditional roles of men and women in modern Britain? How are these roles supported and reinforced in modern Britain and to what extent are they changing? (AEB 1978)

6 'Generally speaking, social class and the way one's parents and neighbours vote both have a very strong influence on political leanings. Until quite recently it was usually supposed that people who saw themselves as manual workers, or as coming from a working-class home, would vote Labour, and those who considered themselves middle class would vote Conservative. One of the key facts of British politics is that about one-third of those *who think of themselves as working class* usually vote Tory.' (Crick and Jenkinson, *Parliament and the People*.)

(a) What is the importance of the phrase 'who think of themselves as working class'?

(b) What explanations do sociologists offer for the working-class Conservative voter? (AEB 1978)

7

INFANT MORTALITY IN U.K.

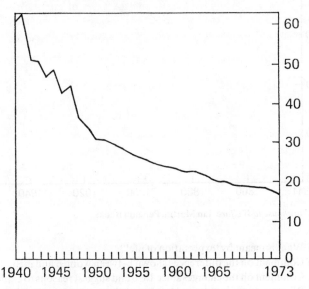

1940 1945 1950 1955 1960 1965   1973

Source: Office of Population Censuses and Surveys

(a) What is meant by the term Infant Mortality Rate?

(b) What changes does the graph show?

(c) What factors have sociologists suggested contribute to these changes? (AEB 1978)

8 A sample survey attempts to gain an accurate picture of an area of social activity by representing as accurately as possible the group of people to be studied. Explain the ways in which sociologists attempt to achieve a representative sample. (AEB 1977)

9   1 Expectation of life

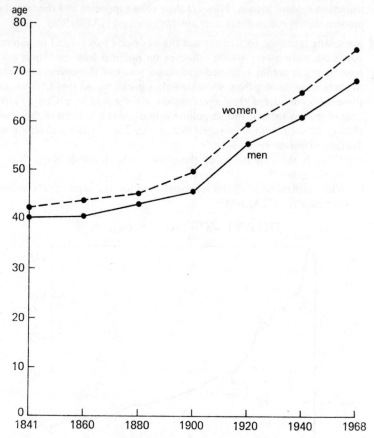

age

From *Workhouse to Welfare,* Ian Martin, Penguin Books

(a) What is meant by 'expectation of life'?

(b) Comment on the differences shown between women and men.

(c) Comment on the changes since 1870 and suggest reasons to explain them.

(d) What problems are caused by changes in expectation of life?

10 'It is because man is a cultural being that sociologists have attached great importance to the notion of socialisation. By this is meant the transmission of culture: the process by which men learn the rules and practices of social groups'.

(a) What is meant by 'cultural being'?

(b) Give two examples of culture transmitted from one generation to the next.

(c) Give two examples of rules men learn in social groups.

(d) If socialisation takes place in all societies why do societies change?

11 Compare and contrast postal questionnaires and personal interviews as methods of collecting research data. (AEB 1978)

12 *The occupied population of Gt. Britain by major occupational groups 1911–66*
Source: Men and Work in Modern Britain Ed. D. Weir

	1911	1966
1. Employers and proprietors	6·7	3·4
2. White-collar workers	18·7	38·3
(i) Managers and administrators	3·4	6·1
(ii) Higher professionals	1·0	3·4
(iii) Technicians and lower professionals	3·1	6·5
(iv) Foremen and inspectors	1·3	6·0
(v) Clerks	4·5	13·2
(vi) Salesmen	5·4	6·1
3. Manual workers	74·6	58·3
(i) Skilled	30·5	28·1
(ii) Semi-skilled	43·4	26·1
(iii) Unskilled	9·6	8·5
4. All occupied	100·0	100·0

(a) What changes in the occupational structure are indicated by the above table?

(b) How would you explain these changes?

13 Imagine a country in which living in families was officially prohibited. Describe the difference this might make to that society.

14 What is a family? Describe some of the different kinds of family organisation you have read about and explain why they are all families.

15 'For others the pressure is more subtle: it is not only economic, it comes through isolation, boredom and the lack of status as well. As the Finer report put it, most women now "fit in" child-bearing between leaving school and having a job. Perhaps because this period is now so short it has become the period in life which confers least status. The achievement of giving birth is only briefly recognised. Many young mothers soon lose their own identity, and come to be regarded (by themselves as much as by others) merely as an extension of their children by day and their husbands by night. So the pressure on women today is to go back to work in order to *participate* in society and not simply for economic reasons.'
Source: New Society, 30th Jan. 1975

(a) What arguments support or refute the author's suggestion that the period of child bearing is '. . . short and confers least status'?

(b) What, have sociologists suggested, are the reasons for women going back to work?

16

Divorce: by duration of marriage

Great Britain   Percentages

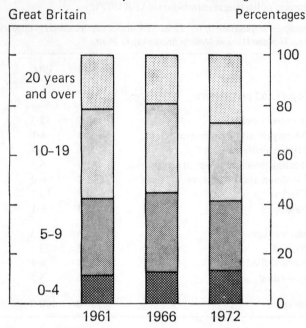

20 years
and over

10–19

5–9

0–4

1961   1966   1972

Source: Social Trends, 1975

(a) What changes does the chart show in patterns of divorce over the period 1961–72?

(b) What effects have changes in divorce law had on marriage stability in modern Britain? (AEB 1978)

17 A primary school situated in the 'twilight area on the fringe of the city' contains 300 children aged seven to eleven. The headmaster is quoted as saying 'Only one in every 100 of my pupils stands any chance of going to university . . . There are two nations when it comes to education . . . That is not the school's fault or the fault of local education authorities.' (Adapted from *Daily Mirror*, April 12th 1973).

(a) To what is the headmaster referring when he talks about 'two nations'?

(b) What sociological explanations can you give for these apparent inequalities in the education system? (AEB 1976)

18 'But if our investment in education is adequate to fulfil the purposes of education we get a long-term return on our money that is second to no other investment'. (M. Hutchinson and C. Young, *Educating the Intelligent*) What are the 'purposes of education'? (AEB 1975)

19 The tripartite system and comprehensive re-organisation were successive attempts to bring about equality of educational opportunity. What changes did these attempts bring about and what problems still remain? (AEB 1978)

20 Explain, with examples, how the occupation which a person follows affects many areas of his life outside of work. (AEB 1979)

21 *Selected differences in terms and conditions of employment. Percentage of establishments in which the condition applies.*

	Factory workers (%)	Clerical workers (%)	Senior managers (%)
Holiday: 15 days +	38	74	88
Normal working 40 + hours per week	97	9	22
Pension—employers' scheme	67	90	96
Time off with pay for personal reasons	29	83	93
Pay deducted for any lateness	90	8	0
No clocking on or booking in	2	48	94

Source: 'Workplace Inequality', by D. Wedderburn, in *New Society*, 9th April 1970

Can you account for the above differences in working conditions?

22 'Work satisfaction' is a phrase which sociologists frequently use. What do sociologists look for when trying to assess the presence or absence of work satisfaction? (AEB 1978)

23 'It has been suggested that the Labour Party represents the interests of the working class and the Conservative Party represents the interests of the middle class. On the basis of this assumption one would expect the Labour Party to win every General Election.'

What explanations are offered for the fact that the Labour Party do not always win General Elections? (AEB 1975)

24 The choice of newspaper which a person reads may be a good example of the fact that an individual only hears or sees what he wants to. Discuss this point in relation to mass communications generally and the effect which they have on people's attitudes and behaviour. (AEB 1977)

25 Why does poverty still exist as a problem in Britain?

26 The Law tells us what constitutes *crime* in modern Britain, but opinions on what is *deviant* may vary. Explain why this is so. (AEB 1978)

27 Do increases in criminal statistics always mean increased social disorder? (AEB 1979)

28 'Many young people are biologically adult by the time they are fifteen. They may not be accepted as socially adult . . . there is a period of years during which the change gradually takes place'. (P. J. North, *People in Society*.)

Discuss this statement in relation to the claim that there is a 'youth culture' in our society. (AEB 1976)

29 'Poverty is not an absolute state. It is relative deprivation. Society itself is continuously changing and thrusting new obligations on its members. They, in turn, develop new needs. They are rich or poor according to their share of the resources that are available to all. This is true as much of nutritional as monetary or even educational resources.

Our general theory, then, should be that individuals and families whose resources, over time, fall seriously short of the resources commanded by the average individual or family in the community in which they live, whether that community is a local, national or international one, are in poverty'.

Source: Peter Townsend, from the *British Journal of Sociology*, September 1962

(a) How does the above extract help us to understand changing standards of poverty over a period of time and in different places?

(b) How can we say that we are experiencing a higher standard of poverty in Britain today than 50 years ago? (AEB 1978)

30 Why are sociologists interested in religion? What kind of studies of religion do sociologists make?

31 'Despite declining church attendance, religious influence in society remains significant.' Discuss. (AEB 1976)

32 Explain the meaning of any three of the following:

(a) status

(b) caste system

(c) social mobility

(d) meritocracy

(e) embourgeoisement

(AEB 1978)

33 Take *two* of the following terms; show that you understand their meaning by giving examples of their appropriate use in a sociological context:

social class   random sampling

alienation   social mobility

automation   pressure group

34 Select any two of the following statements and show why they might be considered misleading.

(a) Poverty is not owning a television set.

(b) A society can solve its problems of overpopulation by introducing birth control.

(c) Bigamy is always a crime and morally wrong everywhere.

(d) net migration refers to the inflow of coloured immigrants

(e) the more available divorce becomes the more broken families are created. (AEB 1977)

35 The following statements are incorrect or misleading. Select three of them and briefly explain why you think each is misleading or incorrect.

(a) all pressure groups rely on strike action to achieve their aims.

(b) The extended family is simply a family with many children.

(c) Bureaucracy is just 'red-tape'.

(d) Comprehensive schools are Grammar Schools containing pupils of both sexes.

(e) Automation involves machines being used by men to make their work easier. (AEB 1975)

Index

Abrams, M., 185
achieved status, 30, 119
Acts of Parliament, 176–7; *see also*
    Children; Criminal; Divorce;
    Education; Factory; Immigrants;
    Legal Aid; Matrimonial; National
    Assistance, Health, Insurance; Poor
    Laws
adults, 119, 228; *see also* parents;
    teachers
affluence, worker, 33–4
age: at marriage, 74, 112; of men, 55;
    of population, 89–91; and religion,
    258; of women, 55, 72, 78; *see also*
    life expectancy
alienation: of housework, 167; in
    industry, 147, 165–6; and politics,
    189–90; in poverty, 208; religious,
    248
ambiguity, status, 152
amplification of deviance, 232–4
aristocracy *see* upper class
Asch, S. E., 64, 267
association, 14–19, 223
attitudes, 9, 37
authority, 136–8
automation, 148–9

babies *see* children; infant mortality
Banbury: class and status in, 27–9,
    101, 202–3; employment in, 3–4, 8,
    11; first study of, 4–7; migration
    into, 4, 10, 12, 85; population of,
    3–4, 12; religion in, 12, 92, 262;
    roles *see* class; second study of,
    7–13; social change in, 4–7; voting
    in, 12–13
Barratt-Brown, M., 153
Becker, H., 62, 229, 267
behaviour: girls', 140; learned, 100–1;
    right, 119–20; wrong, 225

belief *see* religion
Berger, P., 264
Beveridge Report, 210–11
Beynon, H., 166, 267
bias, control of, 63
Birmingham, 85
birth rate, 67–9, 72–5, 79, 83
blackcoated worker, 146, 149–53
Bradlaugh, C., 74
'brain drain', 77
'bulge', population, 67, 74, 89
bureaucracy, 155–7, 165
Burt, C., 221
Butler, D., 38, 179, 182, 267

Cambridge study on delinquency, 224–5
Campaign for Nuclear Disarmament
    (CND), 189–91
campaigns, election, 181
capitalism, 26; *see also* industry; Marx
caste, 25, 96, 101; *see also* class
Census of Population, 10, 35, 46–9, 144;
    see also population
Census of Religion, 49, 258, 263
change: and Census, 49; in divorce law,
    110–12; in family, 102–8; in
    fertility, 73–5; industrial, 86–8, 145;
    in offices, 150–1; population, 67–91
    passim; in women, 103–5; *see also*
    social change
character and education, 137–8
Chibnall, S., 240–2, 267
child-care, 78, 98–9, 109, 140; *see also*
    family
children: cruelty to, 100, 214; and
    divorce, 111–12; in family, 70–3,
    99, 102–3; health, 204–5, 207;
    maintenance of, 98–100; and
    poverty, 214; *see also* family; infant
    mortality; parents
Children's Act, 211